The Humanities in the Age of Science

Dr. Peter Sammartino

The Humanities in the Age of Science

In Honor of Peter Sammartino

Edited by Charles Angoff

Rutherford · Madison · Teaneck
Fairleigh Dickinson University Press

© 1968 by Associated University Presses, Inc.
Library of Congress Catalogue Card Number: 68-10966

Associated University Presses, Inc.
Cranbury, New Jersey 08512

6760
Printed in the United States of America

Foreword

The place of Fairleigh Dickinson University in American educational history after World War II will doubtless be the subject of many studies in and outside of academe, for the university has had a catalyzing influence on both the practice of higher education and the general public's awareness of the need for a new educational approach in the troubled New World.

The prime mover and shaper in the history of Fairleigh Dickinson University has been its first president, Dr. Peter Sammartino, who has just rounded out the first twenty-five years of his incumbency in office and who has relinquished it, to be succeeded by Dr. J. Osborn Fuller.

It has seemed to the faculty, especially the senior ones among us, that as a preliminary token of appreciation of Dr. Sammartino's historic labors, it would be fitting to follow the old and noble tradition of the *Festschrift* with a collection of essays—entirely by teachers who have been closely associated with him across the years—concerned in one way or another with the theme of the Humanities in The Age of

Science. That happens to be one of the areas in which Dr. Sammartino has made a major contribution.

The essays tell their own story about the type of thinking and teaching going on at Fairleigh Dickinson University. They form only a representative group of the many score that could have been available. But the problems of space and variety made a rigid selection, however agonizing, imperative.

CHARLES ANGOFF

Biographical Note on Peter Sammartino

Dr. Peter Sammartino was born on August 15, 1904, in New York City. He earned his B.S. from the College of the City of New York in 1924. Four years later he obtained his M.A. from New York University, and in 1931 he was awarded a Ph.D. by the same University. He has an honorary LL.D. from Long Island University, and from the University of Liberia; also an honorary Litt.D. from Kyung Hee University, Korea. At the time of the establishment of the Peter Sammartino College of Education at Fairleigh Dickinson University in 1966, he was awarded an honorary L.H.D. at a special convocation called by the trustees. He is the author or co-author of the following books: *Survey of French Literature, Emile Zola, French in Action, Grammaire Simple et Lectures Faciles, Avançons, II Prime Libro, II Secundo Libro, Letture Facili, Community College in Action, The President of a Small College, Vivre C'est Chanter, Multiple Campuses, International Conference on Higher Education,* and *The Private Urban University.*

Dr. Sammartino participated in the deliberations of the President's Council on Higher Education, and he was a delegate to the White House Conference on Education. In addition, he was chairman of the eight-town study for the Committee for Economics Development. In 1964 he was president of the International Association of University Presidents, and the following year President Johnson appointed him to the Advisory Board of the Peace Corps.

At the time of the announcement of his impending retirement, Dr. Sammartino received many letters of appreciation. Eight heads of state sent messages and over 200 heads of institutions all over the world sent congratulatory statements. The attitude of the university community in the United States is well expressed by Dr. O. P. Kretzman, president of the Valparaiso University, who said, "Within the framework of Western Culture, you built a school which is unique and significant in many ways." The attitude of the university community beyond our shores was stated by Dr. Rocheforte L. Weeks, president of the University of Liberia: "Fairleigh Dickinson University's rôle in extending the boundaries and influence of the university as part of the World Community is laudable and significant."

Contents

Foreword	CHARLES ANGOFF	
Biographical Note		
Tenderness in American Literature	CHARLES ANGOFF	13
Sufism: Humanism Enters Islam	NASROLLAH S. FATEMI	20
Science and Human Values in the Future of Man	ROBERT THOMAS FRANCOEUR	46
Our First Museum Men	LOYD HABERLY	66
Dewey's Humanistic Legacy	SAMUEL HART	87
The Two Cultures and the Abyss in Between	EMIL LENGYEL	101
Mary Shelley's Frankenstein	FRANK H. MCCLOSKEY	116
Is History a Science?	H. F. MACKENSEN	139
Apollo, Dionysos and the Computer	ANDRE MICHALOPOULOS	154
World War II, a Watershed in the Role of the National Government in the Advancement of Science and Technology	KENT REDMOND	167

Guideposts of Scientific Education	HAROLD A. ROTHBART	182
The Challenge of Technology	HARRIETT SPAGNOLI	197
Pioneers of Social Science and the Humanistic Tradition in America	WILLIS RUDY	213
History, Accidents and Monsters	JOHN C. WARREN	222
On the Origins of Art	GENE WELTFISH	232
Notes on Contributors		268

The Humanities in the Age of Science

Tenderness In American Literature
By Charles Angoff

It has been said that the quality of a culture can be quickly ascertained by the prevalent attitude toward Jews and by the position of women. The United States, most observers would probably agree, scores well on the first count. The Jews form a small minority, some six million out of about 190,000,000. Every one of them with any degree of sensitivity knows he is a member of an "outside" group. One might almost say that a Jew is born with this consciousness of difference. This is probably universally true. There are only 12,000,000 Jews in a world population of more than three billion.

But there is one important difference for Jews in the United States, as compared to their co-religionists in France or Germany or Russia or Italy or even England. Anti-Semitism has erupted now and then in various sections of the United States down through decades of our history as a nation. But never has it had the sanction of the government.

And always it has masqueraded as something else—as a revolt against business chicanery in some individual Jews, as a "corrective" to the inclination on the part of some Jews to "overspend for education" (as happened recently in Wayne, New Jersey), to mention only two specific instances. Those who practiced this kind of anti-Semitism sensed that they were running counter to the American tradition, which from time immemorial has been to a considerable extent philo-Semitic. It is no accident that the line around the Liberty Bell, our central symbol of democracy and the whole American way of life, does not come from Luke or Matthew or any other section of the New Testament. It comes from the Old Testament, Leviticus 25: "Proclaim liberty throughout the land and to all the people thereof." The significant point is that anti-Semitism in the United States has never been a characteristic of the land but rather an aberration. In Germany, one is strongly inclined to say, anti-Semitism has been a part of the philosophy of the nation. The same in Russia. The same, at times, has been the case in France and England.

In the realm of the status of women, the position of the United States is not so clear, certainly not in the field of belles lettres. Women, it is reported, own more property than do men; they are the principal beneficiaries of wills; the mass circulation magazines address themselves almost entirely to them since they are the chief buyers of foods and home appliances; and it has been said that more than fifty per cent of radio and television, as well as newspaper, advertising, has to do with women's needs. There is also a mystique of the adoration of women. Men feel boorish if they don't doff their hats in elevators and if they don't give up their seats to young girls, even when they, the men, are dog tired.

And yet virtually every novelist and every psychologist

(who's a sort of backward novelist) knows that the American woman is unhappy, certainly far less contented than her European sister, who is not the beneficiary of the aforementioned mystique and who hasn't control of all that money.

Perhaps the cause of this paradox can be determined, in some vague way, if one considers the imaginative writings within the United States. The literature of a nation is, all in all, the best reflection of its general attitude toward life, specifically, of its attitude toward women. Writers sense things long before others do. What, then, do American writers sense about the position of women in the American community?

Our first poet of any importance, Anne Bradstreet, wife of Governor Bradstreet of the Massachusetts Bay Colony, admitted that she loved her husband but she added quickly that she loved God more. This was hardly a compliment to her spouse—after all, there are varieties of love—but her expressed sentiment did indicate what she missed in her relationship with her husband. Hester Prynne, in Hawthorne's *Scarlet Letter,* is portrayed as a woman of valor—she never reveals the name of the father of her child, Pearl—, but the important point in this regard is that nowhere in the novel does Hawthorne have anything to say about the quality of the relationship between Arthur Dimmesdale, the preacher, and Hester, who was married to another man. Indeed, Hawthorne doesn't reveal anything about the relationship that had existed between Hester and her lawfully wedded husband. Was it tender? Did it satisfy a mutual need? Did it enhance their joy in life? Did it ennoble their days and light up their nights? Did it bring them closer to the God of Creation? Hawthorne doesn't think it necessary to comment on any of these matters.

Not one of the Bearded Poets of New England experienced

any pressure to say more than did Hawthorne about the man-woman relationship. In fact, they revealed less. Hester did give in, as the vulgar saying goes, to the call of the wild in her being, and what went on between her and Dimmesdale was a high pledge of unconditional surrender to the urgencies of primal being.

What of William Dean Howells? Perhaps he was the first of the major American realists, as some academic critics maintain, but his realism managed to skirt the reality of woman's yearnings and hence falsified man's yearnings as well, for generally what woman truly desires man wants profoundly to give. Emotional hunger often is a two-way affliction. In not one of his novels, not even in *The Rise of Silas Lapham,* where there is the celebrated triangle (the two Lapham girls and the rich young man, who is assumed to love one but really loves the other), does Howells infuse full-bodied tenderness, so to speak, into the man-woman relationship.

Stephen Crane, who heralded the mature democratization of American fiction, was more concerned with the sociological background of the downtrodden than with what went on in their hearts. The heroine of *Maggie: A Girl of the Streets* is, truth to tell, little more than a girl who made a "mistake." She has no other being. She carries along a fictional documentary. At the time such a girl in more or less popular fiction was most unusual. But she is remembered largely as a symbol of her background, not as a person and a woman in her own right.

With Dreiser the man-woman relationship, in the last analysis, is not so much different than it is in Stephen Crane, with one exception. Sister Carrie is a conniver and a maneater. She is incapable of tenderness. Her various lovers are also incapable of tenderness. They desire her, and they need her for sexual comfort or as a show-piece, but they do not wish to be gentle with her, to be abidingly kind to her. The same with Jennie Gerhardt. The one exception just referred to is Aileen in *The Financier.* There is a woman who, as the saying goes, would kill for her man, and Cowperwood often gives her the only thing she wants in return: love that includes desire but that also includes joy and release in her company and a compulsion to give her adoration compounded of tenderness and delight.

Henry James's women generally make little sense as people or as women. So many of them seem to be educated and animated manikins. Perhaps the most successful of them is Isabel in *Portrait of a Lady,* a woman of principle who throws away her life on a bounder. In a profound sense she made pretty much the same mistake that Maggie did. It is never clear what she wanted from the inferior man she married, but it is altogether too clear what he wanted: money and "position." The relevant point is that she didn't consciously seek for tenderness, which is a misreading of the eternal woman by James— this is, incidentally, perhaps his greatest deficiency. James didn't know what she wanted, what any woman wanted. A novelist must *know.* Not that a novelist knows any more answers than do "ordinary" people. The most important problems in the world have no answers. The *ding an sich* about men and women remains impenetrable. But it's the function of the literary artist to elaborate the mystery. Such elaboration constitutes a form of illumination.

Hemingway merits no serious attention as a perceiver of the man-woman relationship. He remained all his life a senile adolescent in his attitude to women. His women are either instruments for sexual gratification or manikins. The woman in *The Snows of Kiliminjaro* is a lump of jello draped with a skirt for a few moments. Catherine Barclay in *A Farewell to Arms* is no more a woman than the marble slab her body lies on in the last page of the novel. Maria in *For Whom the Bell Tolls* is a Spanish Maggie who hasn't yet discovered her "mistake." With Fitzgerald the situation is only a trifle better. Fitzgerald was more mature emotionally than was Hemingway. But while Nicole in *Tender is the Night* is more a woman than any of Hemingway's females, she is not depicted as one who needs what every woman needs, and what every man yearns to give her: tenderness. Of course, Nicole has a mental malady to contend with, but in between her "seizures" she's all woman, and there Fitzgerald fails her. The thought occurs that perhaps Fitzgerald was at his most tender with a "real" woman, Sheila Graham. In other words, he succeeded best in his "real" life, but came a-cropper in his fictional creations.

What about American playwrights? They have not been more successful than have the writers of prose fiction. Nina in *Strange Interlude* is O'Neill's inept attempt to get on the stage his misunderstanding of Freud. The play has many values—O'Neill couldn't make a list of telephone numbers without somehow getting dramatic tension into it—, but one value it hasn't got is the authentic depiction of woman's heart vis-à-vis the man of her choice. But is Anna Christie, in the play by the same name, any better? Hardly. Of course, Mrs. Tyrone in that classic, *Long Day's Journey,* is a woman of substance and stature. But as O'Neill saw her, he really had no reason for probing too deeply into the eternal woman in her. In a sense she wasn't a woman at all. She apparently never enjoyed giving herself to her husband—as it is ordained woman should enjoy it—, she had almost no need for tenderness. The only tenderness she seemed to desire was that flowing from the crucifix on the wall of a convent.

Arthur Miller's *Death of a Salesman* and *A View from the Bridge* contain women: in the first, the understanding wife of a failure, and in the second, the young girl who is insanely desired by her guardian while she actually loves an Italian immigrant. Perhaps the real tragedy of Willy's wife is that she is called upon to be the man of the house: she has to give tenderness to the man she has a right to expect to give it to her. The young girl in the *Bridge* is only a young girl who unwittingly causes a lot of trouble. She is not a character at all, only a prop. The poor, bedgraggled wife, who is deprived of her rights of the bed, is more woman than the girl, but Miller virtually throws her away as a character. He only hints at what is going on within her.

There are only two other major playwrights in contemporary America who are worthy of discussion in this respect. But both Edward Albee and Tennessee Williams appear to to be allergic to women as fictional material. Virtually all their women are caricatures, so loathsome and troublesome and neurotic are they. All of them appear to be in a state of constant hysteria, or they are floating in a pre-natal haze. They roll in drunken stupors on beds or they wallow in domestic filth or they shriek at their men (who are no more men than they are woman)—and they almost invariably collapse in despair, at the same time exhausting and bewildering and offending the audience.

American fiction is a fiction without universal women. We have no one even remotely approaching the stature of Anna Karenina or Emma Bovary or Becky Sharp. Our writers do not seem to be able to get into the mystical and mysterious loveliness that God ordained should exist between man and woman. Love, gentleness, tenderness—above all tenderness—seem to be alien facets of life to our short story writers and novelists and playwrights. It's love, gentleness, and tenderness that are the central fountains of all the arts and at the very heart of Humanism. Nothing that is human should be alien to the civilized man. But where there is no tenderness, there is only defective humanity.

Sufism: Humanism Enters Islam

By Nasrollah S. Fatemi

One of the greatest contributions of the Muslim thinkers to humanity was the idea of Sufism. It originated as a rebellion and reaction to the formalism and corruption of the Islamic church and the tyranny of the rulers. Sufism was the antithesis of the arrogance, intolerance, demogogism, hypocrisy, and corruption of the Medieval society.

Few terms in the dictionary are as imprecise as the term *sufi* or *sufism*. Its very mention quite often provokes debate about its meaning, its evaluation, and its purpose. To the orthodox and traditional Muslims, it stands for qualities deeply distrusted and despised; to the enlightened and liberal, it connotes humanitarianism, generosity, harmony, a protest against rigid dogmatism, love of mankind, and a challenge to achieve excellence. To some, Sufis are dreamers, rebels, and meddlers, who interfere with the serious business of state and religion; to others they are the conscience of society and "the antennae of the race." They exhibit in their activities a pronounced concern for humanity and a deep interest in the core value of society.

While the Muslim church of the ninth and tenth centuries tended to be absorbed in the pursuit of power, and on ways and means to exercise tyranny over the minds of the people, the Sufis felt the need to resist "the Establishment," to ridicule the rich and the mighty, to exalt the low and the poor. They tried to go beyond the superficial religious teachings and to penetrate into the realms of the "inner thoughts and values." They protested against the cruelty of their society, and they exhibited an unusual sensitivity to the sacred, an uncommon reflectiveness about the nature of their world and the rules which govern it.

The first question they asked was, "Is God the object of formal worship or of love?" Is the purpose of religion to unite, to comfort, to improve, and to bring all races and peoples of the world together in love and brotherhood or to divide, to tyrannize, to exploit, to shed the blood of innocents, to mesmerize, and to commit every crime in the name of Allah who is all love, compassionate and merciful?

The ninth and tenth centuries were the "Golden Age of Islam." A great empire extending from the Pyrenees to Pamir and stretching from the Nile to the Indus had been created. Baghdad was the center of wealth, learning, power, commerce, crime, and corruption. A strong clergy under the leadership of the Caliph exercised both temporal power and spiritual influence. They had abandoned the pietistic tendency of early Islam. The piety, poverty, and popularism of the first four decades of Islam were replaced by the power, privilege, and despotism of the Abbassides Empire. It was in this environment that Sufism showed its face.

II

The origin of the word *sufi* has been the object of much dispute in the past. Some Sufis maintain that it is derived from the Arabic word *safa* meaning purity. Others contend that it is an historical allusion to Ashabus-safa or to the people of the bench, referring to the fact that the early Sufis spent most of their time debating the Muslim clergy on benches at the porch of the temple.[1] However, most scholars have come to agree that the name is derived from *suf* (wool). The Sufis adopted coarse wool as their dress in imitation of Christian monks, from whom was borrowed also the practice of celibacy which Islam discouraged.

Beginning simply as an ascetic life, sufism in the tenth century developed into a great movement, borrowing many ideas from many philsophers and prophets. Later on it absorbed many elements of theosophical and pantheistic doctrines.

In Sufism there is the fundamental conception of God as not only almighty and all good, but as the sole source of Being and Beauty, and, indeed, the one Beauty and the one Being, in whom is submerged whatever becomes non-apparent, and by whose light whatever is apparent is made manifest. Closely connected with this is the symbolic language so characteristic of these, and, indeed, of nearly all mystics, to whom God is essentially "the Friend," "the Beloved," and "the Darling"; the ecstasy of meditating on Him, "the Wine" and "the Intoxication"; His self-revelations and occultations, "the Face" and "the Night Black Tresses" and so forth. There is also "the exaltation of the subjective and ideal over the objective and formal, and the spiritualization of religions and formulae, which has been already noticed amongst the Ismailis, from

---

[1] John A. Subhan, *Sufism Its Saints and Shrines,* Lucknow Publishing House, Lucknow, U.P. (1960), p. 6.

whom, though otherwise strongly divergent, the Sufis probably borrowed it." [2]

The Sufis believed in world brotherhood and complete tolerance. Their motto was "The ways unto God are as numerous as the number of people living in this world." (*Tariqatallah Kal-addadi nufusi Bane Adam*)

When Abu Said Ibn Abul Khaya, one of the founders of Sufism, was asked to define his doctrine, he replied, "To lay aside what you have in your head, such as pride, desire, hostility, arrogance, jealousy, greed and hatred and to give away what you have in your hand, and to flinch not from whatever befalls you."

"The veil between God and thee," he told his students, "is neither earth nor heaven, nor the Throne nor the Footstools; thy selfhood and allusions are thy veil, and when thou removest these thou hast attained unto God."

The Sufis also rejected the doctrine "fear of God, the wrath of the day of Judgement, the fury of Hell and the promise of Heaven." The mainspring of sufism is love of God:

I love thee with two loves, love of my happiness and perfect love, to love thee as is thy due. My selfish love is that I do naught but think on Thee, excluding all beside; but that purest love, which is thy due, is that the veils which hide thee fall, and I gaze on Thee, no praise to me on either this or that, nay thine the praise for both that love and this.[3]

III

As we have already mentioned, the Sufis being men of an emotional, mystical temperament, or as they called themselves,

---

[2] Edward G. Browne, *A Literary History of Persia,* Vol. II, London, T. Fisher Unwin, (1906), pp. 267-268.

[3] R. A. Nicholson, *Literary History of the Arabs,* 2nd. ed., Cambridge University Press, Cambridge, (1930), p. 234.

"men of heart," "men looking behind the veil," "men rebelling against formalism, organized church, tyranny and the divisive forces which divide human race," naturally borrowed the best of any religion and ideology. They developed their doctrines with the aid of Christians, Jews, Buddhists, Zoroastrians, and especially Greeks. The Neoplatonic metaphysics was popularized by Sufi leaders such as Al-Ghazzali, Shibli, Junaid, and Zunnun. They identified the Allah of the Quoran with Neoplatonic Being, the one, the Necessary being, the only Reality "the Truth," "the Infinite," which includes all actual being, good and evil, the First Cause, source of all action, good and evil alike.

According to their theory the Infinite includes all being, evil included, but as this is not consistent with the goodness of Allah, evil is said to proceed from not being. Similarly St. Augustine said evil was a negation.

The pantheism of Sufis as is expounded by the Gulshan Raz is very different from that of European Pantheism of today which, according to Bossuet, "makes everything God except God himself." The Sufi pantheism is an amplification rather than a minimification of the idea of the Divinity, infinite, omnipresent and omnipotent.

The aim of Sufis is to achieve perfect union with the divinity. Like Plotinus, they assume the reality of the supernatural over against the material world. The Sufi has to show on the one hand the relation existing between the Divine and on the other hand the means whereby he may ascend. The one watchword in this philosophy is continuity. There shall be no impassable gulf dividing God from man, spirit from matter. Self-control, self-sacrifice, patience, and boundless trust in God were the virtues that any Sufi had to possess.

"Sufism was a child of the soil, called into being by the deeper and truer religious spirit which the dry monotheism and stubborn orthodox dogma had stifled."

IV

Al-Ghazali (d.1084), the great Sufi teacher, introduced into sufism the doctrine of emanation. "He speaks of the unitarian seeing things as a multiplicity, but he sees the many as emanating from the one, the Supreme, and again he states that God is the first in relation to existent things, since all have emanated from Him in their order."[4]

Al-Ghazali, like Plotinus, states that the first emanation from God was the universal mind (*Al Aql al Awwal*). "When God wants to bless his creature, he makes use of the First intelligence, universal mind becomes the teacher and the sanctified soul the taught."

The First Intelligence is a pure light outpoured upon all things, for it is the spirit of all and by the gnostics it has been called the Heart of the Universe." [5]

From universal mind emanates universal soul (*Nafsi Kul*), which in its turn gives rise to individual soul. According to Al-Ghazali, the relation between universal mind and universal soul is the same as the relation between Adam and Eve. "When universal soul takes possession of a body, its presence there is called a human soul." He believed that human soul belongs to the spiritual world and is the highest self, divine and rational.

The Sufis also talked about "the Reproaching Soul" (*Al Nafs ul Lawemah*). This is the inner voice or the conscience which strives to save man from temptation and the downward pull of flesh. The scolding soul steadily and strongly opposes the irrational and capricious soul (*Alnafs ul Ammarah*) which represents the greediness, the arrogance, the cruelty,

---

[4] Al-Ghazali, *Ihys ul ulum*, trans. by Margaret Smith in her book *Al-Ghazoli*, Luzac & Co., London, p. 106.
[5] *Ibid.*, p. 106.

the caprice, the anger, and the ugliness of human nature.

The Sufis also borrowed the terms of darkness and light from Zoroastrians. "Ignorance," says Al-Ghazali, "is like a state of blindness and darkness, and knowledge is like vision and light." He refers to existence as light poured out upon the universe from the light of God, who is the light of all the universe. The light to Sufi is the ultimate truth. The Sufi God is not only the God of light; He is also the God of love and beauty. "It cannot be denied where beauty exists, it is natural to find love. The greater the beauty, the greater the love, and since complete and perfect beauty is found only in God, He alone can be worthy of true love."[6]

The Sufis tried to destroy religious prejudice and to introduce the idea that all men are children of God, who would not judge us according to color, creed, or race but according to our deeds. Al-Ghazali has a story that somebody asked God whether a Jew could enter Heaven. God's answer was: "If this servant in spite of his weakness, did not deny Us, how should We deny him our Grace?"

The Sufis' theory of knowledge is very interesting. They make distinction between the knowledge which can be acquired by study (*Ilm*) and the knowledge of understanding (*marifa*) which is given, not acquired, and through which man can learn about his creator, his fellow creatures, and the true value of a happy and useful life. They took issue with the orthodox *ulama*, whose only concern was the outward rituals and the letter of the law. "You have taken your knowledge from the learned in outward ceremonial, a death thing from the dead, but we have taken our knowledge from the living one, who does not die."

The Sufis also introduced music and dance, against very

---

[6]Margaret Smith, *Al-Ghazali,* p. 109.

strong opposition on the part of the orthodox clergy. They contended that even animals like to listen to good music and enjoy it. "When the heart is moved by music what is manifested is only what it already contains as from a vessel there drips only what is in it."

They divided the people who follow the "path of sufism" into three groups:
1. The seeker (*murid*) who is a novice striving to find the truth.
2. The traveller who is on the right path doing everything possible to get closer to his Beloved.
3. The attainer (*murad*) who has attained the stage of ecstasy and submission to his Beloved (*tamkin*).

He has made his peace with himself, his creator and his fellow creatures. He has reached the stage of self-obliteration, has destroyed all his animal desires, and is completely absorbed in the contemplation of God (*shahid·ul Haqq*).

Any man who succeeds in following "the path of truth would then receive the fruits of God's grace. These are patience, gratitude, understanding, hope, love, faith in his fellow men, kindness, self-effacement, contentment, trust in God and man, unification with the divine, service, justice, tolerance, meditation, contemplation, and finally Love."

Love, according to Al-Ghazali, is the final stage of the sufi way and its goal; only the true man of God is able to love and to overcome the evils of envy, jealousy, prejudice, bigotry, hatred, lies, sensitivity, selfishness, lust, greed, and desire. Once these evils are conquered, then love would take over and transfer him to Abraham, Buddha, Jesus, or Muhammed.

Any "seeker" of the "path," according to the Sufis, has to travel through seven stages:
1. Obedience (*ubudiyyat*), characterized by repentance.

In this stage the traveller attempts to purify his soul and prepares himself for the subsequent stage. This stage has been called by the Sufis "the awakening of the soul from the slumber of indifference to the awareness of its evil ways and a sense of contrition for past sins."

2. Love (*ishq.*). As a result of the wide influence, the "seeker" of the "path's" soul is inclined toward the love of God. This stage is also characterized by contentment and poverty, for if the Sufi's longing for God is truly intense, there is no room in his heart for any worldly desire. Thus by contentment and poverty, the Sufis mean not only the absence of wealth, but also the absence of any greed or desire for wealth.

3. Renunciation (*zuho*). This stage has two levels. At the first level the Sufi must purify his soul from all sensual desires. After this is accomplished, he enters the second level where he renounces all but God.

4. Gnosticism (*marifat*). In this stage a man turns away from all his inner thoughts so that he may contemplate the nature and the attributes and the work of God.

5. Ecstasy (*wajd*). This stage again is one of contemplation accompanied by prayers and ritual dance. Through this ecstasy, the Sufis believe that the "individual self is lost and the universal self is found."

6. Truth (*haqiqa*). The Sufi now is able to see the true nature of God and decides to put his trust in him and to become dependent upon his will.

7. Union (*wasl*). This is the stage of satisfaction because the Sufi submits himself to the will of God. At this stage he decides to serve God as his divine beloved and to devote his life to the service of mankind. It is in this last stage that the Sufis claim to experience meditation, nearness to God, love, hope, longing, service, intimacy, tranquility, contempla-

tion. The Sufis, like Calvin, believe that the "states" descend from God in the man's heart, and thus the seeker experiences only through "states" which God chooses to bestow upon him. After completing each "stage" of the "path," the Sufi is transformed from "seeker" to "knower" and reaches a new plane of consciousness which the Sufis call "gnosis." Gnosis is not related in any way to acquired knowledge. It is a natural understanding of the divine knowledge of God and people based upon meditation, contemplation and revelation.[7]

V

Neither space nor the scope of this article allows me to give a detailed account of the evolution of sufism, its philosophy, its purpose, and its practice. Suffice to say that the Sufis humanized rigid formalism of orthodox Islam. They left a profound impact not only on Persian literature but on Arabic and Indian literature as well. They advocated many unpopular and controversial ideas and, as a result, hundreds of them died a martyr's death. The following are a few of the many contributions of the Sufis.

1. God is the ultimate because of all beings He is Transcendant yet is Immanent. He is a Living, Personal God. He is the creator of truth, light of lights, perfect goodness, and the only object of beauty and love. Thus, those whom God loves are His friends.

2. Man's soul is able to receive direct knowledge of God and to enter into direct fellowship with Him. You need no prophet or saint to appeal your cause before God and to wash away your sin. No soul in this world is lost. The

---

[7]John A. Subham, *Sufism—Its Saints and Shrines,* Lucknow Publishing House, Lucknow, U.P., pp. 68-73.

sinner at any time can free himself from the shackles of greed and hatred and the bonds of his lust and ambition and return to the state in which he was one with the Divine.

3. Any man by blazing the "path" of humility, love, contentment, friendship for his fellow man and fellowship of his God can free his soul from the veils which hinder it from seeing God and obtaining eternal happiness and peace of mind.

4. By accepting man as a manifestation and the image of the Divine, the Sufis discarded the theory of original sin and put man on a pedestal and asserted that through his will power he can promote himself to the highest place. Furthermore, they contended that since man possesses will power and reason, given proper education, he would be able to understand and follow the path of truth, and use his mind and will power in the service of God and humanity.

5. The Sufis were the only group amongst the Moslem sects that believed that love was the guiding star of man. Rabia had thought that man could only be reformed, purified, and saved through unselfish love and dedication to the cause of his brethren. The Sufi's love was an all-absorbing passion.

6. The Sufi "state" of mystic ecstasy meant that man is so absorbed in his Beloved that he abandons self (Fana) and becomes conscious only of his God. It was in this "state" that Bastami and Hallaj claimed that they were one with God. Hallaj, walking through the Baghdad streets, told his audience to stop wasting their time and money by making pilgrimages to Mecca in search of God. He admonished them for their hypocrisy and for their dishonest business deals, and accused them of robbing orphans and old

women. He advised them to spend their money on the poor and the sick, and look for God in their hearts. "Cleanse your heart, dedicate yourselves to the service of your people," he shouted, "and there you will find truth and tranquility." When Hallaj was brought before the Inquisitor for punishment, he asked him to repent. His answer was, "I am He whom I love and He whom I love is I; we are two souls indwelling in one body. If thou seest me thou seest Him and if thou seest Him thou seest us both." In 922 Hallaj was crucified for claiming identity with God and henceforth Sufism became openly and frankly pantheistic.

7. The Sufis avoided any rigid or dogmatic doctrines and tried to make their ideas and beliefs a mode of thought and feeling. They discarded most formal Moslem religious rituals, replacing them by chanting and mentioning the name of God alone in their meetings. (*dkịkr*) For these free thinkers, Islam, however they might lean upon it, was a broken reed. Scorning the barren virtues of dogmatism and orthodoxy, condemning the hypocrisy of the clergy, opposing the intolerance and bigotry of the fanatics, ridiculing the established church, accepting no Saviour but a pole star of the divine transitory illumination, the Sufis rendered a great service in checking the power of the "religious establishment" and weakening the tyranny of the fanatics.

8. Throughout the Islamic world the Sufis established convents, "orders," and "brotherhoods." Some of these "orders" went to the extreme of placing Gnostics above the law and tradition of religion. They considered themselves free not only of ritual, but of moral precepts. "What, then," they asked, "could the statutes and demands of society, what the tenets of this or that specific faith mean

to Him who had seen through the meaningless mirage?"[8]

On the other extreme, some "orders" tried to add Saint and Miracle to the human typology of sufism. The Saint, according to them, was a perfect man whose intimacy with God enabled him to work miracles. He was chosen to be the governor of his kingdom, had ordered him to manifest his actions, and had favored him with different kinds of miracles, and had purged him of natural corruptions. These doctrines were vehemently challenged by many of the Sufi leaders. They denied special privileges and miracles, and they asserted that all good men are friends of God. Abu Said, the recognized leader of the Sufis, was told about these saints and how they could walk on the water, and how they could fly, and how they could in the twinkling of an eye travel from Cairo to Baghdad. His answer was, "The frog can swim and the swallow can skim the water, the bird and the fly traverse the air and the devil can pass in one moment from east to west. These are of no great importance," he continued, "the happy man is the one who lives in harmony with his fellow men, associates and works with them, shows restraint and control in his deeds and in his words under the most difficult circumstances. He is dedicated to serve, he is humble, tolerant, and will never hurt anybody, and would never bring sorrow or unhappiness to those whom he works with."

9. The Sufi world was a universal world. According to one of the leaders, the ideal and morally perfect man should be of Persian culture, Arabic in faith, Babylonian in education, Hebrew in insight and sagacity, a disciple of Christ, in conduct, as pious as a Syrian monk, a Greek in the in-

---

[8]Gustave Von Gruenbaum, *Medieval Islam,* University of Chicago Press, 1946, p. 137.

dividual sciences, an Indian in the interpretation of all mysteries, but lastly and especially, a Sufi in his whole spiritual and intellectual life." [9]

VI

A characteristic feature of Sufism was its adaptation to the earthly language of love, beauty and passion to express ecstatic communion with the Divine Lore. The best presentation of pantheistic Sufism is found in the mystical poems of the great Persian, Arabic, and Indian poets. Because of lack of space, I intend to mention here only a few of the most celebrated names in this branch of thought and literature.

1. Abul Alamaarri (d. 1005) is a great figure in the world of Moslem thought and Arabic literature. He was the blind poet who, with all his wealth, lived an ascetic life, wearing a coarse cloak, allowing himself only bread and water. He had an open house and whoever arrived in his town could stay at his mansion as long as he wished. Once a friend asked him why, since God had bestowed on him all this wealth, he gave it all away to the people and did not enjoy it himself, to which he replied, "Man is not entitled to anything more than he can eat. The rest he has to give away to those who need it."

The following are two specimens of Maarri's verse:

Within Jerusalem was rife between Christ and Mohammad bitter strife;
This with Adhan (call to prayers) and that with blare of bell doth summon man to prayers:
Each seeks to prove his doctrine true; but which is right?
Ah, would I knew.

---

[9] T. J. DeBoer, *The History of Philosophy in Islam,* London, 1903, p. 95.

We love, but foolish is our joyless mirth;
Tears best befit all dwellers upon earth,
Beneath fortunes we break like brittle glass
Which no fresh mould shall ever restore, Alas! [10]
I am able to love my God for the sole reason that He has
Given me freedom to deny Him whenever I desire.

2. The second great Sufi poet named Baba Tahar (d. 1058) was once summoned before the reigning monarch of Iran. When the king told him that whatever his wishes were they would be granted, Baba's answer was, "I have one wish and that is to be left alone by you." The king asked him for advice and his reply was: "Be just and magnanimous to your people because you are here to serve them, not to suck their blood." Baba always protested against the injustice and tyranny so prevalent in his time. In many of his poems he takes God to task.

Oh, God, although for fear I hardly dare to hint it,
All this trouble, springs from Thee.
Had'st Thou no sand or gravel in Thy shoes
   (if you had played everything straight with us)
What may Thee suffer Satan willingly?
Things were well if Thou had'st made the lips and teeth
Of the Khata Turk beauties not so fair to see,
With cries of 'On' thou bid'st the hound pursue;
With cries of 'On' thou bid'st the deer to flee.[11]

3. Abu Said (d. 1049) was the first master of theosophic verse, and the first to popularize the quatrain as a vehicle of Sufi thought and "to make it the focus of all mystic-pantheistic traditions."

---
[10] Brown, *Literary History of Persia*, Vol. 2, p. ....
[11] Brown by mistake attributes this verse to Nasir Khusraw.

Sufism: Humanism Enters Islam

Oh, God 'blame me not if wine I drink,
Or spend my life in striving wine and love to blend,
When sober, I with rivals sit but when beside myself
I am beside my Friend.

To gladden one poor heart of man, is more, be sure,
Than temples a thousand to restore;
And one free man by kindness to his slave is better
Than to free of slaves a score.

My countenance is blanched of Islam's hue;
No honor to a Christian dog is due
So black with shames my visage that of me
Hell is ashamed and Hell's despairing crew.

4. In Jalal ud din Rumi, the Persian mystical genius Sufism found its supreme expression. Viewing the vast landscape of Sufi poetry, he stands out as a great and revered mentor. The influence of his example is felt through all the succeeding generations; and any literate Persian has read and paid homage to the work of this respected "prince of faith."

For Rumi "the word is non-existent," states Reynold A. Nicholson, "and he will not study the unreal; like the compass he circles ever round a point, in which he finds actions and very being depend; he cannot stray from his course any more than a star can leave its orbit. Hence mystical writings are the record of one spiritual experience and are pervaded by a single over-powering emotion. The language of all mystics is the same. How often do Law, Emerson, and Shelley remind us of Rumi? Juan de la Cruz has indited lyrics which it would be easy to mistake for translations from the Rumi Divan."[12]

---

[12]Brown, *Literary History of Persia*, Vol. 2, p. 524, translated by R. A. Nicholson.

Jalal ud Din Rumi's works are poetry of a very high order. His Masnawi is commonly called in Iran the "Quoran in the Persian language." Its author describes his work as "the discovery of the mysteries of reunion and sure knowledge of God."

"It is," he continues, "the supreme science of God, the most resplendent law of God, and the most evident proof of God. It is the paradise of heart abounding in fountains and foliage."

Rumi's literary work is as stupendous in magnitude as it is in sublime content. It consists of the very last collection of mystic poems, perhaps as many as twenty-five hundred, which make up the Divan; the Masnawi, six books of about twenty-five hundred rhyming couplets; and the Rubaiyat which are quatrains.

Rumi also was responsible for founding a Mulavi order which exercised a great power throughout the Middle East. The most characteristic feature of this order is the celebrated whirling dance. This ritual has as its purpose the achieving of an aesthetic experience.

The following lines are a few translations from Rumi's works, illustrating different phases of his poetry:

Lo, for I to myself am unknown, now in God's name what must I do?
I adore not the cross nor crescent; I am not a Zoroastrian nor a Jew.
East nor West, Land nor Sea is my home; I have kin not with Angel nor gnome.
I am wrought not of fire nor of foam; I am shaped not of dust nor of dew.
I was born not in China afar, not in Saqsin and not in Bulgar;
Not in India where five rivers are, nor in Iraq nor Kurdistan I grew.

Not in this world nor that would I dwell; not in Paradise neither in Hell.
Not from Eden or Heaven I fell; not from Adam my lineage I drew.
In a place beyond uttermost place, in a tract with shadow of place.
Soul and body transcending live in the soul of my loved one anew.[13]
From the depth I come to the height,
I was seeking that lovely beloved.
I had friendship with that one in the world of souls,
And I return whither I came.
I was an unthreaded pearl and suddenly I came into the breast of flint
The sun of His mercy warmed me back from the place I appeared in time.
Once I had private converse with the universal reason
And again I wandered demented in the desert.
One hundred thousand years and centuries without number
Even before Adam and Eve I was.
Once I drew breath with the silent ones.
From that silence I have now become a speaker.

Oh, gracious Lord, with whom disguise is vain
Mask not our evil.
Let us see it plain but veil the weakness of our good desire
Lest we lose heart and falter and expire.

Rumi feels that so far as evil exists in us, its source is in our hearts, and it is "selfishness" which separates us from God. In the following story he tells us: "Purge the heart of self, and evil disappears."

---

[13]*Ibid.*

"The lion took the hare with him; they ran together to the well and looked in. The lion saw his own image; from the water appeared the form of a lion with a hare beside him. No sooner did he spy his enemy that he left the hare and sprang into the well. He fell into the pit which he had dug; his inequity recoiled on his own head. Oh, Reader, how many an evil that you see in others is but your own nature reflected in them? In them appears all that you are—your hypocrisy, inequity and insolence. You do not see clearly the evil in yourself, else you would hate yourself with all your soul. Like the lion who sprang at his own image in the water, you are merely hurting yourself; oh, foolish man, when you reach the bottom of the well of your own nature, then you will know that the wickedness is in you." [14]

5. Omar Khayyam (d. 1123) we find a mystic poet, with the outstanding qualities of courage, sincerity, gaiety, gay cynicism, indifference, humor, and a gift for parody. The most remarkable, but most frequently overlooked, feature of Omar's verse is his sheer sense of fun and humor. It is this last quality, and enough of it is shown through the translation of Fitz-Gerald, which keeps the *Rubaiyyat* so popular.

When the local theologian in Omar's home town (Nishapur) accused him of infidelity, Omar sent him the following quatrains:

> Will those brave stupids, two or three,
> Who in their folly are so wise
> They know, what we scarce realize,
> They only know the world, not we.
>
> Thou'st better be an ass as well;
> For they're so sunk in assishness

---

[14]Rumi's Diran, translated by R. A. Nicholson.

That they call every man, unless
He be an ass, an infidel.

Omar's quatrains could be classified under six headings:

1. Complaints against "the Wheel of Fortune," which is responsible for injustice, inequality, suffering, hardship, toils and tribulations of the majority of mankind. He laments man's limited faculties, and condemns the fact that man's fate and future is pre-ordained.

2. Satires on hypocrisy, the impiety of the so-called pious, the ignorance of the secular and spiritual leaders, the stupidity of men of power and wealth, and the perverse attitude of his own generation.

3. Love poems on the sorrows of separation and the joys of reunion with the beloved.

4. Poems in praise of nature.

5. Irreligious and antinomian utterances, charging the sin of the creatures to the failure of the creator, scoffing at Heaven and Hell, singing the praise of wine and pleasure, and preaching the gospel of eat, drink and be merry for tomorrow we will all die.

6. Addressing the Deity in the language of a Sufi, bewailing sins and imploring pardon, craving deliverance from selfishness, greed, intolerance and conceit, and finally pleading for union with "the eternal Truth," or Deity, as conceived by the mystics.[15]

The following are examples of Omar's way of thinking:

> The world's affairs or so they seem,
> Nay, the whole universe complete
> Is a delusion and a cheat,
> A fantasy, an idle dream

---

[15] E. H. Winfield, *The Quatrains of Omar Khayyam,* Yale University Press, New Haven, 1952, p. 133.

O sky wheel! all base men you supply
With baths, mills, and canals that run not dry,
While good men have to pawn their goods for bread:
Pray, who would give a fig for such a sky.[16]

O unenlightened race of human kind,
Ye are nothing, built on empty wind!
Yea, a mere nothing, hovering in the abyss,
A void before you, and a void behind! [17]

We come and go, but for the gain, where is it?
And spin life's woof, but for the ways, where is it?
And many a righteous man has burned to dust
In heaven's blue rendure, but their smoke, where is it?

If Allah wills me not to will aright,
How can I frame my will to will aright?
Each single act I will must needs be wrong,
Since none but He can make me will aright.

Ah, my Beloved, fill the cup that clears
To-day of past regrets and future fears:
To-morrow—why, to-morrow I may be
Myself with yesterday's seven thousand years.[18]

Oh, Pontif, you go more astray than I
Although to drinking I give way:
I drink the blood of grapes, you that of men:
Which of us is the more bloodthirsty, pray?

Though I drink wine I am no libertine,
Nor am I grasping since, save of cups of wine;

---
[16]*Ibid.*, p. 185.
[17]*Ibid.*, p. 185.
[18]Fitzgerald translation.

You ask me why I worship wine? Because
To worship self, like you, I still decline.[19]

We are associated with the wine and women,
You are destined to live in monastery and temple;
We will be sent to Hell, and you are going to reside in
  Heaven.
Tell me what did I have to do with this fate
On the day of eternity? The Divine engraver so inscribed
My destiny upon the tablet of predestination.

Heaven multiplies our sorrows day by day,
And grants no joys it does not take away;
If those unborn could know the ills we bear
What think you, would they rather come or stay?

You know the secret of this life, my dear!
Then why remain a prey to useless fear?
Bend things to suit you since you cannot; yet
Cheer up for the few moments you are here!

Some for the glories of this world; and some
Sigh for the prophet, paradise to come;
Ah, take the cash, and let the credit go,
Nor heed the rumble of a distant drum.[20]

Oh Fortune, you are absorbed in your own tyranny;
You are immured in the temple of injustice or oppression:
You cherish and pamper the wicked and cause agony and
Anguish for the righteous.
My deduction is that either you are an ass, or a dotard.

After my own desire and yearning, sorrow I would
If I had any power over destiny, I would mould it

---

[19]Winfield translation.
[20]Fitzgerald's translation.

Obliterate wholly from the world, and replace it by joy
And gladdness which would raise me to high Heaven.

Drunkards are doomed to Hell, so men declare
Believe it not 'tis but a foolish scare;
Heaven will be empty as this hand of mine,
If none who love good drink find entrance there.

Was e'er man born who never went astray?
Did ever mortal pass a sinless day?
If I do ill and thou requite with ill,
Wherein does our behaviour differ, pray? [21]

Ah Love, could thou and I with Fate conspire
To grasp this sorry scheme of things entire?
Would not we shatter it to bits—and then
Re-mould it nearer to Heart's desire? [22]

Musleh ud Din Sadi (d. 1291), is the sage poet of Persia. He spent thirty years of his life in acquiring knowledge. While at Baghdad he came under the influence of the eminent Sufi Sheikh Shahab ud Din, of whose deep piety and unselfish love of his fellow creatures Sadi speaks in one of his anecdotes in the Bustan.

In 1226 Sadi left his home town of Shiraz and for some thirty years he travelled in the Muslim Empire. When in Syria he was taken prisoner by the crusaders and put to digging ditches in Tripoli. After his return to Shiraz in 1257, he published his poem the "Bustan", and a year later the "Gulistan", a collection of anecdotes with ethical reflections and maxims of worldly wisdom based on ancient traditions of India, Persia, and Arabia.

---

[21] Winfield's translation.
[22] Fitzgerald's translation.

The way in which Sadi used his combination of knowledge, experience, and human understanding gave him his unique character as the "savant of Shiraz." Sadi believed that the truth is simple and can always be made accessible to everyone.

He blamed all the world conflicts on the stupidity of the kings, judges, priests, and princes. He called upon the world to eliminate such uncivilized features of the cruel Mongolian society as intolerance, superstition, tyranny, torture, and hatred. He invited mankind to accept the fundamental principle that:

> The sons of men are members in a body whole related,
> For of a single essence are they each and all created.
> When fortune persecutes with pain one member sorely surely,
> The other members of the body cannot stand securely.
> O you who from another's troubles turn aside your view,
> It is not fitting they bestow the name of "Man" on you! [23]

Sadi believed that man is the measure of all things. He seeks excellence and personal happiness in this world. Whatever helps him to achieve this excellence and happiness is good; whatever hinders him from doing so is bad. Sadi had a very strong social consciousness and he believed that service was the basic standard.

"Religion consists alone in the service of the people; it finds no place in the rosary, or prayer-rug, or tattered garment. Be a king in sovereignty and a devotee in purity of morals. Action, not words is demanded by religion, for words without action are void of substance."

The pain of love is pleasanter than health: the kingdom of poverty is more attractive than that of wealth. Wisdom is re-

---

[23] Sadi Gulistan, translated by Cuylor Young, Princeton University, Princeton, N. J.

garded as the best of created things, but gnostics assert that intoxication (divine ecstasy) is better.

Egoism arises from (the possession of) wealth and position, but renunciation of self is superior to selfhood.

Arise, and let us keep the vow of fidelity to "our trust" (and) atone for our past sins by means of service (to God).
It was an act of folly on our part to humble ourselves before men: henceforth let us practise humility at the door of the Divine Majesty.
The door of the Hospital of penitence is not yet closed, so that we may (still) cure the disease of sin by reparation.
We turned away from God, towards all people, but it was all in vain: it would be better to turn to God from everyone else.
Let us put aside lust and desire and the heart's vain passions: let us bend double the back of devotion with a single heart,
It is a pity that the hearts of men should get into the power of the Devil, how long shall we surrender the home of the Friend to the enemy?
Since (even) the exalted rank of the angels is below our position, why should we yield so humbly to Satan's power?
Base silver (hypocrisy) only brings shame and an evil reputation: arise, O Sage! so that we may seek the elixir (of Truth).
O, Sadi! the rich journey (far afield) for purposes of trade, while we, like beggars, offer prayers at the door of the Beneficent One,
O God! lend us Thine aid, for favours and forgiveness are befitting to Thee, while our deeds are worthy of us.

Each day the wind carries off a rose from the garden, and wounds the poor nightingale's heart.

He who is accustomed to the society of contemporaries ought to exercise forbearance over the tyranny of Time.

For this falcon of Death carries off in his talons, like a pigeon, everyone that is born.

O friend! set not your affections on this present world: undisturbed security is impossible here.

No edifice has been erected on the earth that has not sooner or later undergone a change.

The deceitful world is (really) foul of aspect (though) it impudently displays a (seeming) beauty every morning.

Yesterday the garden and the pleasure ground and tulip bed were full of delight, and a clamour arose in the orchard through the warbling of birds,

While today the mimosa thorns have drawn their swords and you might even say that a rose never bloomed in this garden.

The world is but a bridge that leads to Eternity and people of discernment do not make their home on a bridge.

Science and Human Values in the Future of Man

By Robert Thomas Francoeur

Between the two infinities of the unimaginably immense reaches of space and the inscrutably minute world of atoms, modern man seems to have lost his footing. Insecure, anxious, and even fearful, man faces the future reluctantly. Gone forever, perhaps, is the youthful enthusiasm of the Renaissance man, the joy of conquest that spurred man at the dawn of the Industrial Age.

Two centuries ago mankind embarked on the path of technology and science with all the vigor of a venturesome explorer. Today man hesitates with all the indecision of a voyager who suddenly panics at the possibility that he may have taken the wrong path. Caught up in the inexorable advance of technology modern man often experiences a helplessness akin to that of primitive man confronting the impersonal forces of nature. Adding to the confusion is a remorse that modern man has created the very situation he now fears. Like

Pandora, we wonder whether we should or can close the doors opened by science in this atomic age.

In the Greek and Roman empires and deep into the times of Dante and Aquinas, one day followed another with little if any noticeable change. Generation after generation grew up secure in a world that suffered only superficial changes in one's way of life and thought. In most cases a father could leave to his son a small plot of land or job he had gained during his life, and thus also to his grandson. There were problems, of course. In a society where most men lacked material comfort and any opportunity for education, human existence was often subject to the whim of the feudal lord or invading barbarian. Man's control over his environment was only marginal. Still, a certain sense of security permeated the thinking of pre-Industrial man. Whether it was a pagan in classic Greece and Rome or a serf of medieval Christiandom, the fixed world image common to all ancient cultures gave man the security of hope. Man's time on this earth was seen as a "period of testing," an interval with no real intrinsic values of its own. Perilous as this life might be for some, when it was over, each man would be rewarded or punished by the gods or God for his observance of certain specific laws and rituals. The promise of a future life and reward, in some timeless empyrean, made the injustices and trials of this life bearable and even unimportant.

But the fixed world image of Aristotle, Ptolemy, and Dante has gradually dissolved as man gained more and more control over his environment. Discovery of the New World tore the veil of ignorance from the "Sea of Darkness"; no longer a "Mare Incognita" but a hemisphere filled with dry land, animals, and people. For a while Jerusalem and Rome might remain the center of the earth, but their demise was already assured by wandering explorers. Then the telescopes of Copernicus and Galileo set our earth itself in motion around the sun. Our earth became but a minor planet hurtling around a very minor star lost on the edge of a galaxy itself lost among millions of other galaxies. Even the solid earth beneath man's feet became fluid. The "eternal hills," so we now know, are constantly molded and reshaped by frosty blades and the soft caresses of wind and water. Even the surety of man's creation at 9 A.M. of Saturday, the 30th of October in the year 4004 B.C. has fallen to a blurred ancestry reaching back some two and a half million years to the enigmatic puzzles of *Homo habilis* and the Australopithecines.

Considering the fact that this shift from a fixed world image to that of a dynamic evolutionary and ever-changing picture touches every detail of our life and thinking, it is small wonder that mankind seems to have lost its footing and orientation.

"A ridiculous atom, lost in an inert and immeasurable cosmos, man knows that his feverish activity is but a tiny, ephemeral, local phenomenon, without meaning and without aim. . . . Fending off the fruitless vertigo of the infinite, deaf to the frightening silence of space, man will force himself to become non-cosmic just as the universe is nonhuman; fiercely turned in upon himself, he will dedicate himself humanly and earthly to the achievement of his poor intentions, which he will pretend to treat with the same seriousness he would show if they were directed to eternal goals."[1] Such is the lost pessimism expressed by the noted embryologist Jean Rostand. There is in his view all the cynicism of Cyrano de Bergerac, and a touch of deep irony; a nostalgia for a paradise lost, a fear of the doors we have opened and a longing for the secure world mankind has thoughtlessly left behind as he entered the age of technology and science.

---

[1] Jean Rostand quoted without reference by Paul Chauchard, *Teilhard et L'Optimisme de la Croix,* Paris: Editions Universitaires, 1965, p. 2.

The basic question modern man must ask himself is this: does our modern insecurity, our hesitancy and scepticism over the progress of man and science really have a basis in fact, or is it perhaps the myopic illusion of a mankind just entering its adolescence?

This question can, and perhaps should, be expressed in other terms to plumb its full meaning. Is the advance of science and technology really opposed to the true nature of man and his deepest personal values? Does the modern scientist actually exist in an ivory tower all his own whence he can manipulate the fate of other men? Is the world of science and technology really so inhuman, so impersonal and despotic? Or more fundamentally, does a real dichotomy exist between the two cultures of science and the humanities, the one inhuman and the other human?

In his *Dialogue on the Two Chief World Systems,* Galileo faced this question obliquely in the discussion between Salviati and Sagredo. In a more recent dialogue, *The Abacus and the Rose,* Bronowski is more direct. In highlighting the essential unity of all man's activities, this noted biologist claims it is impossible to separate art and science into two opposing worlds. To emphasize this point, Bronowski has his scientist, Dr. Potts, recite for his humanist friend, Sir Edward, a poem composed by a fellow scientist:

> I, having built a house, reject
> The feud of eye and intellect,
> And find in my experience proof
> One pleasure runs from root to roof,
> One thrust along a streamline arches
> The sudden star, the budding larches.
>
> The force that makes the winter grow
> Its feathered hexagons of snow,

> And drives the bee to match at home
> Their calculated honeycomb,
> Is abacus and rose combined.
> An icy sweetness fills my mind,
>
> A sense that under thing and wing
> Lies, taut yet living, coiled, the spring.[2]

One motivation, that of the pilgrim mind, underlies all human activity. One spring, and one spring alone, gives thrust to the scientist's study of things and the poet's winged ecstacy. Neither the scientist nor the technologist becomes less human, less a person, or less inspired by his attempts to master the earth, for the radically human character of technology was divinely set in Eden. There the Lord God pronounced his blessing on man, "Fill the earth, and make it yours; take command of the fishes in the sea, and all that flies through the air, and all the living things that move on the earth." In a very real way, technology then becomes an essential component in man's sense of the eternal and his need for self-transcendence. The scientist's urge to master the earth is part and parcel of man's divine vocation to become fully human. If technology becomes inhuman it is not because the modern scientist has set himself up as a despot in an ivory tower. Rather it is because mankind as a whole has lost or blurred its orientations towards the personal and human.

All too often art, poetry, philosophy, and religion are honored as the staunch defenders of man's eternal values, his hope in the future, his sense of self-transcendence and his committment to the future—and this in opposition to science

---

[2] J. Bronowski, "The Abacus and the Rose," from *Science and Human Values,* New York: Harper & Row, 1965, p. 119.

and technology. Yet, how often in the history of mankind has a whole artistic tradition disappeared from view? How often has a whole philosophical culture been lost for centuries on end? Is it possible that these steadfast defenders should be so frail and perishable? On the other hand, science and technology have, by their very nature, unceasingly fostered and encouraged man's striving for the future and for perfection in human life. Unlike art, philosophy, and religion, the history of technology exhibits a unique consistency and unity. A technological invention does not remain inert; it spreads among men everywhere until somewhere, sometime, a creative mind improves on it to produce a better tool. Technology has an evolutionary history without missing links.[3] "There are no final achievements in art, upon which all subsequent periods will build such as we find in technology where new inventions can always accumulate on the tremendous base of the development of a hundred thousand years."[4] Whereas catastrophies, floods, and wars may spell death for an artistic or philosophic tradition, much to the detriment of mankind, the development of technology is irreversible. "Philosophers and theologians have paid too little attention to this unique phenomenon of steadiness and progression in technical development and to its inherent tendency for integration, universality, and catholicity as distinct from the dialectical aimlessness and particularity in other fields of the human spirit."[5] (Perhaps this inexorable progress of science as contrasted with the unexpected intangible frailty of art, philosophy, and religion so accentuated today is another cause of modern man's uneasiness.)

---

[3] R. R. Landers, *Man's Place in the Dybosphere,* Englewood Cliffs, N. J.: Prentice Hall, 1966, pp. 21-24.
[4] Andre Varagnac, "Das Altapalaolithicum," in: *Der Mensch der Urzeit,* 600,000 Jahre Menschheitgeschichte, 2:52.
[5] Ernst Benz, *Schopfungsglaube und Endzeiterwartung,* Munich: Nymphenburger, 1965, p. 146.

In recent decades the inherent universality of technology and science has been greatly enhanced by advances in communications that have, as Marshall McLuhan has noted, turned our world into a global-sized village of instantaneous knowledge.[6] At the same time, travel and communications have highlighted the variety and particularity of cultures, the African, oriental, and European-American most of all. Unlike art, the unity and universality of science is immediate, overwhelming and all-embracing. An American must *learn* to appreciate the native art of Africa or the orient, jazz or folk music. In contrast, true science tolerates no barriers of culture, race, creed, geography, or political persuasion.

The universality of science and technology arises, as Teilhard de Chardin noted, from the fact that man is a creature characterized by both hands and a brain; he is *"cérébro-manuel." "Les mains, c'est le machinisme; les machines sont trouvées par l'individu; l'outil est passé de l'individu au groupe. Alors apparaît cette entité de machinisme dont les développements sont tellement solidaires que morale et machine ne peuvent progresser l'une sans l'autre."* [7] The progress of technology and industry is not something accidental or peripheral to either human or cosmic evolution. It constitutes rather an organic outgrowth of man's very nature rooted in the earth. It is the fruit of an evolution become conscious of itself, taking into hand the very control of nature.[8] Modern l'Homme du Mecanisme de l'Evolution," *op. cit.*, p. 322.
technology is, in fact, the only human creation to attain anything approaching a global universality, for art, literature,

---

[6]Marshall McLuhan, *Understanding Media: The Extensions of Man,* New York: McGraw Hill, 1964.

[7]Pierre Teilhard de Chardin, "Place de la Technique dans une biologie général de l'humanité," in: *L'Activation de L'Énergie,* Paris: Éditions du Seuil, 1963, pp. 164-165.

[8]P. Teilhard de Chardin, "Transformation et Prolongement en

philosophies and theologies are still too entangled in the chains of local cultures and traditions.

A second characteristic of modern science and technology adds weight to our argument that this aspect of human life is truly human and does not constitute a true danger to human values. This is the eschatological dimension of science and particularly technology.

In the early centuries of Christianity, the eschatological hopes for the future were expressed in terms of the future Kingdom, complete with all the comforts of a secure and perfect pastoral village.[9] With the dawn of the Industrial Revolution this image changed drastically to fit man's new image of life. Expectation of the coming Kingdom of God was transformed into a technological utopia. In the earliest of these technological utopias, those, for instance, of Thomas More, Thomas Campanella, Samuel Colt, Johann Valentin Andreae, and Francis Bacon, we find a harmonious blending of the traditional expectation of perfection the perfect life or salvation at the end of time with the image of a perfect urban society blessed with all the technological advances predicted by their authors.[10]

Francis Bacon beautifully details this relationship between Christian eschatology and a technological utopia. His ideal state, the New Atlantis, is presented as the true Kingdom of God, not in contrast to the heavenly Jerusalem of the Book of Revelations but rather as a natural development of that image. Spiritual knowledge is seen as the highest degree of scientific knowledge. The Christian virtues are directly related to man's technological domination of nature. Many of the

---

[9] E. Benz, *op. cit.,* pp. 1-34.
[10] Thomas More's *Utopia* (1515), Thomas Campanella's *Civitas Solis* (1602), Johann Valentin Andreae's *Christianopolis* (1619), Francis Bacon's *New Atlantis* (1625), and Samuel Golt's *Nova Solyma* (1648).

technological predictions made by Bacon have lost their utopian character in today's world, only to be replaced by new visions. Even so, the technical aspects of these transitional utopias still arouse enthusiasm among modern technicians. Lewis Mumford, the well-known city planner, for instance, speaks with great admiration of Andreae's *Christianopolis* (1619) as the ideal for a model city.[11]

These early technological utopias, and those of today as well, have only transplanted the early Christian eschatology into an industrial and scientific setting. They are the modern version of biblical eschatology, corresponding to an advanced stage of Christian consciousness of history and time. In this new vision man is no longer a helpless player in God's world; he becomes rather a worker and cooperator in the vast process of creation. Creation, in fact, now becomes an ongoing process in which man, each man, has a unique and essential role to fulfill.[12]

The transition from these early technological utopias to our modern scientific world passes through the social utopias of the nineteenth century. In Saint-Simon's *Nouveau Christianisme* (1825), for instance, the coming industrial state is described and characterized by a strict hierarchical organization of industrial functions. Building on the structure of medieval Christianity, Saint-Simon suggests that the intellectual and moral authority held by the clerics in the Middle Ages will pass to researchers and scholars. The supreme human authority will be a type of social high priest, or industrial pope, and the whole social structure and life will be permeated by the spirit of a reasonable and rational Christianity.[13]

---

[11]Lewis Mumford, *The Story of Utopias,* London: 1923.
[12]Wayne W. Parrish, *Outline of Technocracy,* New York: Farrar Straus, 1933; Caspary, *Die Maschinenutopie,* Berlin, 1927.
[13]Ernst Bloch, *Das Prinzip Hoffnung,* Frankfurt, 1959, pp. 601ff.

Extreme as Saint-Simon's Utopia may seem in the light of medieval Christiandom, it is impossible to deny to our modern technological revolution its eschatological roots. It is this fact among others that accounts for the true humanistic character of modern science. "If you read modern literature about the ideological basis of technology, you will be surprised to find how strongly technical utopians are influenced by ethical and idealistic motives. This is particularly true of literature written by technicians and inventors and not by philosophers and theologians whose sole connection with technical matters is their license to drive an automobile." [14]

This leads us to a consideration of a third important, and likewise often ignored, aspect of modern technology and science. In a singular and unparalleled way the body of scientists exists as a unique society. "The dizzy progress of science, theoretical and practical, has depended on the existence of a fellowship of scientists which is free, uninhibited and communicative. It is not an upstart society; for it derives its traditions, *both of scholarship and of service,* from roots which reach through the Renaissance into the monastic communities and the first universities. The men and women who practice the sciences make a company of scholars which has been more lasting than any modern state, yet which has changed and evolved as no Church has. What power holds them together?

"In an obvious sense, theirs is the power of virtue. By the worldly standards of public life, all scholars in their work are of course oddly virtuous. They do not make wild claims, they do not cheat, they do not try to persuade at any cost, they appeal neither to prejudice nor to authority, they are often frank about their ignorance, their disputes are fairly decorous,

---

[14] E. Benz, *op. cit.,* p. 148.

they do not confuse what is being argued with race, politics, sex or age, they listen patiently to the young and to the old who both know everything." [15]

At this point the reader might object that the virtues mentioned by Bronowski can be applied to scholars in general and are not the sole prerogative of scientists. This is true, but the real values and ethics of science derive not from the virtues of individual scientists nor from the watchful eye of fellow scientists who keep us on the right path. The human values and virtues of science have grown out of the practice of science. Science simply cannot be practiced without certain virtues being respected and practiced by the whole community: dissent which is the surface mark of freedom, originality which is the hall mark of independence of the mind, and a tolerance for both dissent and originality that is based on true respect and honor for others.

"The society of scientists must be a democracy. It can keep alive and grow only by a constant tension between dissent and respect; between independence from the views of others, and tolerance for them. The crux of the ethical problem is to fuse these, the private and the public needs." [16]

In speaking of values, ethics and morals in the scientific world, non-scientists commonly confuse science with a conglomeration and collection of objects. Science is more than an inanimate mechanism, it is part and parcel of human progress. It is not a set of dry facts and data, but a search for them. To confuse the ethic or value neutrality of these facts and data with the practice of science is dangerous if only because it ignores the integral relationship that must exist between men who practice science and the community of

---

[15] J. Bronowski, "The Sense of Human Dignity," in: *Science and Human Values, op. cit.,* pp. 58-59.
[16] *Ibid.,* pp. 62-63.

man as a whole. Within the scientific community individual scientists must constantly make use of one another's work and data. More often than not new scientific theories and experiments are worked out in a collaboration that reaches around the world. But the same collaboration exists to some extent between the scientific community and that of the non-scientists.

The scientist and the scientific world are well aware that they cannot play the benevolent despot who sets up the standards and decides what is best for mankind as a whole. On the other hand, many non-scientists would like to force this role on the scientists or scientific world, feeling that perhaps the scientists are better equipped to decide ethical problems connected with our technological society than our elected public and governmental representatives. *The practice of science is but one aspect of a very complex and pluralistic human society; its ethical implications can only be dealt with by the whole community of man acting together, in freedom, dissent and respect.*

In order for the progress of science and our modern technological society to promote true human values it is absolutely essential that the whole community of man knows what is going on in the laboratories. Unless the channels of communication are wide open between the scientific and general communities of man, any ethical decision reached regarding the application and use of new technological advances will be partial and liable to the myopic distortion of a single privileged subgroup.

In the context of human convergence and an accelerating psycho-social evolution, man will in the future place more and more emphasis on cooperation and communication within an ever-tightening social net. Faced with the growing complexities of modern life, individuals are relying more and more on national and international programs aimed at coping with poverty, ghettos, air and water pollution, care of the aged, and education of the underprivileged. In this process industrialization and organized research teams will play an ever-increasing role. In our industrial society today it is imperative that even the ordinary man in the street have some acquaintance with technology and science if he is to survive in the new world. In subhuman societies the premium is placed on brute strength; in today's global-village the premium rests not on family position or background but on our ability to adapt to an ever-changing and ever more technological culture. In such a society there is much more room for personal variability and non-conformity than ever was in the tightly knit but small rural societies. (The cries of inhumanizing, depersonalizing technology only betray an ignorance of the demands of our modern culture.)

Amid the many fascinating prospects for tomorrow's technological utopia perhaps none is more disturbing than that now being explored in the area of human embryology and reproduction. Certainly, no area of human technology arouses more debate, emotion, and questioning than the experiments now going on in the laboratories of experimental embryologists and developmental geneticists.

Fetology, the science and control of human development in the uterus, has only recently received its proper name. The field is only a few years old but already there are indications that it may raise far more crucial and penetrating questions than any other aspect of our developing technology and control over nature. Already we have evidence of how man may in the very near future have control over the whole reproductive cycle, to the point of being able to determine the sex and other characteristics of a human fetus, modifying these at will and even controlling the genetic make-up of the child.[17]

Today a doctor can check on the development of a human fetus in many ways. He can, for instance, take a sample of the amniotic fluid which bathes the baby in the uterus. By checking cells found floating in that fluid, cells sloughed off by the fetus, the doctor can tell the sex of the child long before birth. In certain cells a dark-staining body just below the surface of the nuclear membrane, the "Bar body," indicates an inactivated X chromosome characteristic of a female. More important the doctor may find in these cells an extra chromosome, an indication that certain enzymes are being manufactured in superabundance by the child's organs. In the near future it may be possible to ascertain just what enzymes are being over-produced, either by computer analysis of chromosome maps or sophisticated biochemical tests. Once the situation is diagnosed, enzymatic medication might eliminate forever a number of defects such as mongoloid idiocy which have already been traced to supernumerary or damaged chromosomes. Following amniocentesis (sampling of the amniotic fluid) and analysis, the doctor may find complications arising from the Rh factor conflict between child and mother. Until recently, a radical solution to this complication involved complete transfusions of the fetal blood beginning as early as the 22nd week of intrauterine life. A much simpler solution is now being developed that involves immunizing the mother with injections of anti-Rh gamma globulin. Once immunized with the foreign anti-bodies, the mother's Rh negative system will no longer respond to the antigenic effect of the fetus'

---

[17] R. T. Francoeur, "The Challenge of Utopian Biology," *Frontline* (Baltimore), 2:1 (Summer 1963), 8-21. Francoeur, R. T., *Perspectives in Evolution,* Baltimore: Helicon, 1965. Jean Rostand, *Can Man Be Modified?* New York: 1959.

Rh positive blood leaking through the placenta. Amniocentesis and intra-uterine photography may in the near future allow doctors to diagnose and perhaps even correct certain sex-linked defects like hemophilia and delayed or ambiguous genital development, muscular dystrophy and the congenital blindness and severe mental deficiency associated with pseudoglioma.

Experiments in semi-delivery have already proven successful with lambs, dogs, and monkeys. In this process a surgeon draws an arm or leg of the fetus through the uterine and abdominal wall of the mother out into the open where he can operate on it to correct malformations such as polydactyly (six instead of five fingers or toes) before they become irreparable.

This newly acquired ability to modify the developing human fetus within the uterus is only a starting point. Dr. Rollin D. Hotchkiss, a molecular biologist at Rockefeller University, told the 1965 meeting of the American Institute of Biological Sciences that within perhaps five years man will be able to reach down to the bedrock of the gene and modify man's very heredity. One approach to this "genetic engineering" could be through nanosurgery, a technique that relies on the electron microscope and laser to perform operations on the molecular level, 10,000 times more delicate than the microsurgery now performed by pediatricians. A second approach might involve modifying the chromosome and genetic content by administering altered DNA to replot the genetic code of the fetus very shortly after conception. Dr. Hotchkiss has already succeeded in modifying the genetic content of bacteria in this way. Conceivably in the not too distant future such gene manipulation could also be applied to eggs or sperm used in ectogenesis or artificial fertilization and testtube babies. Conceivably also virus bearing specific genetic information may be injected into a pregnant woman, ultimately being incorporated into the hereditary pattern of the developing child. To reach this state, of course, will require much more detailed information about genetics and human heredity, an area we have only begun to explore.

While genetic engineering may be far off, other possibilities in bio-engineering are much closer to reality. Scientists have already made important advances in developing a practical "artificial womb." With such a machine it would be possible to induce a very premature delivery in a mother prone to miscarriage. Her child, born perhaps only one or two months after conception, might then be placed in the artificial womb where it could develop without any danger of miscarriage. In time this practice might prove advisable even when no danger of miscarriage exists. A serious problem already under study is involved in this procedure, namely the *psychological* effects it might have on both child and mother.

The fact that man is a mammal walking erect has had serious implications for human embryology long ignored. An erect posture brings with it considerable alterations in our anatomy. Our spinal column is S-shaped rather than arched as in other primates. Our pelvis has become massive enough to support the whole weight of our body and the internal organs have also shifted in the abdominal cavity. These changes may account for the fact that the human female is the only mammal to bear her offspring with intense pain and suffering. Birth is a very important biological milestone and for life to continue it must be as safe and functional as possible. Yet in human childbirth, both mother and child are laid open to infection, disease, and the definite risk of death. (Only a century ago up to twenty percent of the mothers giving birth in hospitals died of infections.) Is it illogical then to believe that as man gains more control over the situation, we will come to view an "artificial" womb pregnancy as part of the ordinary course of affairs?[18]

Other more exotic and sometimes bizarre possibilities are within reach of modern man. Embryologists have known for some time that the head of the human sperm bearing the X chromosome is oval in shape and reacts differently in an electrical field than the round-headed Y-bearing sperm. If an X-bearing sperm fertilizes a human egg (which can only carry an X chromosome), the child will be a girl; if the sperm carries a Y chromosome, a boy will develop. In the future it might be possible to sort out the sperm of a husband and use only those of the desired sex for artificial insemination. (This has been done in Russia for over twenty years with cattle.)

Countless experiments have been performed with success in the area of artificial fertilization and insemination. Healthy and normal children have been born with the use of frozen sperm. Given an effective artificial womb it may be possible in the near future for a child to be conceived and carried full term to "birth" without any biological dependence on the mother. An egg donated by a fertile woman might also be fertilized by sperm from the husband of a sterile woman and the developing zygote implanted in her womb. It is now common practice for animal breeders to stimulate a champion ewe to release hundreds of eggs at a time rather than the one or two normally produced. These eggs can then be fertilized with frozen or fresh sperm from a prize ram, implanted in a pseudo-pregnant doe rabbit and shipped to distant lands. When the rabbit "incubator" arrives, a team of veterinarians removes the developing sheep embryos and transplants them

[18]Theodosius Dobzhansky, *Mankind Evolving*, New Haven: Yale Univ. 1962, pp. 335-36.

into the wombs of ordinary ewes that have been tricked into pseudo-pregnancy by hormone injections. The end result is a flock of prize sheep produced in one breeding season.

Even more exotic is the possibility arising from the classic experiments of Briggs and King in nuclear transplants. Working with frogs and salamanders, these embryologists have removed the nucleus of an egg and then transplanted into this ennucleated egg a nucleus extracted from another older embryo. In many cases a normal, full-grown frog developed. Such nuclear transplants have been successful in varying degrees even when animals of *different species* were used! In a similar vein Dr. Steward of Cornell University has taken single isolated cells from the leaf or stem of a carrot plant and grown a full mature plant. In the future it may be possible for scientists to take a single cell from the skin of some genius or artist, place it in the proper medium, and end up nine months later with a fully developed human baby!

Experiments like these raise some very serious legal and moral questions, but the fact that they are possible and in some cases already a reality makes it imperative that mankind face and discuss them rationally.

As man's science advances, the selection pressures against certain biological handicaps naturally decrease. In ages past few people with diabetes mellitus survived to marry and have children. Today with insulin shots and other drugs, a diabetic can lead an almost normal life. The result has been a sharp increase in the frequency of diabetes. In coming generations men may take insulin tablets and other drugs much as we take aspirin today.

Drugs and medications have their limitations, so that one of the serious problems mankind must come to face soon is the question of genetic control. At the 1966 meeting of the American Association for the Advancement of Science, Theodosius Dobzhansky, one of the world's leading geneticists and a great humanist, called for the adoption of a program in negative eugenics. This proposal would seek to prevent perpetuation of readily identified genetic defects within the human race.

One area where a program in negative eugenics has already been considered is that of sickle cell anemia. This disease affects the Negro race while similar anemiae affect people coming from areas where malaria is common, Italians, Turks, Greeks, Sicilians and Asiatic Indians, and Africans frequently suffer from this disease. Occasionally the gene for normal red blood cells mutates to a condition producing rigid, fragile cells that easily break down and form clots. If oxygen is scarce these cells assume a sickle-shape instead of the normal round form. Under ordinary conditions, natural selection would eliminate this harmful mutation from the population since many of the diseased children would die before reproducing. Yet in malarial infested areas, the gene not only survives, it increases in frequency. The reason is that while sickle-cell anemia is harmful, malarial parasites seem to have little effect on a person with normal blood if he is a "carrier." A carrier has one gene for normal blood cells and the other for sickled cells. Blessed with a "hybrid vigor," carriers survive in a malarial area while people with two genes for normal blood are killed off by the malaria. Thus the defective gene is perpetuated.

Recently Charles F. Whitten, a doctor on the medical faculty of Children's Hospital in Detroit, suggested a program of negative eugenics for the public high schools aimed at abolishing sickle cell and similar anemias or at least drastically reducing them. Basically this program would involve genetic counseling, a type of preventive medicine that could easily be done by the family or school doctor during high school years. The first step would involve detection of carriers whose blood cells sickle when subjected to very low oxygen pressure and people with both genes for the disease whose cells are sickled under ordinary conditions. These children would then be advised of their condition and counseled against marrying someone with a similar condition. If two carriers marry, one-half of their children will be carriers and one-quarter will be seriously anemic. If two persons with the disease marry all of their children will have this defect. Whether such a program can actually be introduced into our high schools is a question yet to be answered, but we might recall that we already have laws requiring pre-marital blood tests, chest X-rays, and urine analysis aimed at preventive medicine.

Prospects for man's future are fascinating and breathtaking. But there is also the unmistakable challenge utopian biology holds not just for the scientist but even more so for the whole human race. The scientist cannot alone decide the morality or value of any of the prospects we mentioned here. This can only be decided by the human community as a whole. To reach any judgment in this area the scientist must first make the non-specialist aware of what the possibilities are. At the same time, those who do not spend their days in research laboratories must make an effort to learn what the future holds for us. As mentioned before, it is becoming more and more evident that survival tomorrow will require an openness to a life-long educational process and a growing awareness and appreciation of the technological world of constant change we live in. Only in this setting of dialogue, world-wide communication, the freedom of dissent and respect, can mankind look to the future with grounded faith that the technological utopia of today and tomorrow will lead to the fulfillment of man and mankind, the highest development of human values.

Our First Museum Men

By Loyd Haberly

PIERRE EUGENE DU SIMITIERE, 1737-1784

Science got off to a bad hindstart in an America which the Mayflower and her subsequent sisters peopled with theologians and Latinated schoolmasters and local political philosophers.

Here and there a mild eccentric who read the new books or explored the ancient forests collected curious rocks and shells and stuffed the rare birds that fell to his fowling piece. These stood for Natural History. Anthropology was an Indian pot or two and a handful of chipped points. Water wheels, spinning wheels, and cider presses were science in action. Experimental science was a kite sent up by a printer to tempt a thunderbolt.

But while Cotton Mather worried about bewitchments, a new breed of Europeans had begun to discover the Wonders of the Visible World. Truths of botany and biology and geology and a fossilized past peeped out of curio cabinets at amateur gentlemen of science to whom they were translative and awesome as religious revelation had been in the days of the Mystics.

Of the last generation of these enthusiastic amateurs was Pierre Eugene Du Simitiere of Geneva. In 1757, when he was twenty years old, he left Europe to devote his life to the Civil and Natural History of the New World.

Precariously supported by the painting of second rate miniatures he searched the West Indies and our Atlantic seaboard for the curiosities of Natural and Civil History. He taught himself taxidermy, and how to pickle fish and press flowers and pin up butterflies. He copied out of books and newspapers. He took rubbings of New England tombstones. He counted the carriages in New York. So when the right time came, he was ready to found the first American Museum.

"A very curious man," as John Adams called him, he was already well known in Philadelphia when the other Founders gathered there to write the ideal form of government for their new nation. Singly and in groups, Du Simitiere enticed them into his Chestnut Street lodgings to look at his cases of minerals and birds and fish and plants and shells. Also he showed them the most complete collection of pamphlets, dispatches, and newspaper comments on the outbreak, progress, and final triumph of the Revolution. Hopefully they would realize that Natural History and Civil History were equally worthy of study by men with a sense of destiny.

No public move was made to support his collection, which by this time had impoverished him. Bowing to bitter necessity Du Simitiere dropped his last proud pretense to gentility and became our original Showman of Science. The *Pennsylvania Journal* for July 12, 1782, carried the announcement that his AMERICAN MUSEUM would be open to the public three days a week at an admission charge of half a dollar.

An American Museum handbill listed these exhibits:

"NATURAL CURIOSITIES"

MARINE PRODUCTION. A very large and Complete Collection of the most rare and beautiful Shells, Sea-eggs, Corals, Sea-plants, Fishes, Tortoises, Crabs, Sea-stars, and other curious animal productions of the sea.

LAND PRODUCTIONS. Rare Birds, and parts of Birds and Nests; a variety of Snakes, Lizards, Bats, Insects, and Worms, the most of them from different parts of the West Indies.

FOSSILS. Ores of various metals, Platina, and other mineral substances, Agates, Moccos, Jaspers, Cornelian, Onyx, Chrysolites, Chrystals, Sparrs, Quartzes, Asbestos, and other curious and rare-figured, pellucid and diversely coloured pebbles.

PETRIFACTIONS, of various kinds of wood, Plants, Fruits, Reptiles, Insects, Bones, Teeth, and of those subjects that once belonged to the sea; such as Shells, Sea-eggs, Sea-worms, Shark's-Teeth, Corals, and Madrepores. As also curious concretions of petrified waters, and stony incrustations over several kinds of bodies, natural and artificial.

Likewise, Fossil substances produced by the eruptions of Volcanos.

BOTANY. A very considerable Collection of the most curious Plants of the West Indies, together with the several productions of those Plants; such as their Wood, Fruits, Pods, Kernels, and Seeds, all in the highest preservation.

ARTIFICIAL CURIOSITIES

Antiquities of the Indians of the West Indies, and of the North American Indians. Ornamental Dresses of the modern Indians of North and South-America, with their Weapons and Utensils. Curious ancient European and East-Indians Weapons; also a valuable curiosity from the Island of Otaheite. Various weapons, Musical Instruments and Utensils of the Negroes, from the coast of Guinea, and the West-Indies. A Collection of curious Paintings in Oil, Crayons, Watercolours, Miniature, Enamel, China, with specimens of the ancient and modern transparent painting on glass, and a curious deception of perspective. Besides a number of miscellaneous Curiosities of various kinds"

It is to be regretted that a nine-by-six-and-a-half-inch handbill lacked space for Du Simitiere's collection of butterflies and coins and medals and paper currencies. It did not mention by name his exotic toucans and flamingos, his bittern and his rare cross-bill. Nor did it even hint at his vast treasury of old books and documents, and all his laborious transcripts from ancient records.

When the Marquis de Chastellux of the French Army and the French Academy saw these rarities he facetiously wrote in his diary: "This small and scanty collection is greatly celebrated in America where it is unrivalled; it was formed by a painter of Geneva called Cimitiere, a name better suited to a physician than a painter."

Hard times and Du Simitiere's utter lack of practical shrewdness condemned his museum to failure. He and his few loyal friends vainly tried to commit the state of Pennsylvania to carry it on after his time. When he died, on November 23, 1787, in his 47th year, his Natural History exhibits were broken up in a sale by auction. Somehow the bulk of his bound copybooks and correspondence has survived in two collections, one now in Philadelphia's Logan Library and the other in the Library of Congress. Engravings of Du Simitiere's miniature portraits of Founding Fathers were pirated abroad as designs for dishes and draperies and enamel doorknobs. Some of these last are to be seen in the Metropolitan Museum. He had the good fortune to be a friend of Thomas Jefferson—whose daughter he could not teach to draw. And he had the misfortune to be a devoted friend of Major Andre, who shared his interest in Natural History and Indians, and who had studied art under Du Simitiere's old master in Geneva. All that ended when the gay and gifted young Major stepped out of an American Army cart into nowhere with a noose around his neck.

The purchaser of some of the American Museum's curios was Charles Willson Peale, who built this nucleus into Peale's Museum which was for decades the best known of Philadelphia institutions.

GARDINER BAKER, ?-1798

After the Revolution there were rumors that the Society of the Cincinnati, open only to former officers, would become an American hereditary nobility of eldest sons. As a counterfoil, the New Yorkers who had shouldered muskets and marched barefoot in the Revolutionary ranks formed a-man-on-the-street fraternity styled The Society of Saint Tammany.

Still flush with patriotic fervor, this society in 1791 set up the Tammany Museum to show America's vast and varied resources. It was put under the management of a democratic shoemaker named Gardiner Baker who was the Society's Wiskinski or doorkeeper. Established in free premises in the Old City Hall—just vacated by the National Congress—the infant museum accepted "articles in the historical and natural lines, highly deserving the notice of the curious."

Tirelessly Gardiner Baker tramped New York and New Jersey in search of additional curios. To learn the anatomy and chemistry a taxidermist needs, he enrolled in the medical classes at Columbia College. Requiring larger quarters, the Tammany Museum was moved to the city-owned vacant Exchange Building where it took over some cheerful rooms above an arcaded ground floor market at the foot of Broad Street on the lower East Side. There, in an illuminated formal opening on the evening of Columbus Day, bustling Gardiner Baker, "a snub-nosed, pock-pitted, bandy-legged, fussy, good-natured little body," showed the following exhibits, listed in the *Daily Advertiser* for November 4th, 1793:

"LIVING ANIMALS"

"A Porcupine from the East Indies, the only one ever seen in America; his quills are very long and formidable, and is considered as a great curiosity.

"The Ant Bear, from the coast of Patagonia, a beautiful animal and the only one ever brought to this country.

"The American Grey Squirrel, in a machine in which he grinds pepper for his living.

"Also, a number of other animals.

"LIVING BIRDS"

"The King of the Vultures, from South America—this remarkable bird is near the size of a turkey; the head and neck are beautiful, and resemble the head of an Indian when painted and decorated in an elegant style.

The American eagle very large and gay.

"Two beautiful Doves, from the Bahama Islands.

"PRESERVED ANIMALS"

"The male and female Ourang Outang, or Man and Woman of the Woods, with a perfect fœtus of the same preserved in spirits, from Africa, all in a fine state of preservation; the greatest natural curiosities in America.

"The American Buffalo in his natural standing position while alive.

"The Brazil Porcupine.

"The Armadillo, from Terra del Fuego.

"Several American Alligators.

"A number of Monkeys of different species.

"The Sloth, from South America, said to be the most slothful of all animals.

"A lamb, with two perfect heads and necks complete, and but one body, from Brunswick, New Jersey.

"The head of a Sea Lion, from Faulklands Islands.

"A tooth of the American non-described Animal, called the Mammoth, supposed to be four or five times as large as the modern Elephant. This tooth is upwards of seven inches through, and four thick: weighs upwards of four pounds, was found in April 1792, at the great Salt Licks, near the river Ohio, in Kentucky.

"Also, a great variety of other animals.

"PRESERVED BIRDS"

"A large and beautiful collection, among which are the following:

"The celebrated English Pheasant, Partridge, Ruff, and two beautiful Owls.

"The Gold Cock, from South America.

"The Toucan, or Bill Bird, from Africa; this is a remarkable bird, its bill being nearly as large as its body.

"The Sea Gannet, a welcome sight to the mariner after a long voyage.

"The Penguin, from the Faulkland Islands.

"SNAKES"

"A large number of snakes, very remarkable, amongst which are,

"The Yellow Snake, from South America, 18 feet in length.

"The American Rattle and Hoop Snakes.

"The Glass Snake, from South Carolina.

"FISHES"

"A large number of fish and parts of fish, amongst which are the sword, saw, and thrasher, which are formidable enemies of the whale.

"The Dolphin, flying fish, porcupine fish, and Seahorse.

"An uncommon large jaw and teeth of a shark, and a knife that was found in him when taken.

"Also, corals of various kinds, and a large number of fossils and minerals.

"A large and beautiful collection of shells, and other marine productions.

"A large collection of beautiful butterflies and other insects from St. Criox, together with a large number of curiosities from the universal garden of nature.

"ARTIFICIAL CURIOSITIES"

"A large collection of Mr. Bowen's celebrated wax figures (in full stature) among which are the American divine, philosopher, the statesman, the hero, the venerable, the artist, the beautiful, and the ugly.

"The celebrated aeronaut Mr. Blanchard.

"Two beautiful Mandarines from the East Indies, dressed in the modern style of that country.

"A transparent monument (in clay) designed and executed

by the celebrated Italian artist in statuary Mr. Ceracchi. This monument is intended to perpetuate the memory of American liberty, by alluding to events which have been completed to our present situation, and to most probable future incidents.

"A transparent monument (placed in the center of the room) sacred to the memory of Christopher Columbus, who discovered to Mankind this Western World, on the 12th October, 1492.

"A number of Indian ornaments and dresses from different countries.

"Sundry African warlike instruments and ornaments.

"Also several Chinese instruments of war and other curiosities.

"An excellent electrical machine and apparatus.

"An air gun made in this city by an American artist. This gun when properly charged, will discharge about twenty bullets successively, without renewing the charge—for several times it will discharge a ball to do execution at a distance of sixty yards.

"And a considerable collection of coins and medals.

"DESCRIPTION OF THE ROOM"

"The room in which the Museum is contained is 60 feet by 30, with an arch of 20 feet high, upon which is elegantly painted a sky blue, and inter-mixed with various kinds of clouds in some of which are naturally represented a thunder storm with flashes of lightning. On the walls are elegantly painted a number of trees from various parts of the world, some of which are as large as their natural growth, among those are the celebrated bread fruit tree from the Pacific Ocean, and the delicious mangoston from the same country,

&c. &c. These trees or plants are surrounded by small ones of the same kind, forming beautiful groves which have a fine effect. Also on the walls of the room are painted a number of beautiful birds, from various parts of the world, among which are the spoon bill, the Bird of Paradise, Flamingo and Ostrich, together with a great variety of foreign animals, among which are the rhinoceros, zebra, hyœna, leopard, hippopotamus, or river horse, camel, cameleopard, lion, &c.

"The above paintings were copied from the best historical prints, and are universally allowed to be excellent imitations, with respect to color and form."

On week-days the Museum was open from 10 to 1, and from 3 to 5. It was open on three evenings a week for candle-light showings. The admission charge was two shillings for adults and one shilling for children.

When warm weather came, Gardiner Baker moved his livestock to a vacant lot on the corner of Pearl Street, fronting the Battery. This "menage," as he called it, was America's first zoo. He now hired and began showing "the largest collection of Birds, Butterflies, Insects and Beatles in America," a collection which a notice in the Weekly Museum for 26 July, 1794, numbered at six hundred stuffed birds and above two thousand insects.

The Tammany Society was now far in arrears on Gardiner Baker's small salary, which he had been augmenting by operating a shooting gallery, and by making buttons from New Jersey mussel shells. To clear off this uncomfortable debt to its own likeable Wiskinski the Society deeded its collections over to Baker on the condition that he continue showing these and that he keep alive the name of the Tammany Museum.

On his own at last, Gardiner Baker engaged in a whole series of dramatic ventures which are recorded in the Columbia University diary of his admiring young friend, Alexander

Anderson, who gave up medicine to become an amazing pioneer of wood-engraving—a craft he learned by conning the prints in Baker's public library of Science and the Arts.

Now the Tammany Museum was making Science understandable and Art acceptable. In its galleries, average Americans peered through telescopes and microscopes, saw electricity sparkle, and heard little metallic automated musicians beat drums and tootle trombones. Waxworks showed the living likeness of great worthies, along with lovely waxen belles dressed in what the well-groomed lady ought to wear. For the Washington worshippers there was the authentic portrait of the General by Joseph Wright, designer of our first coinage and son of Patience Wright who left a New Jersey farm for London where she became the world-famous waxworker and a contradictive converser with George the Third.

Nothing indelicate was ever shown in that Tammany Museum. But outside it, herds of pigs scavenged the garbage-littered street, and Yellow Fever mosquitoes buzzed the cesspools. Gardiner Baker sent a questionnaire to New York's doctors and druggists to find out what they did with Yellow Fever patients. He was planning to write a book on that dread disease, which sent downtown people out to the country camping-place called Greenwich Village when the sickly summer heat began.

Aware of the vast distances of their continent, Americans were already daydreaming of aerial flight. A poet promised the Gods of Olympus to "visit them soon and forsake this dull ball with coat, shoes and stockings, fat carcass and all." As a showman of Science, Gardiner Baker was the man to get Manhattan aloft. Though a family man of small means, he now put everything he had into sponsoring a lighter-than-air flight by Blanchard, a Frenchman who brought his balloon to this country to barnstorm and earn what he could by airmanship. Baker was to go up with Blanchard to look after "the barometer, thermometer, hydrometer, electrometer," etc., and to drop overboard several small animals from his menagerie that would parachute down.

Meanwhile the Baker family moved out to an expensive, rented property on the Broadway Road where workmen were putting up a hangar for the baby-blue balloon, and alongside it an amphitheatre for spectators. At the last moment calamity struck. Alexander Anderson's diary records it as striking on September 14, 1794—a tornado that tore hangar and amphitheatre to splinters and ruined the balloon.

Back in the Museum, Gardiner Baker recovered his enthusiasm for electrical therapy as the new cure-all. But calamity struck again—this time at his own hearth. He found his wife unfaithful, and in manly anger prosecuted a French friend of the family for Criminal Conversation with her. But innate charity changed his mind and he took her and the little Bakers and a cargo of exhibits to Boston where he was invited to make use of the Museum showrooms of his long-time friend Daniel Bowen.

Yellow Fever went North with the tragic family. Stricken by it, Gardiner Baker died in Boston on September 13, 1798.

After his death his widow kept the Tammany Museum alive for a time by selling its curios to visitors. Then she too died, and the remaining exhibits were auctioned off to a grocer, who sold them to the artist Edward Savage, who sold them to John Scudder, a tobacconist with a genius for taxidermy. Scudder built these exhibits up into New York's famous American Museum. Bought by Barnum, it became in his hands the biggest in the world. Never again has a single museum contained an aquarium of whales and sharks, along with a monkey house, a zoo, a snake pit, a Chinese wing, a natural history floor, a waxwork display, a machinery hall, a three thousand seat theatre, a Midway of sideshow freaks and a National Gallery of Portraits!

When *The New York Times* for July 14, 1865, devoted its full first page to the total destruction of the American Museum by fire, its reporter lamented the loss of collections unmatched in any other age or country.

DANIEL BOWEN, 1760-1864

When the American attack on British-held Newport fizzled out in the rain, an elite rifle company calling itself General Sullivan's Bodyguard stood fast at stone wall after stone wall to cover the retreat of the Rhode Island Militia. Eighteen-year-old Daniel Bowen was one of the elite riflemen.

A spirited young man of good connections, he managed then to get daredevil Silas Tallot to take him privateering on the twelve-gun sloop Argo. As recorded in *An Historical Sketch of the Life of Silas Tallbot, Esq.* the Argo rashly ran afoul of an eighty-four gun British warship. In a hairbreadth escape the Argo took some heavy fire. One of her wounded was Daniel Bowen, who carried the honorable scar of that day down into the Presidency of Franklin Pierce.

As the Bowens came from Rehobeth, Massachusetts, known for skilled counterfeiting of British banknotes, it was natural for them to work with type and presses. Abel Bowen would in due time become one of Boston's best-known engravers. But his uncle, Daniel Bowen, first appealed to the literate public with "A Collection of Funny Moral and Entertaining Bon Mots" published by himself in 1787 in New Haven where he belonged to a printing partnership.

His next venture was into waxwork showmanship. A star-spangled hero could enter that calling proudly, for fine art in wax was America's own. From modeling her New Jersey farm neighbors in butter, amazonian Patience Wright had gone on to glory in London, where her waxwork of Lord Chatham is still on view in a case in the Crypt Museum of Westminister Abbey. A German bomb cut off his Lordship's head, which miraculously escaped injury and remains there at his feet, with its waxen brow wrinkled in apparent puzzlement at not being put back where it belongs. Besides her Promethean modeling, Patience Wright was also believed to be the best of our London spies, having access to Buckingham Palace through her daughter's husband, the artist John Hoppner, who was sponsored by George the Third with what gossips hinted was a paternal interest.

After the Revolution, Wright waxworks were shown in New York by another daughter. The prize piece was a waxen George Washington. Its original had been a life mask taken by Patience Wright's son Joseph, who became so agitated by the General's impatience to get the clay off his face that he dropped and broke it. When mended, it served well enough as a modeler's model, though something is said to have been queer about one of its ears.

With profit as well as patriotism in mind, Daniel Bowen bought this whole lot of waxworks for the sake of the striking George Washington. Exhibiting up and down the country, he had such a good reception in Boston that he set about building a museum there that would more than match Peale's Philadelphia Museum or the Tammany Museum in New York. While it was going up on what is now Tremont Street, along Boston Common, Bowen taught himself to model in wax and busied himself with the collection of curiosities. As Robert Edge Pine's romanticized portraits of the Revolution were going a-begging, he bought these. All of them would go up in flames later, except an idealized painting of George Washington which escaped with slight blacking and blistering. It hangs now in Dreyfus Hall of Fairleigh Dickinson University's campus at Madison, New Jersey.

The first of the several showplaces that Daniel Bowen was to set up in Boston stood ready and stocked for an official opening on December 3, 1795. Called the Columbian Museum, it displayed waxworks and Pine paintings, along with a few stuffed birds and an Indian scalp. A blind pianist played in the ninety by twenty-eight foot exhibition hall while the proprietor sold fifty cent tickets at the door and imported prints in the basement. He also sold jewelry, musical instruments, and exotic cheeses, and employed his natural eloquence in auctioneering. He modeled in wax and printed handbills in his house called Bowen's hill out in Brighton where Yellow Fever mosquitoes were few.

As an active apostle of the Washington worship which he was helping to establish as the American religion he packed his museum on Washington's birthday with Bostonians who heard him deliver to the General's wax likeness such eloquent tributes as these: "Immortal Washington—may thy days be cheered with felicities, countless as thy virtues, pure as thy mind, and brilliant as thy exploits. And when in some remote period of time thou art translated to thy native Heaven—may thy mantle be caught by some future son of thy beloved Columbia, who, emulating thy character, shall deserve the eulogy of a grateful country, and the applause of an admiring world."

The New York Historical Society has one of Daniel Bowen's broadsides of this period. Headed by mean looking engravings of a lion, a chained bear and a porcupine, it lists many historical paintings by Pine, Copley and Trumbull, then goes on with the Columbian Museum's Science Section:

"AUTOMATION AND MUSICAL CLOCKS"

"A Canary Bird which sings a variety of elegant songs, Minuets, Marches, &c. and which appears natural as life. A Company of Figures which dance to the music of a harpsichord. Three figures which play the harpsichord and hautboys in concert. A Chimney Sweep and his boy. Three Figures which strike the hours and quarters. A butcher killing an ox. King Herod beheading John the Baptist, and his daughter holding a charger to receive his head."

"NATURAL CURIOSITIES"

"Great Snake 25 feet long, 20 inches around. Diamond Beetle. A large fish, 12 feet in length, caught in Boston Harbor. Rattle snakes. A large collection of Birds in fine preservation; among which are, a Peacock which spreads its plumage 15 feet in circumference, in a large case, Humming Birds and their nests, Butterflies, Insects, &c. &c. too numerous to mention."

In 1801 Bowen went to London to buy curios in a bargain market. Sir Aston Lever's collection which had filled sixteen rooms in Leicester House was being broken up and sold by the man who won it with a two guinea ticket in a lottery. Mr. Perryman, the glass-grinder of St. Martin's Lane, was offering bullfinches trained to pipe God Save the King. Brooke's menagerie had for sale an incomparable Nyctalopess and a serpent that swallowed both cattle and men.

Back home again, Bowen married Mary Ruggles Paine, of a Boston merchant family. In the Columbian *Centinel* for February 10, 1802, his museum advertisement announced "a large and valuable collection of Curiosities, consisting of Birds, Beasts and Insects, in the best preservation . . . many extraordinary Animals, in particular the head of a black leopard, exhibited for several years (with other beasts) in the Tower of London.

A family man now, he was showing a family waxwork scene—"the fair Desdemona, in bed asleep—Othello, her husband, stands at the side of the bed holding a dagger . . ." There was a year of prosperity for the Bowen newlyweds. Then, on January 15, 1803, the Columbian Museum caught fire and burned to the ground in so fierce a conflagration that almost nothing could be saved from it.

In spite of his huge loss, Daniel Bowen got a new Columbian Museum going on Milk Street only four months after the fire. In it he operated a Physognotracetes which cut precise, tiny black silhouettes of sitters, "free of expense." Outdoors he had a new menagerie of animals, snakes, birds, and a pair of ostriches.

But the Milk Street premises were small and, as a subsequent eulogist said in the New York *Evening Post* for February 9, 1807, "Mr. Bowen was desirous to place his establishment on a scale which should give greater scope to his intentions, and afford room for an assemblage of natural and artificial productions, which should justly become an object of interest to the community and reflect some credit on the country where it had been so liberally patronized."

So Daniel Bowen and his museum assistant William Doyle joined in partnership and built a third Columbian Museum on Doyle's property off Tremont Street, next to the burial ground behind the present Kings Chapel, in 1806. The *Independent Chronicle* for December 29th described it and its contents:

"The building is the largest and most convenient for the repository of the productions of nature and art, of any in the United States, the dimensions of which are 107 feet in length, 30 feet wide, and 70 feet in height, to the top of the figure of Minerva upon the Observatory.

"NEW COLLECTION, in addition to the former.

"In the large hall—Among the Wax-figures are several interesting scenes from Shakespeare's plays—a variety of beautiful females of America, England and France, large as life, and handsomely drest; with black scenes of gardens and fountains, which have a fine effect. Also a large collection of Paintings and Prints arranged on a Gallery, which appears both novel and pleasing.

"At the end of the Museum Hall is placed a large interesting painting of the celebrated Fountain at Versailles, with upwards of 100 figures of French fashion and taste; also a beautiful glass fountain.

"A great variety of natural curiosities, consisting of Birds, Beast, Serpents, Fish, Insects, Corals, Shells, Minerals, &c. too numerous to mention in particular.

"The Lower Hall contains a large collection of natural and artificial curiosities, viz.—The Mammoth,. Wax Figures, Statuary, Paintings of Beasts, &c. &c.

"In this room the Phantasmagoria, consisting of a great variety of transparent moving figures, are exhibited at precisely 8 o'clock, every evening, to accommodate those who may wish to view this curious exhibition, which is seen to the greatest advantage when the room is in total darkness."

At this time the Columbian was also projecting a show of all the most modern British textile machinery, secretly reproduced in miniature and spirited out of England to show Yankee craftsman how to compete in an industrially revolutionized world.

Among so many exhibits, the one nearest to Bowen's patriotic heart was surely the eerie Phantasmagoria scene called The Apotheosis of Washington, in which the Museum Hall was "illuminated instantaneously in a very surprising manner."

During the chill small hours of the morning on the sixteenth of January, 1807, the phosphorescent chemicals employed for this illumination ignited spontaneously, setting off an explosion which filled the hall with fire.

The crowd which quickly assembled around the burning building managed to carry a considerable part of its contents out of reach of the flames. Newswriters of those days took for granted the work of experienced volunteer firemen, whose promptness and zeal that night saved enough of the new Museum to justify its reconstruction. But a Columbian *Centinel* reporter who was there recorded the tragic collapse of a section of the Museum's south wall. Toppling far out, the weakened masonry crashed down over the adjoining burial ground, where a crowd of excited teenagers was climbing the tombstones to look over the cemetery wall into the lower windows of the burning building. Some escaped with fractures and a battering but six young lives were crushed out.

Crushed out with them was Daniel Bowen's last chance for a secure livelihood and for an honorable place among Bostonians. Undaunted, he joined with Doyle in an immediate announcement that the Columbian would soon be operating again, with every fire-proofing precaution built into its reconstruction, and every possible vigilance employed to guard it thereafter from "such an accident as has recently occurred."

But sincere assurances such as these came too late to save six dead boys. And they could not clear Bowen from angry condemnations whose justness he admitted in a solemn promise that the restored Columbian would be used "for the sole purpose of a Museum." He knew his fault. The spectacular Phantasmagoria had more business to be in a circus sideshow than in what his own advertising had termed "a spacious and elegant building in one of the most central and pleasant situations in this Metropolis."

Financially ruined by this second fire, Daniel Bowen tried

for a while to go on operating the restored Columbian as a servant of his creditors. Beaten by the Depression of the Embargo days, he had to accept the charity of friends at a Benefit Night advertised for him.

At this muddy ebb of our nation's history and of his own fortunes the broken showman set himself to glorify new heroes of the War of 1812—American ships and American seamen. Joining in partnership with his nephew Abel Bowen —now a skilled engraver—he helped bring out a trumpet-toned patriotic book advertised as *The Naval Temple,* containing an account of all the battles that have taken place between the Navy of the United States and that of Great Britain, during the late war between the two countries; with twenty elegant engravings.

After once more trying to set up a museum—this time called the Phoenix—Daniel Bowen in 1817 admitted failure and moved to Berwick in the Pennsylvania wilds where his wife had inherited some property. With a Revolutionary pension of thirty dollars a month, and such newspaper work as he could get in towns on the Upper Susquehanna he went on quietly for many years.

Then, at the edge of eighty, he resolved to restore his name of long ago—as a man of spirit and resource and abounding public eloquence. Returning to Philadelphia, where his daughter Lucy Anne was now the wife of Isaac T. Jones, a solid merchant, he set about the single-handed composition and printing of a unique book which must still excite the envy of all Chambers of Commerce.

To this illustrated, handsomely produced, multi-colored volume he gave the following comprehensive title:

A History / of / Philadelphia, / with a notice of Villages, / in the vicinity, / embellished with Engravings, designed as a guide to Citizens and Strangers, / Containing a correct account / of the / City Improvements, / up to the year 1839; /

an Historical account / of the late war, / including the names of over two thousand patriotic officers, and / citizen soldiers, who volunteered their services in defence / of this city, / when threatened by an hostile Army. In 1812, -13, & 14 :/ Philadelphia / Printed and Published by Daniel Bowen / 1839"

For some years thereafter, Bowen and his wife Mary enjoyed the Philadelphia hospitality of the Jones household; apparently it was during this period that the artist John Kyle painted the only known portrait of Boston's first Museum man.

Kyle's vigorous oil gives Daniel Bowen a look of bigness and strong solidity. His wavy hair is still thick and dark, his eyes are deep and imaginative under a high forehead and heavy brows. His chin is square with stern determination, but the mobile face and eloquent mouth might well belong to an actor or a spellbinding Senator.

The Philadelphia *Public Ledger* for the first of March, 1856, printed this death notice:

"On the morning of the 29th ult., Daniel Bowen, aged 96 years. (Boston papers please copy.)"

What was the accomplishment of these three unqualified and unsuccessful men who first introduced science to the public of the three largest American cities of their time? They were awakeners. Their museums bred museums everywhere— in small towns, on canal boats, in frontier trading posts. Thus the look of minerals was made known to homesteaders, along with the names and ways of wilderness things. Miniature models of spinning machines and smokeless stoves and suspension bridges showed natural inventors what to turn their minds to. Out of museum cabinets came swarms of those Wonders of the Visible World that are at once the comfort and the terror of today.

Dewey's Humanistic Legacy

By Samuel L. Hart

Unlike particular sciences such as physics, chemistry, and biology which have a definite subject matter, the subject matter of philosophy is more elusive and indeterminate. To a certain extent we could say it is constituting itself in the process of thinking, the result rather than a starting point of intellectual endeavors. These endeavors are manifold. To say that one is more important than another one is to give a biased description of philosophy. Philosophers themselves are prone to one-sided appraisals of their doings. Some preoccupied with linguistic and logical analyses proclaim that such an activity is the sole aim and justification of philosophy; others predominantly interested in social and political issues are inclined to view other problems as unimportant; those who dwell on the salient features of man's consciousness frown upon nonphenomenological approaches which transcend introspective, immediate data.

The various philosophical activities may be reduced to three: scientific, logical, and moral. The scientific function rests with an integration of knowledge gleaned from various studies of nature and man. Such an integration is imperative for a proper understanding of a given issue, and for finding a workable solution. There are no philosophical problems but philosophical approaches to a problem. One of the essential characteristics of these approaches is a well-founded coordination of various aspects, for no human issue is an isolated, discrete phenomenon to be dealt exclusively by a particular science. The philosopher realizes the synoptic nature of a genuine issue such as peace and war, social disintegration and social cohesion, the glaring injustices in reality and the ideal of a pervasive justice. A constructive solution to these persistent problems depends upon a thorough acquaintance with various studies of nature and man, with physics, psychology, sociology, and economics. There is a consensus of opinion that the great issues of any period are eminently philosophical in their nature. By that we mean that their scope transcends any given discipline, that their solution requires an unbiased thinking, a disentanglement of uncontrolled fancy from reasoning guided by reality, a shifting of tradition as to its obsolete and vital elements, and a scrutiny of entrenched ideologies and theories of man which could commend themselves to reason and experience.

Next to the task of integrating knowledge, the logical function is of great importance. Clarity of language and logical vigor have always been desirable traits of philosophical thinking. In the absence of both there is confusion, rambling sophistication, talking past each other instead of talking together. Logic, as its founder Aristotle saw, is an organon, an instrument, not an end in itself. Norms of correct thinking are not self-certifying principles. They are presuppositions of any meaningful discourse.

Great philosophers of the past and the present have never

neglected the third aim of philosophy, the moral task. The quest for the better, a more comprehensive and richer ideal of justice has been the driving force in their thinking, a quest which could not be affected by the rather poor social progress of man, and the many skeptical beliefs rationalizing the evils man metes out to man as innate aggressiveness or opaqueness of human nature to reason.

While the three philosophical aims are interdependent, not all of them have been pursued with the same vigor by most philosophers. The emphasis shifts with the personality of the thinker and the period in which he lives. Dewey puts the greatest emphasis on the social and moral task. Unless we keep this in mind, his peculiar type of pragmatism, called instrumentalism, is bound to be misconceived and misinterpreted. For Dewey, knowledge is not an end in itself. It is a power to be used for change of conditions for the better, an instrument for reconstruction of the individual and society. Ideas and principles are plans of action. It is not their genesis but their consequences they bring about which certify them. Philosophy for him is social in its origin and in its effects. Man does not create in a social vacuum. He thinks in a socially saturated medium. He partakes of this medium and enlarges it. He echoes the needs and desires of many people, and he engenders new needs and aspirations. For Dewey "the distinctive office, problems, and subject matter of philosophy grow out of stresses and strains in the community life in which a given form of philosophy arises, and that, accordingly, its specific problems vary with the changes in human life that are always going on and that at times constitute a crisis and a turning point in human history."[1] Since these stresses change from time to time, from place to place, there

---

[1] J. Dewey, *Reconstruction in Philosophy*, New York: Mentor Books, 1950, p. 8.

are no perennial issues for Dewey. New challanges call for new responses. If a man is too traditionally minded he may re-employ responses which were useful in the past and which have become obsolete in the present. Turning to the past may invoke a false sense of security with a complete retreat from reality. Dewey speaks of social responsibilities of philosophers. They ought to endeavor to free man from all kinds of irrational beliefs, from narrow-mindedness, from bias and prejudice. Like any great predecessor, Dewey extolls the power of reason, the faculty of deliberation, the might of intelligence. But the intelligence he espouses is a scientifically oriented one. Its domain is an objective study of facts with the aim of reconstructing social institutions to answer man's desire for a more pervasive happiness which comes from freeing and promoting capacities "of human individuals without respect to race, sex, class or economic status. And this is all one with saying that the test of their value is the extent to which they educate every individual into the full stature of his possibility. Democracy has many meanings, but if it has a moral meaning, it is found in resolving that the supreme test of all political institutions and industrial arrangements shall be the contribution they make to the all-around growth of every member of society." [2]

Dewey does not write as a skeptic who in advance questions the possibility of a warranted knowledge related to social, moral, and political issues. Neither does he write in the spirit of an ethical neutrality, so highly characteristic of the majority of social scientists who avoid value judgments and value commitments as violating scientific objectivity. Societal phenomena are studied in their genetic sequence, as they arise "from group-inclusion or group-exclusion, and

---

[2] *Ibid.*, p. 147.

manifest themselves in institutions, customs, and mores . . . ethical norms, goals, and values are treated as if they were of the same importance and of the same validity."[3] Dewey does not accept the ethical neutrality, for it fails to do justice to man's aspirations for self-realization. Norms of behavior are socially conditioned, but what certifies them is their role in guiding, and promoting, the kind of experience man cherishes as congenial to his nature. Dewey's instrumentalism cannot be understood unless we view it as stemming from a value commitment that self-fulfillment of men is a desirable goal. The moralist Dewey is motivated by this noble ideal. Fully aware of the innumerable injustices man has in store for man, he is deeply convinced that they are avoidable. As a reformer, Dewey is guided by the vision of a better, more intelligent, and more cooperative humanity. Such an ideal may prevent a thinker from an unbiased investigation of facts. If this happens, the reformer becomes a dreamer who takes refuge in utopian projections incongruent with reality. This does not happen to Dewey. As a tough-minded philosopher, he looks at reality in all its dimensions—good and evil, just and unjust, rational and nonrational. As a pragmatist he knows that a retreat from reality is a retreat from reason. The ideal of a moral humanity predicated on self-realization of each individual, of an ever-expanding experience of common, sharable goods inspired Dewey to acquaint himself with a wealth of empirical data so utterly neglected by a moral skeptic or dogmatic. These data, no matter how diversified they may be, were for Dewey no facts to be collected and categorized, no affairs to acquiesce in, but affairs to be reconstructed, to be remedied. Nobody can accuse Dewey of being blind to the seamy sides of existence. The pre-

---

[3] S. L. Hart, "The Sociology of Values" (in the *Frontiers of Social Science,* London: Macmillan & Co. 1955, p. 177).

cariousness of life is one of the main themes in his writings. But this precariousness did not invoke in him a mood of despair, for he was aware at the same time of the many qualities of existence which nurture and intensify our zest for living.

Dewey's philosophy is extremely varied to fit into one single type or movement. Hence the many isms applied to it: pragmatism, naturalism, humanism, empiricism, instrumentalism, and pluralism. It is difficult to discern any single, dominant idea in his writings, still more difficult to identify what is most original. The emphasis on progress is the legacy of the Age of Reason; his aversion to speculations is in the good tradition of the critical empiricism of Hume; his operationalism as as method of defining true and meaningful concepts goes back to Peirce; his emphasis on intelligence as the unrivaled authority in examining and directing conditions of life is as old as when man began to free himself from reliance on myth and magic. Dewey's uniqueness or greatness does not rest with a single idea. It rests with his unparalleled gift of making us grasp the power of great ideas, their function in concrete, problematic situations. To make them into efficient agents in our quest for an enhanced life, we must take care of the necessary conditions without which ideas cannot operate. Most seminal ideas in Dewey's extensive writings relate to the continuum of man and nature, freedom and control, the individual and society, the real and ideal, mind and matter, facts and values. One cannot help noticing the influence of the Hegelian dialectic based on sublation and not rejection of oppositions.

Being experience-centered Dewey rejects the Kantian claim of effecting a Copernican revolution "by treating the world and our knowledge of it from the standpoint of the knowing subject."⁴ For Dewey neither the mind nor reality is a discrete entity. They are reciprocal factors in a continuous process of transaction. Indefinite interactions are taking place "within a course of nature which is not fixed and complete, but which is capable of direction to new and different results through the mediation of intentional operations. Neither self nor world, neither soul nor nature (in the sense of something isolated and finished in its isolation) is the center, any more than either earth or sun is the absolute center of a single universal and necessary frame of reference. There is a moving whole of interacting parts; a center emerges wherever there is effort to change them in a particular direction."⁵ Experience is not something which occurs to us. It is basically a result of doing—affecting us and our environments.

Contrary to the popular caricature of Dewey, he is not an iconoclast or rebel who delights in discarding or disparaging tradition. For him tradition and innovation are not opposing but complementary forces. Continuity of ideas and not discontinuity is the lever for any progress in all fields—in science, philosophy, art, and religion. Intellectually cumulative experiences of the past enrich the present. Dewey wants us to use tradition as a storehouse for ideas able to fructify new ideas. Such a usage depends upon a mature, courageous intelligence unperturbed by many social pressures which disguise entrenched interests of a group as a legacy of the past not to be criticized or changed. Dewey himself would be the last to deny how much he owes to his many predecessors—to Plato, Aristotle, Bacon, Hume, Kant, J. S. Mill, Darwin, and Hegel. Their ideas were seminal to him as his own ideas have become seminal to us.

---

⁴J. Dewey, *The Quest for Certainty,* New York: Capricorn Books, 1929, p. 287.
⁵*Ibid.,* p. 290ff.

The individual and society comprise a continuum. Man cannot find self-realization unless he is immersed in a larger group. Living together engenders the most gratifying needs and aspirations. Even bare survival is predicated on cooperative efforts of many. Society is not a hypostatized entity, having its own structure and goals apart from the members who constitute it. For Dewey morality is private and public. Like Aristotle, he tells us that moral traits require constant employment and reemployment in all institutional and public life. Without opportunities to act they become extinct. Empirical findings reveal that human nature is more flexible than social customs which as a rule promote the interests of one group at the expense of another one. "The greatest obstacle to a harmonious social life, to a life of abundance and fulfillment, is not the hidden beast in man, but rather the inertia of social customs and institutions which disregard blatant facts related to man's needs and mainsprings of action." [6] "The unalterability of human nature is a myth invented and adhered to by people who hide their selfish interests behind the sanctity of an outworn tradition. Slavery, caste system, feudal serfdom, discrimination, inequality of races, and wars are not grounded in a primordial, pugnacious human nature. They are rooted in customs and institutions which employ innate capacities to promote and foster social discord." [7]

Freedom and control or discipline are for Dewey no antithetical entities. They are interdependent, reciprocal factors in man's behavior. Dewey is against one kind of discipline, an authoritarian one, which instead of guiding growth cripples it. He is for a rational control of potentialities, for an organization of man's desires and energies with the end in view of

---

[6] S. L. Hart, *Ethics, the Quest for the Good Life,* New York: Philosophical Library, 1963, p. 15.
[7] *Ibid.,* p. 15.

greater maturity, greater satisfaction. As a pragmatist, Dewey shies away from speculations centering on a metaphysical freedom of will. It is not as he states, such a freedom men cherish or fight for, but a concrete liberty, which includes "efficiency in action, ability to carry out plans, the absence of cramping and thwarting obstacles .... capacity to vary plans, to change the course of action to experience novelties . . . and the power of desire and choice to be factors in events." [8] In all these forms of freedom, intelligence acting upon a thorough knowledge of conditions, of antecedent and consequent factors is the highest asset. The function of such informed intelligence is to guide our passions and desires, so that we can not only preserve but expand freedom. A mere licentious behavior deprives us of deliberation and foresight, the most potent agents against acting on a mere impulse, the main source of evils we commit against our fellowman.

Just as freedom and control are interrelated, so too the real and ideal. Dewey is against visionary projections which do not arise from a scrutiny of facts. He is for ideals which are suggested by facts themselves. Those ideals are not ready made waiting for our grasp. They are visions calling for implementation. "Man is a transcending being. Never content with given states of affairs, he conceives ideas of better, more propitious forms of life. Out of such cravings culture developed. Life is activity, and activity, as Whitehead says, is emergence into the future. To be concerned with the future means to dwell on possibilities and potentialities." [9] Having ideals is a feature of man's existence. "Although imagination is often fantastic, it is also an organ of nature; for it is the appropriate phase of indeterminate events moving toward

---

[8] J. Dewey, *Human Nature and Conduct*, p. 303.
[9] S. L. Hart, *Treatise on Values,* New York: Philosophical Library, 1949, p. 51.

eventualities that are now but possibilities. A purely stable world permits of no illusions, but neither is it clothed with ideals." [10] For Dewey the ideal world is not "a haven in which man finds rest from the storms of life" . . . but a world of "imagined possibilities that stimulate men to new efforts and realizations." [11] The better for him is an instrumentality of action, and not an entity to contemplate in reverie. Such ideals are objectives of planned, intelligent actions. Their workability depends upon their concatenation with reality. Dewey sees a dire need for such visional projections, for an intelligence divorced from aspirations succumbs easily to paralyzing, fatalistic beliefs.

For the moralist Dewey, knowledge of facts does not entail a passive acceptance of these facts. Morality is concerned with desirable usages of facts. It is a function of intelligence when to conform to facts and when to change them. When facts enter "into a medium of human activities, of desires and aversions, habits and instincts," [12] they become value phenomena. Only sentient beings experience values and disvalues—objects, events, qualities which we call good and bad, beautiful and ugly, worthy or unworthy of being preserved and augmented or discarded. Preferential behavior is a feature of man's existence. "Without a cultivated sense of values and disvalues man could not survive, still less enhance his life. Survival on a mere physiological plane is predicated upon a proper grasp of objects which answer to our basic needs. Our enhanced life depends upon tested appraisals of objects which minister to our higher psychological and social drives, such as affection, freedom, security, belonging, self-esteem and

---

[10] J. Dewey, *Experience and Nature*, Chicago: Open Court Publ. 1925, p. 62.
[11] J. Dewey, *Reconstruction in Philosophy*, p. 103.
[12] J. Dewey, *Human Nature and Conduct*, p. 299.

regard for others. Our sentient nature registers events as pleasing and unpleasing, agreeable or disagreeable, gratifying or frustrating. Our cognitive nature looks for objective constituents of values and disvalues. Of the innumerable qualities of objects, we are primarily interested in the actual and potential efficacies related to our needs, basic and derivative." [13]

For Dewey the most urgent problem is to narrow down the cultural lag, the discrepancy between our scientific beliefs about nature, and our rather vague, speculative beliefs about values. As we contemplate the almost miraculous achievements in nuclear physics, man's moral and political issues appear insignificant. Yet while man's knowledge of nature surges ahead he is still unable to find solutions to social evils. Man rationalizes the cultural lag. He ascribes it to the impossibility of a reliable knowledge of man on the basis that his behavior reveals a pattern of multiple causations; he attributes the lag to a discrepancy between powerful passions on one hand, and a feeble reason on the other hand.

That our moral, political, and social ideas trail behind our scientific ideas is a brute fact we cannot deny. This fact need not be if we have intellectual courage to critically examine the many forces which preserve and reinforce the continuous cultural lag. This is the message Dewey has for us. He is not only pleading for a scientific approach to man's vexing problem of values and valuations, but he also clarifies for us the necessary steps we must take to implement this goal. We can fully agree with him when he says that "when theories of values do not afford intellectual assistance in framing ideas and beliefs about values that are adequate to direct action, the gap must be filled by other means. If intelligent method is

---

[13] S. L. Hart, *Ethics, the Quest for the Good Life*, p. 62.

lacking, prejudice, the pressure of immediate circumstance, self-interest and class-interest, traditional customs, institutions of accidental historic origin, are not lacking, and they tend to take the place of intelligence." [14]

Dewey is not concerned with the status of values, although his naturalism would reject the two common, extreme views: subjectivism and absolutism. Values are for him neither mere mental states nor Platonic immutable nontemporal entities. He puts the primary stress on valuation. In ordinary speech valuation stands for both prizing and appraising. In prizing "emphasis falls upon something having definite personal reference, which, like all activities of distinct personal reference, has an aspectual quality called emotional. Valuation as appraisal, however, is primarily concerned with a relational property of objects so that an intellectual aspect is uppermost of the same general sort that is found in 'estimate' as distinguished from the person-emotional word 'esteem.'" [15]

If all our desires and interests could always be fulfilled, there would be no need for appraisal. In this case objects we prize would be proper values. Since our desires and enjoyments are often frustrated, the intervention of reason is necessary to evaluate desires and enjoyments. "Enjoyments that issue from conduct directed by insight into relations have a meaning and a validity due to the way in which they are experienced. Such enjoyments are not repented of; they generate no after-taste of bitterness. Even in the midst of direct enjoyment, there is a sense of validity, of authorization, which intensifies the enjoyment. There is solicitude for perpetuation of the object having value which is radically different from mere anxiety to perpetuate the feeling of enjoy-

---

[14] J. Dewey, *The Quest for Certainty*, p. 265.
[15] J. Dewey, *Theory of Valuation*, p. 5.

ment."[16] The desirable and enjoyable are desires and enjoyments which have a solid foundation in nature, and as such make objective, predictive claims. What we desire is a matter of fact but the desirable is a matter of value. Valuational standards are for Dewey not intruders from outside. They are results of learning from experience. "The 'desirable,' or the object which should be desired (valued), does not descend out of the a priori blue nor descend as an imperative from a moral Mount Sinai. It presents itself because past experience has shown that hasty action upon uncriticized desire leads to defeat and possibly to catastrophe. The "desirable" as distinct from the "desired" does not then designate something at large or a priori. It points to the difference between the operation and consequences of unexamined impulses and those of desires and interests that are the product of investigation of conditions and consequences."[17]

Norms of appraisal arise from experiences and are tested by experiences. They are not self-certifying principles independent of, and superior to, actualities. Like scientific hypotheses, they are being confirmed by the consequences they entail.

Dewey's lasting contributions relate to solid foundations of a scientific humanism. The term humanism came into usage in the Renaissance. Here it refers to a rediscovery and intense study of the Greek and Roman classics. Today humanism has many meanings. To clarify the various meanings we have to contrast humanism with supernaturalism. All types of humanism center on the notion of an immanent fate; supernaturalism is predicated on a transcendent fate. Immanent fate implies that whatever man's aim of a gratifying exist-

---

[16] J. Dewey, *The Quest for Certainty*, p. 267.
[17] J. Dewey, *Theory of Valuation*, p. 32.

ence may be, he can achieve it by his own endeavors. A transcendent fate implies that in the final analysis man's destiny is beyond his control. For humanism and supernaturalism man's intrinsic end is self-realization. Humanism looks for self-fulfillment in this worldly existence; supernaturalism projects such a state in an otherworldly existence. In humanism religious values enhance man's morality; in supernaturalism ethical values are subservient to religious values. The ethics of humanism is naturalistic in its base, and idealistic in its aspirations. In supernaturalism it is spiritual in both. In naturalism human nature is to be developed in all its dimensions; in supernaturalism it is to be curtailed. In humanism ideals are not intruders from outside; in supernaturalism they are transcendent principles to curb rather than to liberate and sublate human nature.

Reflecting upon the creed of humanism, we find that all its major ideas and principles are recurrent themes in the history of philosophy. It is, therefore, not a particular idea for which Dewey can claim originality. The uniqueness of Dewey's philosophy rests with his endeavors to give to the humanistic creed a scientific foundation, and a scientific respectability.

In the light of the rather bleak human history, with continuous strife on the national and international scene, Dewey's optimistic faith in humanity is inspiring. His unwavering faith stems from his belief in science on one hand, and the realization that man's intelligence has not been equally applied to his social, political, and moral problems. In the age of a threatening catastrophe of an atomic war, we cannot afford to attack his legacy for reasons of some subtle logical or semantic flaws. It calls for a constructive appraisal. In that spirit I have written my essay.

The Two Cultures
and the Abyss in Between

By Emil Lengyel

Observing salient, contemporary problems from the heights of a modern Zarathustra, the British scientist and novelist C. P. Snow espies two divergent "cultures": those of the natural scientist and of the literary intellectual. The former deals with measurable natural phenomena, the latter with intangibles of the human mind. In spite of this divergence, they seek to achieve parallel results, expressed in a single word—*cultus*, which, paradoxically, means both to "cultivate" and to "worship." The common origin of the same word illustrates the two cultures, the one which may be diverted to till the devil's fields, while the other one bends to God's will. The small book setting forth the ideas of Snow on these subjects entitled *The Two Cultures*, containing his "Rede Lecture" at Cambridge some years ago, is on the way to becoming a classic. In that respect it may share the fate of a series of lectures delivered by Thomas Carlyle, *On Heroes, Hero-Worship, and the Heroic in History.*

C. P. Snow himself dwells in two cultures, and therefore is the right person to point to the antinomy and thus ring the tocsin. The scientist follows one set of guidelines embodied in the curiosity nature elicits in him and is so wrapped up in his attempts to crack nature's hidden code signals that he may lose sight of the relationship between his findings and their value to humanity. The literary intellectual, on the other hand, the humanist, social scientist, is mainly concerned with nature's mysteries within himself and the social organizations. He has little scholarly interest in the physical universe.

The vast difference between the rates of speed between the two cultures is of course axiomatic. We have long called it the "cultural lag." In our own days the placid term "lag" is no longer sufficient. The humanities—social sciences, anchored in traditional terminologies, the language which refuses to absorb sudden changes, institutions which are too ponderous to be pushed into new orbits—continue on their plodding ways. We understand Shakespeare and he would understand our tongue, too, deformed thought it is compared with his own. The sciences, on the other hand, have experienced an outburst of energy which may be expressed, perhaps, in the most complex computer language, but not in any dictionary words. Even "The Admirable Doctor," Roger Bacon, would be out of his depth in a dialogue with an average high-school student of today.

Nature guards its secrets with jealous care. One of the greatest secrets was concealed in the atom, so infinitely small that not its size but only its emanations could be measured. Not long ago scientists of genius broke the code and found that the infinitesimally small atom, a micro-organism, was in reality a macro-organism, containing replicas of the entire cosmos, the universe. More than that, the scientists learned that the endlessly complex organisms could be made to perform immense tasks set for them by man—tasks of construction of indescribable magnitude or of destruction capable of blowing up the earth.

That was only the beginning. The sequel promises—or threatens—even vaster scientific breakthroughs, an infinity of choices, branching off into more selections of infinite variety.

So the cultural lag has found the scientist at an immense distance from the humanist and the social scientist. Yet, the scientist, capable of penetrating into secrets kept in the womb of time for billions of years and found for the first time, was not capable of solving some of the simple social problems—what to do with these discoveries? His mind, in most cases, was equipped to deal with natural phenomena, not with social institutions.

There was then the fork of the road. Angels stood guard at one of the forks "Selig der Liebende . . ." as the choir of celestial creatures sing in Goethe's *Faust:* "Blessed those who love . . ." and who have stood the test. And at the other fork, Mephistopheles: *"Ich bin der Geist, der stets verneint. . ."*—I am the spirit that always says "nay."

One road may lead to the gates of Utopia. Our scientists have achieved far more than the medieval alchemists and dreamers ever fancied. They dreamt only of transmuting dross into pure gold. Our scientists have found the means by which the world's vast deserts can be made to bloom—in the Biblical word—like a rose. They found the means which if properly applied could feed the hungry people of our globe, make literate all the illiterates, and heal the sick.

Meanwhile, with the aid of the new insights of our scientists it is possible—at least in our part of the world—to control nature in a way we need not fear the holocaust of mass epidemics. Our problem is no longer that we should not have enough food, but that we have too much. The most prominent edifices in our country are the schools. Our colleges are filled with sophisticated teaching aids of all sorts. In a remarkably short time, life has become not only easier to bear but also more colorful and if we have dull moments they are our faults.

At the same time there is a great threat. It revealed its real nature over two cities. We know that the force which incinerated thousands of people was puny in comparison with the new punch it has acquired since then. At the end of this road is the global charnel house.

The question: Is there what India's people call the *darshan*—a celestial emanation, a blessing on man's handiwork in unleashing nature's hitherto secret force? And so C. P. Snow asks what are we to do? Can the two cultures meet? Will they teach one another, or will they lead their separate existences resulting in the great immolation?

The scientists say that the humanists are wrapped up in the contemplation of beautiful words they string together in verse and prose. They also admire their handiwork in finding ingenious explanations of the operations of the human mind— the philosophers—each of them a different explanation. They love the incomprehensible jargon of sociology containing a plethora of words and a dearth of thought, showing how easy it is to make simple social phenomena appear complicated. Failing to understand contemporary physical science, these social scientists exert little influence over the thinking and behavior of the average man. They provide no clue, for instance, to the social application of the significant technological developments of relativistic physics.

Many of the natural scientists themselves have not done any better. One of the pioneering nuclear physicists, Niels

Bohr, for instance, made things easier for his ilk and more difficult for others by holding that human relations, too, are subject to the laws governing natural scientific phenomena. He looked upon concepts of justice and love in human affairs as complementary notions, phenomena also observable in particles of the atom.

One of the cultures—science—dealing with physical phenomena affects human life, obviously, more closely than the other one—humanities. Muted voices are sometimes heard from the science camp about great decisions affecting all mankind. Such a voice has reached the layman's world in a notable book relating the development of the atom and hydrogen bombs, *Brighter Than a Thousand Suns,* by Robert Jungkh. This is the story told in a chapter of the book:

The Bomb may have never been developed to haunt the world if there had been communication among scientists on both sides of the fighting front during World War II. According to Jungkh, the German nuclear physicists in the Third Reich were anti-Hitler almost to a man and were loath to place the "ultimate weapon" in the hands of the madman obsessed with "ultimate solutions." The scientists in the Reich were dragging their feet. Luckily, the top Nazis lacked the imagination to see the bomb in the proper light. Many American physicists had been associates and friends of the German scientists. Because war severed communications between the belligerents, the American scientists were not aware of the acts of sabotage of their German confréres. On the contrary, they assumed that Germany, ahead in the game in the past, maintained her initial momentum. "If only these German scientists had made a determined effort," Jungkh writes, "to let their American and English colleagues know of their decision! Then, Western scientists could have followed the example of their German colleagues, and the American

A-Bomb project would have bogged down, as the German one did."

We may assume that in that case the Soviet project would have bogged down, too.

The signals were not given in Germany, because that was impossible on account of the war. Apart from that, could it be expected that scientists on the threshold of a major breakthrough—for good or bad—would abstain from pursuing experiments leading to a new light, even if it was to sear mankind to cinders?

It would be Utopian to expect the scientists to provide the answer. Let us therefore look at a broader spectrum, offering a more disseminated solution.

This very question was broached, laterally, many years before the Two Cultures concept of C. P. Snow had gained currency, by Albert Einstein in an interview he gave to the author of this essay (published partly in the Magazine section of *The New York Times*).

The time was the summer of 1930, and Einstein was a resident of Germany. He had his pleasant villa in a suburb of Berlin. Visiting him in his house, it was interesting to observe the lack of "tools" of the great scientist. His working alcove, adjacent to a spacious living room, was barely furnished: a desk, a chair, a couch, on which, he said, he liked to take naps on hot summer afternoons. And a few etchings on the walls—his heroes, Hertz and Faraday.

On the desk, sheets of paper covered with what seemed to be mathematical formulae, and the stub of a pencil. That was the only "instrument" in sight. There was a slender shelf with books from American publishers, hoping for endorsements.

"What instruments do you use, Professor Einstein?"

Looking at the interviewer with his dilated eyes—the eyes

of a child, some people said, the eyes of a genius—he tapped his head:

"My only instrument. There is no need for more."

Then the questions and answers. Professor Einstein spoke of the "two cultures," which he called "art" and "science."

His head, he said, was basically that of an artist. He had an idea, coming to him in a flash sometimes—when shaving, early in the morning, waking during the night, boating on Zempliner See, the small lake at the foot of the hill on which his house was situated.

"Just an idea," he repeated, "not based on facts, as yet. An inspiration, if you like, an intuition. An artistic concept. A scientific concept, too, since the two are interlinked. A scientist must be an artist, if he is creative. This should be the other way around too, I presume. Then my real work begins. This may sound absurd, a roof without supporting walls. Then the foundation, the walls, if the roof is right.'"

"So you start working like an artist. What then?"

"Then the lake, if the sky is blue, as it is today. I get into my boat, just in a pair of trousers, not even a shirt. In the boat I have my 'tools,' a pad of paper and the pencil stub."

Frau Einstein now joined the conversation.

"Yes," she said smiling, "my husband is a real artist. He actually runs up fever when in the process of creation. That is not so good for our little *ménage*. Sometimes, I invite guests, close friends. Albert is in the house, but ages away from us. Still, he is gentle and descends the staircase to greet the friends. There he sits, lost to the world, his head filled with what he considers the most beautiful work of art—mathematical formulae."

"Artists are the people who penetrate into the secrets of nature whether they write poetry, novels, or papers on the unified field theory," Professor Einstein added.

Here then was a man, a great man, who combined the two cultures in his own person—he called them art and science. And he was hoping that this combination was advancing the welfare of man. Without such hope his interest in his work would be less ardent. There was a third element in his work—the saving grace, the connecting tissue.

"I have been seeking, as you may know," Einstein added, "a simple formula for a unified field theory in physics. It cannot be right if it is not simple. It would explain light, magnetism, radiation in one mathematical picture. Perhaps I will find it, this unified field theory in physics. But I have already found another unified field theory," he added with an apologetic smile, "in human relations. You have two components of it—art and science. There is also a third one. Luckily in human relations we can engage in speculative adventures. It is not so easy to catch our mistakes."

"And what is that third element?"

"You see, I am a religious man. The anti-Semites of this country keep on publicizing the fact that I am a Jew. I am not a synagogue-going Jew, however. Yet I consider myself a pious man. I follow the particular kind of religion my fellow Jew, Baruch Spinoza, sought to explain. With him I believe that God is not only in heaven. He is everywhere, and the entire universe is filled with His presence. Call Him the World Order, if you like. I call him the Incarnation of the Ethical Principle. At this point we have found the third factor in my humanist unified field theory—ethics—next to art and science. Any activity—the work of the artist and scientist—becomes worth while if it aims at the realization of an ethical principle, a new insight, pure science at present, a help to people in the future. Spinoza's God has hidden secrets all over His Universe. Some of the secrets harm man, others help him. Life is good and bad. The bad is there to be combated, to serve as challenges. Our universe is kept in balance through the interplay of the equilibrating forces—harmful and useful. I try to seek out the forces that may eventually help my fellow man."

Nuclear physics was in its infancy in those days and Einstein did not have it in mind. He was thinking of other things.

"In the late world conflict,"—he was referring to World War I—"many colleagues conducted bacteriological experiments. Others engaged in the study of toxic gases. I was not asked to work in these fields. Had I been asked, I would not have accepted the invitation. That type of work was contrary to that third factor I mentioned—the Ethical Principle.

"You may think I am naive. As I take my writing pad in the morning, posing my pencil, I lift my eyes heavenward. To that extent I am a traditionalist. An elderly Jew, I might say. Ask these young nationalists who draw swastikas on my house."

Eventually Einstein left Germany, moved to the United States; the Nazis assumed power in the Reich. About a decade after this interview took place, Einstein wrote his historic letter to President Franklin D. Roosevelt, a letter that was to become the birth certificate of the atomic age. Where was the Ethical Principle?

Sometimes the Ethical Principle demands that a scourge be eliminated. The virus and the bacillus that kill people would have no right to appeal to Ethical Principles. Einstein shared the fears of his physicist colleagues, many of whom had come from the Reich, that the Germans had been working on the "ultimate solution." They thought that such a weapon in Hitler's hands would lead to the *Goetterdaemmerung* of our culture.

The Nazi maniac did not have the Bomb, and his Reich

collapsed. Now Einstein and some of his colleagues faced the Ethical Principle, as they saw it, in a new guise. They believed that Japan was already on her knees and that no demonstration of the apocalyptic power of the nuclear force was needed. Several scientists formed a "Committee on Social and Political Implications" which advised against the bomb being dropped on Japan and recommended a harmless demonstration of its power, far from human habitations. Later, some scientists joined the "Society for the Social Responsibility of the Scientists," in which they gave prominent place to Einstein's Ethtical Principle. Leo Szilárd, who had launched the "nuclear revolution for defense" now advocated a "science lobby," supported by humanists and humanitarians, to divert the energy to peaceful uses.

The scientists today keep on feeling their responsibility in the presence of the power they unleashed and of new ones they may unleash in the future. They have expressed their concern in the *Bulletin of Atomic Scientists,* founded in the "year of the bomb," in 1945. And many of them have filled shelves with books they have written on the subject of science and morality.

One of these is Nobel Prize winning Albert Szent-Györgyi, whose specialty is submolecular biology. He, too, shares the concern of the scientists for their role in the nuclear world and expresses his views strongly in a collection of essays characteristically entitled *Science, Ethics and Politics.*

"Human relations are decided by morals, and our present troubles may be due to the fact that scientific and technological development has outstripped moral development. Man has had no time to adjust his moral code to the new conditions created by science, and science cannot help, simply because it has no moral content. But is this really so? Has science really nothing to do with morals? It depends on how we look at it and what we think science really is. Religion, if cleansed of church imperialism, is, in essence, identical with science; it is a search for truth and understanding. It differs from science only in its methods and approach. But why give preference to artistic thought and deny science a moral content because it works with more reliable tools? And what is science? And what are morals? Morals are the simple rules which make living together possible. They are the foundation on which human societies are built. They have no intrinsic content, vary according to conditions, and have a meaning only in relation to society."

Carrying this thought of the dichotomy of "unbridled" science and reticent ethics Eugene Rabinowitch, a nuclear scientist himself, writes in his book *The Dawn of a New Age* a collection of essays:

"I believe that the basic cause of the predicament into which the discovery of nuclear energy has brought the world lies not in the inadequate ethical standards of the scientists or in the difficulties of communication between them. Rather it lies in the low ethical standards of national governments and the difficulties of communication between them; and this, in turn, is the consequence of the stubborn survival of an obsolete organization of mankind, its division into separate sectors which require—and receive—full and exclusive loyalty from their members . . ."

The conflict between loyalty to his scientific ethics, Rabinowitch continues in substance, and loyalty to his nation weighs as heavily on the conscience of the atomic physicist as it does on that of a farmer, worker, lawyer called into military service. It is not because of indifference to human suffering or high monetary rewards, that scientists do not walk out en masse from the weapons laboratories. It is because they, like others, are trapped in an antiquated structure of mankind. They are parts of a humanity divided into fractions, each enforcing a moral code within it but acknowledging no such code for its relations with other countries. "Scientists cannot hope to change dramatically this situation through passive non-cooperation of individuals, but they could—and, in my opinion, should—contribute individually and collectively toward a gradual reform of the world structure, ultimately to make possible a unified, harmonious humanity."

". . . The most important plea I would like to make," the same author says, "is the necessity to provide future generations not only with general understanding of science as such, but, most of all, with the capacity to appreciate those aspects of science that affect the future of man, the impact of science on public affairs, on the fate of our nation and of mankind as a whole."

Science should be taught not as a separate body of technical facts, or as an autonomous system of ideas, but in relation to other disciplines that traditionally mold the attitudes of growing generations toward the society and the world they will have to live in: history, philosophy, science, sociology—religion, too.

Inevitably, this leads us to education. It is not only the education of humanities for the scientist, and science for the humanist, but above all, education for the majority of people, those in between, the citizens, the voters. Theoretically, it is they who decide what new sources of energy should be employed for what purposes. Our source of reference, C. P. Snow, supports the proposed solution. "The chief means open to us," he writes in discussing the two cultures, "is education, mainly in the primary and secondary schools, but also in colleges and universities." And we might add: in newspapers and books, too; on the radio and television, on the lecture platform and the political hustings.

But then—a thought. Education at one time appeared to be almost a specialty of Germany and look what happened? A Walpurgis Night of bloodsoaked orgy. And this not in the land of Genghis Khan, but in the country of Goethe and Kant, the most literate nation. Education, evidently, is not enough.

It is not enough, especially not today. Countries impregnated with education are not immune to the enticements of propaganda to destroy—not to construct. Jose Ortega y Gasset pointed to the danger represented by the immature will of the mass man. Frustrated, he pours out his hatred in pugnacity, wars, conflicts. Would there be a mankind today if the impulses of the *Massenmensch* had been humored? The daily newspaper with the largest circulation in the United States is noted for its pugnacity in international affairs. It panders, no doubt, to the "mass man." In publications of this type the apparent will for peace is equated with disposition toward subversion. History demonstrates that those wars in which individual emotions are aroused are worse than those for political decisions. During the Thirty Years War—a religious conflict—Central Europe became a shambles. And what horrors attended the parturition of the Indian subcontinent in the recent past.

Had there been "Gallup polls" throughout history it is likely that wars would have been more numerous and devastating than they actually were. *Noblesse oblige* did obligate the ruling "Establishment" up to a point, assuring the survival of scattered seeds of civilization in a soil predestined for survival.

And so to focus our attention on the contemporary problem of the two cultures and the abyss in between, let us recall: education must be linked to social values, and priorities must be determined by the overriding ethical concerns. A bomb may be devised to eclipse the lethal work of all previous bombs. Should it be constructed just because its construction is feasible—because "it is there," to quote the famous words of the first conqueror of Mt. Everest? But it is also feasible to construct a machine to turn the brine into potable water, fit to fertilize desert wastes, to have the sand replaced by arable land, to feed the hungry billions, and thus reduce the incidence of extreme forms of politico-economic ideologies likely to upset the balance among the nations.

Ethics, obviously, would assign priority to the constructive mechanism—distillation of sea-water. But today our minds do not revolve in that orbit. The relationship between that solution of a human problem and international security is not clear. Today our ethical values assign preference to the Superbomb. We have to learn to formulate our values in terms of the preservation of our breed. Our standards should assist us in bringing about a condition conducive to the solution of human problems and not to a cosmic holocaust. Of course, the humanities should establish closer contact with the sciences, escalating into infinity, and should show greater concern for the prime values of humanity—be more aggressive in propagating the knowledge of their insights. Let us recall that even today, an age of materialism, mankind bends its knees to the propounders of great ethical values—Buddha, Confuscius, Moses, Jesus, Mohammed, and not to the pragmatical scientists. We have to learn not only to worship them, but also to heed their words.

It cannot be repeated often enough: today we have the tools to feed the hungry, clothe the naked, and reduce the tragic toll of disease, ignorance and poverty, to turn the forces found in the depths of the atom into functions of a state of mind. This can be fostered through the educational process, leaning upon our evaluation of ethical values and these are constructive by their natures. The spanning of the abyss may be hard because many vested interests are jealous guardians of the D.I.P., disease, ignorance, and poverty. But the work has to be undertaken. Without ethical standards the very designation "two cultures" is wrong. No culture can exist without them. Man, without them, is bound to find his greatest achievements to serve the purpose of improvidence, instead of Providence.

Mary Shelley's Frankenstein

By Frank H. McCloskey

Recent adventitious attention to *Frankenstein* through the use of the monster—often confused with its creator in television and motion picture stories—has led to some critical studies of the novel and its author. These focus on the book as the most popular and durable of the fashionable "tales of terror," the vogue of which was in its decline when *Frankenstein* was first published in 1817. It was Mary Shelley's fortune not only to be the daughter of the foremost English revolutionary philosopher of the early nineteenth century and of the first of the modern feminists, but also to be the wife of the poet who, in many respects, was more peculiarly the child of the French Revolution than any of his Romantic confreres. Her personality was molded, encouraged, and developed by intimate association also with Coleridge, Byron, the Lambs, Leigh Hunt, Keats, Matthew "Monk" Lewis, Tom Moore, Proctor, Crabbe, Robinson, Holcroft, Landor, Hazlitt, and even our own Washington Irving. It is not surprising therefore to find in her works considerable influence of the spirit of revolt of her times.

Mary Shelley's failure to attain eminence in literature was not for lack of persistent and varied attempts. Viewed quantitatively her output is impressive enough: six novels, two plays in verse, some fugitive biographical sketches, a few miscellaneous tales and articles, two travel sketches, and the notes to Shelley's poems. Of these the world has been mercifully content to forget all but *Frankenstein*, which, though written at the age of eighteen, was unequalled by any of the five subsequent attempts at the genre.[1] In *Frankenstein*, therefore, are to be found most of the significant commentaries she had to make on the rapidly changing concepts and mores of her generation. Naturally many of these were derived from the ideas of her talented parents.

Her mother, Mary Wollstonecraft, was one of the most gifted women of the eighteenth century. Born in 1759, she endured an early girlhood of extreme misery. Her poverty-stricken family was ignorant and tyrannical, entirely unappreciative of the fine, earnest, and courageous spirit so misplaced among them. Her facility with the pen was early manifested, and for years the money which she was thus able to earn was unselfishly devoted to the support of her parents and numerous brothers and sisters. Without doubt the early handicaps against which she was forced to struggle were largely instrumental in convincing her that the women of her time were mistreated and in bringing her to a high resolve to use her talents in every way possible to effect an amelioration of the injustice. She was perfectly conscious of women's intel-

---

[1] *The Last Man,* 1826, has some merit. But the less said about *Valperga, Perkin Warbeck, Lodore* and *Falkner,* the better. By her own admission, Mrs. Shelley took no delight in writing, grinding out the potboilers for the sake of the money they brought in.

lectual equality with man, and, not lacking the necessary courage, she decided to demand openly, in the name of womankind, rightful equality of opportunity for education and social independence. She earned her right to fame by the publication, in 1792, of *A Vindication of the Rights of Woman,* a book which, of its own momentum, started that great movement toward feminine emancipation which is just attaining its goal in our day.

Independence was her creed:

Independence I have long considered as the grand blessing of life, the basis of every virtue—and independence I will ever secure by contracting my wants, though I were to live on a barren heath.[2]

She insisted that . . . "boys and girls be permitted to pursue the same studies together"[3] . . . and that ". . . children will never be properly educated till friendship subsists between parents . . ."[4]

Her untimely death at her daughter Mary's birth deprived the child of the personal influence that such an intelligent and courageous mother would have exerted. But she and her older half-sister, Fanny Imlay, reared in the household of "Godwin and his circle," as growing girls must have been stirred and enlightened (and possibly sometimes amused) by many learned and animated discussions of the *Rights of Woman* as well as the rights of man.

Godwin had arrived at middle age without having married. One of the numerous sons of a country clergyman, he had received a very ordinary education, but had afterwards studied

---

[2] Wollstonecraft, *A Vindication of the Rights of Woman.* Dedication to M. Talleyrand—Perigord, p. 9.
[3] *Ibid.,* p. 183.
[4] *Ibid.,* p. 213.

for the ministry. His ideas on social and economic questions, however, were entirely too unorthodox for this profession; therefore, having a natural inclination and aptitude for writing, he came to London in 1785 and established himself as a writer of political pamphlets. He acquired great experience but little recognition for several years until he published, in 1793, his greatest work, *An Enquiry Concerning Political Justice and Its Influence on Morals and Happiness,* which brought him instant fame. This book was extremely radical for its day, attacking in a scholarly but fiery manner the existing forms of government.

An extreme individualist, Godwin believed in the perfectibility of man. Much of his doctrine he had absorbed from the principles of the French rationalists and Rousseau, amalgamating and harmonizing them. Under these influences he was led to advocate the abandonment of all government, because he believed it to be responsible for the thwarting of personalities. Man's mind must always be free for the reception of new ideas. Political, social, economic, and moral institutions were petrified and thus prevented such instant adaptability. Hence, away with all institutions. Godwin's millennium, the goal of his scheme of social evolution, he describes in this manner:

> The men whom we are supposing to exist when the earth shall refuse itself to a more extended population, will probably cease to propagate. The whole will be a people of adults and not children. Generation will not succeed generation, nor truth have, in a certain degree, to recommence her career every thirty years. . . . Other improvements may be expected to keep pace with those of health and longevity. Disease disappears. Man becomes practically immortal. . . . There will be no war; no crime; no administration of justice, as it is called; no government besides this there will be neither disease, anguish, melan-

choly, nor resentment. Every one will seek with ineffable ardor the good of all. Mind will be active and eager, yet never disappointed.[5]

Political Justice proved to be of almost incalculable influence as the practical genesis of the liberal movement in England.

His views on education would have been uppermost in the mind of his daughter as she wrote *Frankenstein,* deeply concerned as it must have been, with the welfare of her own and Shelley's child. Godwin's meticulous, if somewhat pedantic mind, cast the whole process of man's education in three categories: accident, precept, and political institution. He was sure that a thorough education was indispensable because ". . . a powerful understanding is inseparable from eminent virtue.[6] In considering the first means of acquiring it he rejected the, to him, fallacious "argument in favour of the essential differences we are supposed to bring into the world with us" and maintained that between two people similarly brought up but developing differently" . . . the most trivial circumstance has sometimes furnished the original "occasion of awakening the ardour of their minds and determining the bent of their studies." [7]

The accident of environment determines the earliest potent bent of the person. Thereafter what we call formal education, chiefly because of the fallibility of the preceptor, will be powerless before the corrupting influence of political institutions. He despairs of "rescuing a young person from the sinister influence of a corrupt government by the power of education," for "it is clear that politics and modes of government will educate and infect us all" by subjecting us to

---

[5]*Political Justice,* Vol. I, p. 318.
[6]*Political Justice,* Vol. I, p. 318.
[7]*Ibid.,* pp. 46-47.

"sensuality, ambition, sordid interest, false ridicule, and the incessant decay of that unblemished purity" [8] we enjoyed at the outset.

Education is not advanced by rigorous discipline.

"We mistake compulsion for persuasion, and delude ourselves into the belief that despotism is the road to the heart.[9]

It is clear to him that ". . . instruction which is communicated by mere constraint, makes but a slow and feeble impression; but when once you have inspired the mind with a love for its object, the scene and the process are entirely altered" . . .[10]

To parents of such extraordinary, intellectual endowments, Mary Wollstonecraft Shelley was born on August 30, 1797. On her mother's death Godwin was left with two infant children. With surprising practicality, he set about the task of obtaining for them a stepmother. Unsuccessful in two attempts, he finally succeeded in marrying a Mrs. Clairemont, a typical storybook stepmother—harsh, quick-tempered, unsympathetic, nagging, fretful, and jealous. Mary received from her little of the motherly attention which is the birthright of every young child. She was also neglected by her father. Any attention which he did find time to give to her was probably tinged with his revolutionary ideas, to the child's disadvantage; for, as Profesesor B. Sprague Allen has pointed out, Godwin's age "was an age of educational experiment, and conscientious radicals were eagerly trying novel systems of pedagogy with unsuspecting children." [11] Thus her early youth was spent in poverty and neglect. It is not surprising, therefore, to find her escaping from the confusion and cares of her home, to

---

[8]*Ibid.*, pp. 49-50.
[9]*Ibid.*, p. 44.
[10]*Political Justice*, Vol. I., p. 319.
[11]Allen, "William Godwin and the Stage," *Publications of the Modern Language Association*, XXXV (1920), p. 365.

spend hours at the grave of her idolized mother, with only a book for company.

Very early, she exhibited remarkable precosity. From the diary of Aaron Burr, who was a frequent visitor at the Godwins', after his virtual banishment from the United States, we learn that Mary, then nine years of age, was accustomed to write lectures for delivery by her brother William on such subjects as "The Effect of a Government on the Character of the People." [12]

Godwin's house was the constant resort of many of the literary notables of the day. Probably through contact with such visitors as the Lambs, Mary was inspired with a desire to educate herself, and this, characteristically, she set out to do. She developed rapidly. Godwin wrote of her, as a girl of fifteen:

Mary . . . is bold, somewhat imperious and active of mind. Her desire of knowledge is great and her perseverance in everything she undertakes almost invincible. She is, I believe, very pretty.[13]

At the age of sixteen Mary first met Shelley, then a headstrong boy of nineteen, whose impetuousness and ardent championship of wildly radical principles had already led to his expulsion from Oxford. This disgrace, together with his ill-advised elopement and marriage with Harriet Westbrook, from whom he was even then living apart, had placed him in such disfavor with his father, Sir Timothy Shelley, as to bring about his disinheritance. However, his poetical genius was already beginning to show itself; he was an ardent admirer of Godwin; and he was a possible eventual source of capital for

---

[12] Marshall, *Life and Letters of Mary Wollstonecraft Shelley*, I, p. 87.
[13] Moore, *Mary Wollstonecraft Shelley*, p. 48.

the furtherance of the publishing business in which Godwin was then engaged. All these things made him a welcome and frequent visitor at the Godwin house.

So Shelley, miserable because of his domestic troubles, turned to Mary for consolation. They saw each other frequently, their rendezvous being the grave of Mary's mother, and it was in this sombre, somewhat gruesome setting that they finally confessed their love.[14]

Realizing the hopelessness of a legal consummation of their attachment, they determined to disregard the proprieties and elope. Thus began the union that gave needed steadiness to perhaps the most impassioned of our lyric poets and equally needed encouragement and support to the ever-modest author of *Frankenstein.*

They decided to spend the summer of 1816 in a villa at Geneva, neighbors to Lord Byron. It was here that, by way of diversion during an absence of her husband, Mary wrote the novel.

Mrs. Ann Radcliffe's *Mysteries of Udolpho* (1794) definitely established the tale of terror as a literary vogue. It was followed by hundreds of imitations, each seeking to outdo the others in horror and gruesomeness. Matthew Gregory Lewis's *The Monk,* probably the most crudely horrible and certainly the most popular of all, soon followed.

The Gothic theme fascinated writers of widely divergent talents. Godwin's *St. Leon* is a case in point; Byron tried his hand with little success; the schoolboy Shelley wrote *Zastrozzi* and *St. Irvyne,* "thrillers" which could hardly contain less of artistic merit.

That Mary Shelley, a girl in her 'teens, should succeed

---

[14]Alexander Harvey in his *Shelley's Elopement* makes much of this scene in his would-be imaginative treatment of his theme.

where such men had failed is nothing less than astounding. *Frankenstein* was written in the summer of 1816, and, upon its publication anonymously, was immediately hailed as the finest achievement of Gothicism to date. It won a place in popular esteem which it retains to some extent to the present day. Certain likenesses to Godwin's *St. Leon* were at once pointed out, but Miss Birkhead, in her admirable study of Gothicism, concludes that "the resemblance is so vague and superficial, and *Frankenstein* so immeasurably superior, that Mrs. Shelley's debt to her father is negligible." [15] She is not alluding to Godwin's thematic ideas.

In her preface to the 1831 edition of *Frankenstein,* Mrs. Shelley gives the circumstances by which she determined to write it.

After her union with Shelley, he was constantly urging her to write, but "travelling and the cares of a family" occupied her time. In Switzerland they were neighbors of Lord Byron. At his villa one evening they had been reading together a volume of ghost stories translated from the German. He suggested that they each write such a story, and all agreed. There were five of them—Byron, Shelley, Byron's Italian physician Polidori, Matthew Lewis, famous as the author of *The Monk,* and Mary. Each started such a tale, but Mary's alone was completed. She was diffident about the task of beginning the work and admits that Shelley encouraged and virtually forced her to it by asking every morning if she had thought of a story. The kernel idea itself came to her one night after she had listened to Shelley and Byron in a discussion of the ideas of poet-scientist-doctor Erasmus Darwin, who had already anticipated the general evolutionary ideas of his more famous grandson and talked of the possibility of artificially

---

[15] Birkhead, *The Tale of Terror,* p. 159.

creating life out of inanimate matter. And so, having conceived the outline of a plot, the next day she began her story with the words, "It was on a dreary night of November." [16] At first she planned to develop it as a short sketch but, yielding finally to the importunities of her husband, elaborated it to its present form, of which a brief outline follows.

In a prologue of four letters from Robert Walton, captain of an Arctic exploration party, to his sister in London, we learn that he has rescued and taken into his ice-bound ship, Frankenstein, a scientist, who has nearly perished from cold and hunger in pursuing, over the frozen seas in a dog-sled, a huge figure, travelling in the same manner, which the crew had sighted at a distance the preceding day. After some days, Frankenstein decides to tell his story, and it is given us as if written by Walton at his dictation.

In her first four chapters Mary introduces us in an easy and interesting manner to Frankenstein, his father, his younger brother William, his friend Henry Clerval, and his sweetheart Elizabeth. Frankenstein, the intense, the patient, the indefatigable student lives and moves before us. She presents his discovery of the means of artificially instilling life so deftly and naturally that we are not shocked by its absurdity. The gruesomeness of atmosphere produced by the horrid details of the construction of the Creature from the products of the grave and the dissecting room is effectively developed.

A final scene of horrors shows the monster gloating over the corpse of his last victim just before disappearing into the Arctic night.

Most writers about *Frankenstein*[17] have agreed with Miss Gregory, who says:

---

[16]The first words of Chapter V.
[17]One must include even recent full-length books by Mesdames Grylls, Nitchie and Sparks.

Mary Shelley was the author of several novels which show traces of the influences by which she was surrounded; but their connection with Revolutionism is so indirect as scarcely to warrant us in discussing it.[18]

However, in an age in which "a characteristic phenomenon was the birth of a spirit of ardent discipleship," [19] it would be strange indeed if the writings of the daughter of Godwin and the wife of Shelley did not reflect revolutionary ideas. Revolutionism was more than an academic philosophy. It was a social religion, in the sense that it was to many men their "serious reaction to life as a whole." As one of its earliest and ablest preachers, Godwin was veritably idolized by a great proportion of the radicals of the period. It has been said that "the overshadowing interest in Godwin must always remain his influence upon the great young poets of the time."[20]

Largely guided by the example of their master, whose *Caleb Williams,* and *St. Leon,* were avowedly revolutionary preachments parading under a thin disguise of plot and characterization there sprang up a whole school of revolutionary novelists, the real value of whose works lay, not in their intrinsic merit, but in the illustrations they offered of the practice of revolutionary ethics, as conceived by its sympathizers. Holcroft, Robert Bage, Mrs. Inchbald, Mrs. Opie, Mrs. Charlotte Smith, and many others for a time were busily engaged in writing such tales.

The vogue was short-lived, however, as Miss Gregory points out:

---

[18]Gregory, Catherine, The French Revolution and the English *Novel,* p. 227.

[19]Allen, *"Minor Disciples of Radicalism in the Revolutionary Era,"* Modern Philology, XXI, p. 227.

[20]Allen, "William Godwin and the Stage," *Publications of the Modern Language Association,* XXXV (1920), p. 359.

One of the most striking characteristics of the literature reflecting the French Revolution in England is its apparent inconsistency. In 1789, poets, novelists, and statesmen are touched with a fine glow of enthusiasm for liberty and the sovereignty of the people. A few years pass, and these same ardent friends of the Revolution, all save a few stubborn or courageous souls, have recanted, and are busily engaged in exposing and denouncing the dangerous tendencies of their former doctrines.[21]

Even though Mrs. Shelley's works did not begin to appear until about 1820, by which time even her father and Shelley had been forced to retire somewhat from their earlier position, she was still her father's daughter. In certain prefatory remarks to the second edition of his novel *Caleb Williams,* Godwin shows his intention of making the fiction serve as a cloak to propagandize his revolutionary ideas.

What is now presented to the public is no refined and abstract speculation; it is a study and delineation of things passing in the moral world . . . government intrudes itself into every rank of society . . . it was proposed in the invention of the following work, to comprehend, as far as the progressive nature of a single story would allow, a general review of the modes of domestic and unrecorded despotism by which man becomes the destroyer of man.[22]

The expressed intention of her father to make his novel a social document undoubtedly influenced his daughter to attempt the same in *Frankenstein.* In her preface she wrote:

I have not considered myself as merely weaving a series of

---

[21]Gregory, *The French Revolution and the English Novel,* p. 15.
[22]Godwin, *Caleb Williams,* preface, p. XX. Significantly, this preface, first prepared for the first edition, was cancelled because of Godwin's fear of its adverse reception.

supernatural terrors. . . . Other motives were mingled with these as the work proceeded. I am by no means indifferent to the manner in which whatever moral tendencies exist in the sentiments or characters it contains shall affect the reader.[23]

---

[23] Mary Wollstonecraft Shelley, *Frankenstein or the Modern Prometheus*, p. 5.

Perhaps it was the remarkable emancipation as a woman that she personally enjoyed that led her to draw little upon the revolutionary ideas of her sainted mother. Frankenstein's Elizabeth is rather pallid; she shows little of the spirited resolution of Mary Wollstonecraft. The novel would not have lost in vigor and interest if Mrs. Shelley had made Elizabeth a feminist. Undoubtedly whatever imaginative power her creator possessed came from her mother rather than from Godwin. Hazlitt in his account of his first meeting with Coleridge says, "She [Mary Wollstonecraft] seemed to me to turn off Godwin's objections to something she advanced with quite a playful, easy air. He [Coleridge] replied that 'this was only one instance of the ascendency which people of imagination exercised over those of mere intellect.'"

Nevertheless the mother's independence shines, though feebly, in the work of the daughter. Both reject the extreme tenets of Rousseau. The mother, like William Blake, who illustrated her "Original Stories" in 1796, could not believe that all evil came into man's life from the pressure of environment. "Rousseau," she says, ". . . became enamored of solitude . . . considers evil as positive and the work of man . . . his arguments in favor of a state of nature are plausible but unsound . . . that God has made all things right, and that error has been introduced by the creature, whom He found . . . is as unphilosophical as impious."[24]

---

[24] Mary Wollstonecraft, *The Rights of Woman*, p. 17.

Godwin also insists that Rousseau's attitude toward nature be constantly subjected to the scrutiny of man's reason; and his reason assures him that not *all* the works of the Creator are good.

> In this sense therefore no doubt we ought to follow nature, that is to employ our understandings and increase our discernment. . . . If we would fully comport ourselves in a manner correspondent to our properties and powers, we must bring everything to the standard of reason. . . . Nothing must be sustained because it is ancient, because we have been accustomed to regard it as sacred, or because it has been unusual to bring the validity into question. . . .[25]

Mrs. Shelley, though clearly attracted to Wordsworth's passive mysticism, reflects these views throughout her novel. One illustration must suffice.

The misfortunes and misery of Frankenstein's monster, directly the result of his rejection by society, were ultimately caused by the way in which his creator had formed him. After a year's secret observation of the idyllic life of the cottagers, he tries to reveal himself to them in perfect goodwill.

> At that instant the cottage door was opened, and Felix, Sofie, and Agatha entered. Who can describe their horror and consternation on beholding me? Agatha fainted; and Sofie . . . rushed out of the cottage. Felix . . . in a transport of fury . . . struck me violently. . . . My heart sunk within me. . . . Cursed, cursed creator! Why did I live?[26]

Though the blind father of Felix had just told the monster that "the hearts of men, when unprejudiced by any obvious

---

[25] William Godwin, *Political Justice*, Vol. II, pp. 84-85.
[26] Mary Wollstonecraft Shelley, *Frankenstein*, p. 115.

self-interest, are full of brotherly love and charity," [27] horror and fear have quickly dissipated these kindly virtues.

Like her husband, Godwin, Mary Wollstonecraft was wholly committed to the perfectibilian doctrine.

Rousseau exerts himself to prove that all *was* right: a crowd of authors that all *is* now right: and I, that all will be right.[28]

As a perfectibilian Godwin held that human inventions are susceptible of perpetual improvement.

. . . there is no art that may not be carried to a still higher perfection. . . . If this be true of all other arts, why not of social institution? . . . If we can still further demonstrate it to be a part of the natural and regular progress of the mind, our confidence and our hopes will then be complete.[29]

Mrs. Shelley, the teenager, though she modestly asks in her original preface that nothing in *Frankenstein* be considered "as prejudicing any philosophical doctrine of whatever kind," [30] never avoided reflection of these optimistic convictions. Walton, the explorer, expects to be "wafted to a land surpassing in wonders and in beauty every region hitherto discovered on the habitable globe." [31] Frankenstein, the student, would learn to "banish disease from the human frame, and render man invulnerable to any but violent death." [32] He holds that "the labors of men of genius, however erroneously directed . . . ultimately win [through] to the solid advantage

---

[27]Mary Wollstonecraft Shelley, *Frankenstein,* p. 113.
[28]Mary Wollstonecraft, *The Rights of Woman,* p. 18.
[29]William Godwin, *Political Justice,* Vol. I, p. 119.
[30]*Frankenstein,* p. 6.
[31]*Ibid.,* p. 13.
[32]*Ibid.,* pp. 34-35.

of mankind."[33] Elizabeth, in her letter to Victor, praises the "republican institutions of our country [which] have produced simpler and happier manners than those which prevail in the great monarchies that surround it . . [where even a servant's condition] does not include the idea of ignorance and a sacrifice of the dignity of a human being."[34] Illustrations like these can be found in almost any part of the book.

Man moves toward his perfection in proportion as his actions are guided by the supreme gift of his Creator—his reason. Both Godwins hold this as the capstone of their philosophies and are followed in the well-worn path—though more feebly—by their daughter. To lack of its use, Mary Wollstonecraft attributes all the misunderstandings between the sexes, all the evils to society that grow from depriving woman of her "rights," including the vital one of education. If a woman is not to be educated, she says, "import whips from Russia" for her husband so that he may be "wielding this sceptre, sole master of his house, because he is the only thing in it that has reason:—the divine, indefeasible earthly sovereignty breathed into man by the Master of the universe."[35]

Virtue is shown by the rational behavior of independent persons, for ". . . when any power but reason curbs the free spirit of man, dissimulation is practiced . . ."[36] and one must not . . . "expect virtue where Nature has not given understanding . . ."[37] Thus she lays the blame for the inanities of eighteenth-century Belindas on a society that refuses them education and independence; for "What, indeed, can tend

---

[33] *Ibid.*, p. 42.
[34] *Frankenstein*, p. 55.
[35] *The Rights of Woman*, p. 215.
[36] *Ibid.*, p. 214.
[37] *Ibid.*, p. 215.

to deprave the character more than outward submission and inward contempt." [38]

More persistently, though with less charm and fire, Godwin would subject all considerations given to man and his universe to his "divine," God-given faculty. Reason persuaded him of the necessity for friendly interdependence among us human beings. "Virtue," he says, "consists in a desire of the happiness of the species." [39] And "Right is the claim of the individual to his share of the benefit arising from his neighbors' discharge of their several duties." [40]

Human virtue, therefore, in the view of both sages, is synonymous with rational behavior, lapses from which bring about all the evils of the universe. With this premise "whereon to stand," Godwin moves the world to its perfected Utopia in which *all* evils—including even death and taxes—disappear.

Daughter Mary tried hard to follow faithfully. Her monster was endowed by its creator as a rational being. When first a "convulsive motion agitated its limbs," Frankenstein's irrational emotion was revulsion "at this catastrophe" and he "rushed out of the room." When later that night he "beheld the wretch—the miserable monster," it "muttered some inarticulate sounds, while a grin wrinkled its cheeks . . . one hand was stretched out, seemingly to detain me, but I escaped." [41] Thus Frankenstein irrationally rejected the proffered friendly goodwill of his monstrous creation, rejection which started the creature on its evil path of hate and destruction. As if to underline the significance of the event, the importance of good will in society, on the next page Mrs.

---

[38]*The Rights of Woman,* p. 185.
[39]*Political Justice,* Book IV, Chap. V, Appendix, p. 317.
[40]*Ibid.,* Vol. I, p. xxv.
[41]*Frankenstein,* p. 49.

Shelley has Victor meet his boyhood friend Cherval. "I grasped his hand, and in a moment forgot my horror and misfortune; I felt suddenly, and for the first time in many months, calm and serene joy." [42]

Similarly the successive crimes of the monster result from his repeated rejections by society. In his long dialogue with Victor, recounting his experiences, comprising Chapters 10-17, he says:

Everywhere I see bliss, from which I alone am irrevocably excluded. I was benevolent and good; misery made me a fiend. Make me happy and I shall again be virtuous.[43]

The monster thus describes his first murder, that of Frankenstein's little brother William:

If, therefore, I could seize him, and educate him as my companion and friend, I should not be so desolate in this peopled earth.

Urged by this impulse, I seized the boy . . . he placed his hands before his eyes and uttered a shrill scream. . . . "Child, what is the meaning of this? I do not intend to hurt you. . . ." "Let me go," he cried, "monster! ugly wretch." . . . "Frankenstein! you belong . . . to him toward whom I have sworn eternal revenge? You shall be my first victim." [44]

Essential virtue, crime from rejection.

The monster's other crimes are similarly motivated. His instincts are virtuous. He turns to evil because he is not treated with reason by men, who, despite his origin, are his

---

[42]*Frankenstein*, p. 51.
[43]*Ibid.*, p. 85.
[44]*Ibid.*, p. 121.

fellow-creatures. He is "malicious because [he] is miserable." His "food is not that of man; I do not destroy the lamb and kid to glut my appetite." Reading Paradise Lost, he "many time considered Satan as the fitter emblem of my condition." Thus he is presented as a fallen angel, brought to disaster by the unreasonable pressures of society, from which, in the view of the perfectibilians, all evils of mankind spring.

His education is directed by the Godwinian theses: accident, precept, and political institution. His unreasonable, immediate rejection by his creator was the accident that turned him into his evil path, whereas, shown rational friendliness at this time, he might have as well turned to the path of virtue. His education by precept came from his year-long observation of the idyllic cottagers. The simple virtue of their interrelations made him yearn for similar friendly acceptance.

The old man . . . often endeavored to encourage his children. . . . Agatha listened with respect. . . . I could mention innumerable instances, which, although slight, marked the dispositions of these amiable cottagers. . . . Felix carried with pleasure to his sister the first little white flower that peeped out from beneath the snowy ground . . . he cleared away the snow that obstructed her path . . . he cleared away the snow that obstructed her path . . . he read to the old man and Agatha.[45]

By their wholly virtuous examples the cottagers serve as his ideal preceptors, avoiding the errors of ordinary preceptors who "pique themselves upon disclosing part and concealing part of the truth" and spend labor "not in teaching truth, but in teaching falsehood." [46]

---
[45]*Frankenstein,* p. 96.
[46]*Political Justice,* Vol. I, pp. 47-48.

During an absurd year of secret observation of the cottagers' perfected family life and human relations, the monster's education has been so advanced that he has mastered the language sufficiently to read with complete understanding *Paradise Lost, Plutarch's Lives* and the *Sorrows of Werther*. (Mrs. Shelley fails to avoid absurdity here.) His Utopian education thus perfected, it is now reasonable for him to be accepted by society, despite his horrifying differences from normal man. He therefore reveals himself first to the cottager father, the blind DeLacey, yearning to be accepted into their society. "These amiable people [the cottagers including De-Lacey] . . . have never seen me, and know little of me. I am full of fears; for if I fail there I am an outcast in the world forever." To which Delaney, blind and therefore, in the situation, not subject to the irrational prejudices of society, responds, "Do not despair . . . the hearts of men, when unprejudiced by any obvious self-interest, are full of brotherly love and charity." [47]

But society, represented by the other cottagers who, though not blind physically, are blind to their traditional, irrational prejudices, proceeds to destroy the monster's virtuous inclinations and intentions, by the horror, fury and hate of their instant reactions toward him.

This rejection was the turning point, for "from that moment [the monster] declared everlasting war against the species." To Mrs. Shelley, as to her parents, there are only black and white, no shades of gray. *All* evils come from faults in the social environment, and all evils can be eliminated by their correction through the use of reason. Her novel, from one point of view, may be considered almost a continuous preachment of her parents' revolutionary doctrines.

---

[47]*Frankenstein*, p. 113.

Her account of the relations of Frankenstein with Henry Clerval and Elizabeth Lavenza, his "more than sister," from childhood through maturity, clearly reflects their influence. They are educated together, as Mary Wollstonecraft insisted, against all current practices, that boys and girls must be. And as adults, before the death of Clerval, there is a strong suggestion of the *menage a trois,* intimated in the following passage of Godwin's:

> I shall assiduously cultivate the intercourse of that woman, whose moral and intellectual accomplishments strike me in the most powerful manner . . . [if] other men feel for her the same preference that I do, this will create no difficulty. We may all enjoy her conversation . . . and be wise enough to consider the sexual commerce as unessential to our regard.[48]

Certain similarities between *Frankenstein* and Godwin's *Caleb Williams* have frequently been noticed (flight and pursuit, etc.) but these do not appear to be significant in particular detail. The plot structure in both, however, is mechanical. Edgar Poe, in his "Philosophy of Composition," quotes Dickens as his authority that "Godwin wrote his *Caleb Williams* backwards. He first involved his hero in a web of difficulties . . . and then . . . cast about him for some mode of accounting for what had been done." Obviously *Frankenstein* was not so blueprinted. But the machinery is just as contrived: the artificial envelope of the Walton prologue and epilogue (probably an afterthought prompted by Shelley); the development of the monster up to his character transformation, referred

---

[48] *Political Justice,* Vol. II, p. 511. Miss Elizabeth Nitchie, in her *Mary Shelley,* p. 18, observes that Mary "had fallen in with the plans of Shelley and [Thomas Jefferson] Hogg for a triangular experiment in free love . . . [though] she must have felt relief when the scheme fell through."

to above; and thereafter the successive murders of those people near to Frankenstein, done, as if they were a row of targets in a shooting gallery, in the order of their increasing intimacy with him.

Mrs. Shelley's debt to her father was not in technique but in intention. Godwin frankly announced that his novels were to serve merely as fictional vehicles for the propagandizing of his revolutionary ideas. That his teenaged daughter, born of two revolutionaries, reared in the household which was the sum and source of the nation's revolutionary doctrines, and married to an "ineffectual angel" who had, perhaps more than any other, voraciously swallowed them and tried to put them into practice—that such a young woman, turning to writing, should not have similar intentions would be indeed surprising. *Frankenstein* failed as revolutionary document; few have considered it as one, in spite of the subtitle, "The Modern Prometheus," which its author carefully appended to it. And in her later novels the youthful fire almost completely died. But there can be little doubt that her original purpose, as the book took shape under the friendly encouragement of her husband, was to advance the revolutionary cause of her crusading father, dressing up his radical ideas for his doubting contemporaries under the thin disguise of the "tale of terror," the shocker so avidly read at the time and for which she had so many and so varied examples before her. *Frankenstein*, however, has persisted to our day solely because of its bizarre central situation. Surely its success would have been greater if its author had inherited less of the pedestrian pedantry of her father and more of the clear-eyed foresight, sharp wit, and cordial fire of her talented mother.

Bibliography

Shelley, Mary W., *Frankenstein, the Modern Prometheus,* New York, 1952.
Allen, B. Sprague, "William Godwin's Influence upon John Thelwall," Publications of the Modern Language Association, XXXVII, 1922.
———, "William Godwin and the Stage," Publications of the Modern Language Association, XXXV (1920), 1920.
———, "Minor Disciples of Radicalism in the Revolutionary Era," *Modern Philology,* XXI, 1923.
Birkhead, Edith, *The Tale of Terror,* London, 1921.
Gregory, Catherine, *The French Revolution and the English Novel,* London, 1908.
Godwin, William, *Elopement of Shelley and Mary,* St. Louis, 1911.
———, *Enquiry Concerning Political Justice and its Influence on Morals and Happiness,* ed. Priestley, 2 Vols., Toronto, 1946.
———, *Caleb Williams or Things as They Are,* London, 1835.
Grylis, R. Glynn, *Mary Shelley,* London, 1938.
Marshall, Mrs., Florence A. Julian, *Life and Letters of Mary Wollstonecraft Shelley,* 2 Vols., London, 1889.
Moore, Helen, *Mary Wollstonecraft Shelley,* Philadelphia, 1886.
Nitchie, Elizabeth, *Mary Shelley,* New Brunswick, 1953.
Peck, Walter E., "Biographical Elements in the Novels of Mary W. Shelley," Publications of the Modern Language Association, XXI, March, 1923.
Sanborn, P. B., *The Romance of Mary W. Shelley, John Howard Payne, and Washington Irving,* Boston, 1907.
Shelley, Percy Bysshe, *Complete Poetical Works,* edited by Mrs. Shelley, 2nd ed., London, 1839.
Spark, Muriel, *Child of Light,* Hadleigh, Essex, 1951.
Underwood, S. A., *Heroines of Free Thought,* New York, 1876.
Wollstonecraft, Mary, *The Rights of Woman,* London, 1929.

Is History A Science?

By H. F. Mackensen

This (Hegel's) bold assumption of a world plan leads to fallacies because it starts out from false premises. . . . We, however, shall start from the one point accessible to us, the one eternal center of all things—man suffering, striving, doing, as he is and was and ever shall be.

> Jacob Burckhardt,
> Introduction to *Reflections on History*

Is history a science? The answer to this question has practical and theoretical consequences of fundamental importance.

If history is not a science its methods need not be tested against scientific standards of objectivity and evidence. Impressionistic, individualistic methods may then be admitted in historical research.

If history is not a science claims of universal validity for theories of historical causation and interpretation, on the model of such theories in the exact and natural sciences, cannot be maintained.

If history is a science then its methodology must conform to the objective standards for research and evidence essential to a true science.

If history is a science then theories of causation with regard to the past follow and deterministic prophecies with regard to the future seem possible.

Each of these questions will be examined in turn.

If history is not a science but solely an art, its methods need not be tested against scientific standards of objectivity and evidence. Impressionistic, individualistic methods may then be admitted in historical research.

This was the case in much writing of history until modern times. Herodotus delighted in repeating legends and anecdotes, although he always inserted saving phrases as to their authenticity. Livy based his work on the written accounts available to him, but used them in an uncritical manner and accepted legend as truth. Suetonius, among the least scientific of historians, repeated the gossip of an age and even this is valuable for us. Eusebius, the first church historian, recounted the miracles of saints and martyrs with no questions asked. Everything and everyone were presented according to the strict party (or rather church) line. There was no effort, not even the wish, to be objective. Medieval chroniclers and annalists are notorious for unquestioning acceptance of all statements by official authoritative sources, Christian or pagan. One must wait for the official historians of the modern totalitarian party for anything as systematically one-sided and subjective.

The late Middle Ages and the Renaissance were characterized by the revival of scientific methods and objective analysis of historical evidence. Valla's examination of *The Dona-*

tion of Constantine is a landmark. The Protestant and Catholic historians during Reformation and Counterreformation were not content to rest their partisan arguments on infallible Scripture or popes and Church fathers alone. They presented their carefully slanted interpretations as based on scholarly documentation which they claimed to have subjected to impartial scientific scrutiny.

In recent centuries the demand for scientific methodological standards in writing history increased until it became absolute *à la* Ranke. The writers of history during the Enlightenment sought to maintain a scholarly stance. Voltaire and Gibbon read widely in sources and sought to document, but a great goal was to achieve literary effect.

Only those writers in recent times have preserved their respectability who have used the matter of history in an imaginative, impressionistic manner, namely the historical novelists. Sir Walter Scott opened the chorus. They seem hardly to have cared how far their portraits differed from medieval reality as long as their own impressions of the age were vividly transmitted. This tendency has changed recently. C. S. Forester represents the new school. He imaginatively constructed the fictional career of a Nelsonian naval officer, but no matter how wildly improbable the doings of Hornblower become, his creator guarantees the authenticity of each historical and technical detail by meticulous research. His is a strange wedding of the free, impressionistic use of history in writing romance and the maintenance of strict standards of authenticity in details. Certainly Forester is more enjoyable to read than some pedant's monograph, no matter how useful, on the exact weight of metal fired by *H. M. S. Victory*.

If history is not a science, what happens to those theories of historical causation for which the validity of scientific theories are claimed? Obviously, such claims are no longer tenable. The consequences of this conclusion are profound.

The effort of the individual to rise in his society, or the competition of business corporations for financial domination, or the wars between empire building nations, or the rivalries of races in the creation and preservation of cultures and civilizations can no longer be misinterpreted as Darwinian struggles for the survival of the fittest.

Marxism loses its deterministic and apocalyptic notes. The past history of mankind can no longer be seen as cumulative and inevitable class struggle. Instead the events and developments selected to buttress this thesis can be viewed in natural relation to their own times and places. The future no longer inevitably leads to the worker's paradise, but becomes problematical and open to man's creative imagination and will.

It is surely disconcerting for the devout believers in such theories of history to confess that they no longer have the sure and certain explanation for the past, present and future. But such Post-Marxists and Post-Darwinists find themselves in good company. The Post-Christians are in the same boat. It is hard to believe in a universal plan of salvation activated in history by a God Who is dead. In fact, if the premise is true, the only philosophers of history whose theories remain unaffected are those we might call "The Old Believers."

If scientific validity is denied to theories of historical interpretation then the only theories which retain universal validity are those which are based on religious faith. It is not possible to establish proofs for the operation of Divine Providence in history which will satisfy the scientific historian. Yet history has been written for millennia by believers whose eyes of faith saw the hand of God at work everywhere. Both Old and New Testaments are monuments to such theories of history. St. Augustine of Hippo saw the struggle between the City of Man and the City of God leading from the Garden of Eden to the Final Judgment. Islam sees the fate of men ordained for all eternity by decrees which Allah himself cannot change, once they have been promulgated. Calvin saw the elect predestined to salvation through invincible grace while the reprobates, left to their own devices, were inevitably consigned to damnation.

Whether we consider the "Old Believers" or the modern "scientific" theorists of history, truth is still in the eyes, minds and hearts of the beholders. The fundamental difference between them is that the former rest their theories on inward faith and personal mystical experience while the latter build on empirical evidence conveyed through the senses, subjected to rational analysis by the mind, and arranged according to patterns which fit the theories of selected modern sciences. What *both* types of theorists have in common are unconscious psychological forces at work within which form their religious experiences and beliefs or influence their scrutiny and selection of historical evidence and its arrangement into patterns.

In either case the interpretation of history finally amounts to an act of faith. Or, to cite a third, psychologically determined view, is it a psycho-chemical reflex which permits no freedom of the will? At any rate historical interpretation becomes an act of hope when the historian turns prophet and inevitably forsees arising in the future from the thrust of the past the New Jerusalem, the Pure Aryan Race, or the Classless Society. When this is realized such apocalypses seem more in character and more valid when unveiled by St. John the Divine than by Adolf Hitler or Karl Marx.

We reverse the major premise and ask what the results are for methodology and theory if history is a science.

In that case the methods used for discovering and establishing evidence fall under the same stringent requirements as in the exact and natural sciences. Nothing can be taken on faith, but everything must be tested and analyzed. Carbon 14 tests, archaelogical and numismatic evidence, the comparative and higher criticism of documentary evidence, in fact, the whole arsenal of methods and techniques used in gathering scientifically acceptable evidence must then be required in historical methodology. Even the attitude of the researcher towards his subject must be as objective as his conscious honesty and his recognition of his own unconscious motivations permit. This latter is not easy. It requires great self-control and sympathy ("suffering with" in the original Greek sense of the word). It is the attitude Thucydides sought to attain in writing of the Peloponnesian War. It is the attitude von Ranke tried to inculcate when he emphasized that history's task is to discover and describe *wie es eigentlich gewesen*. Ideally this attitude demands a suspension of judgment until the last bit of available evidence on any question has been uncovered and evaluated. It seeks to let the facts speak for themselves.

If history is a science the consequences in the area of theory are obvious. It must then be possible to establish a scientific theory for historical developments. Even when scientific theories of history differ among themselves, as they do, the assumption is common to all such theorists that one theory must be closer to the truth than any of the others. Most frequently the claim is made that one theory *is* the truth and the others are to be measured against it. It is this attitude which the historians of the Old and New Testaments—St. Augustine, Karl Marx, Houston Stewart Chamberlain and Mao Tse-Tung—have in common.

What conclusions can be drawn from the argumentation so far? It seems to this writer that the second and third hypotheses of the four examined are closest to the truth.

Is History a Science?

History is not a science with regard to theoretical interpretation. The historian, as a theorist, is a philosopher and not a scientist. His conclusions are speculative and tentative. Their greatest value lies in teaching prudence in the widest sense of the word for his own and following generations. On occasion a historical philosopher has the stuff to be a prophet, but prophecy is not simply projection into the future of trends scientifically established in the past. It is the task of a seer, and such crystal ball gazing must never be confused with the reasoned philosophical interpretation of the past which is history.

Theoretical speculations remain fruitless unless they are linked with real life. This is true as well of the considerations which have been advanced. Personal experience gained in encounters with Soviet historians will be used to illustrate the points made.

During a meeting with members of the Moscow Institute of History, on a recent tour of the Soviet Union, the writer sought to discover the reaction of the Soviet conferees to the thesis that the building of the pyramids in ancient Egypt did not represent the exploitation of the masses by the Pharaohs. Instead inscriptions and other evidence definitely indicate that the ancient Egyptians were happy to contribute labor to what was for them a great cooperative act of religious devotion. They worked with the same spirit as the builders of medieval cathedrals.[1]

The answer of the Soviet conferees was strongly negative in character. One insisted that the whole history of mankind was a history of class struggles. Any evidence to the contrary notwithstanding, things had been no different in ancient

---

[1] The statements at this and the subsequent conference are based on notes taken by the writer at the time.

Egypt. Another of the Soviet conferees insisted that if evidence indicated that there had been no class struggle in ancient Egypt then this was due to the absence of real classes. The system of production and distribution had not changed. All were either engaged in agriculture or based their social position on the production of land. As soon as exploitation of the peasants by the nobles reached a certain level they became slaves. The pyramids had been built by slaves.[2]

The writer replied that the point had been completely missed that the Egyptians of the Old Kingdom who actually worked on the pyramids, according to the available evidence, were happy to build what were for them national shrines, like the Mausoleum of Lenin.

A Soviet conferee replied that they had been exploited, whether they had liked it or not.

Some days later at Moscow University the chairman of the Historical Faculty who occupied the chair of party history, the editor of the leading Soviet historical journal and three professors of history participated in the conference.

In order to elicit their reactions they were asked, "When does modern history begin?" This question was asked with the fact in mind that the question of periodization is especially difficult for the Marxist historian. Moreover, some of the Soviet conferees present had in recent months engaged in debate among themselves on this very question in the pages of

---

[2] The view inculcated by the official guide for the middle school course, in which Egyptian history is taught, is as follows: N. V. Andreyevskaya, *Ocherki Metodiki Istorii* (Outline of Method in History), (Leningrad, the Ministry of Education, 1958), p. 29: "The concrete material describing the construction of the pyramids to the students reveals the forced labor of the people,—peasants and slaves, and it underlines once more the powerful authority of the Pharaoh, who, for the sake of a whim, compelled thousands of people to work."

their learned journals. It is not easy to determine even the approximate date at which the bourgeoisie began to win their struggle against the feudality. The traditional dates around 1500 (1453, 1492, 1517) are unsatisfactory from the Marxist point of view and still too early. The date 1789, on the other hand, is a little too late. The answer given by the Soviet historians was: "Modern times begin with the English and Dutch revolutions of the Seventeenth Century."

In reply several objections to this approximate date as the divide between what is medieval and what is modern were presented by the writer. The need to keep in mind the real men and women and the actual events of the period being discussed was pressed. The historian should seek to relive vicariously the lives of persons, whether famous or unknown, who had lived then by reading their diaries, letters, sermons and writings in general. He should study the actual historical sequence of events of those eras as revealed by the documentary and other evidence. He should seek to appreciate the subtle emotional changes during those times by study of their works of art, their music, their fashions and other matters of taste. After he had done these things he should ask, "Were the people of 1500 closer to those of 1600 or to those of 1400 in their whole way of life?" There was a much greater gap between the men of 1400 and those of 1500 than between the latter and any later group until recently. The writer concluded his statement by saying that only since the First World War had groups of men with ways of life arisen which were, as far as he could judge, separated from the men of 1500-1914 by gaps even greater than those which had separated the men of 1500 from those who had lived before them.

In answer the Soviet historians stated that the development of the intellectual, emotional and cultural life of any society was always a reflection of the basic material conditions and requirements under which the people of that society had lived. At the conclusion of their answer one of the Soviet historians stated: "The question of the periodization of modern times is not settled among us Soviet historians as yet." The editor of the leading Soviet historical journal wrily added the comment, which was greeted with uproarious laughter by his colleagues: *K sojaleniu net* ("Unfortunately not"). All, even there, were not agreed on the infallibly true, because scientifically determined periodization of history.

The next question presented to the Soviet historians went a step further. The question was: "What is the importance in the flow of historical cause and effect of the human personality?" This question was asked with the fact in mind that Marx himself had admitted that no other philosophy of history would require a lower estimate of the effects of the human personality upon historical causation than his own. The basic question asked was amplified with a concrete problem: "What was the significance of the personality of Luther, expressive of his inner spiritual development, for the beginning of the Reformation?" It was pointed out, in addition, that the doctrine of justification by faith was a theological atom bomb which, taken entirely in its own sphere of life and realm of discourse, had actually begun the great reorientation of man towards God, towards himself and towards the world which was the Reformation. But all of this had first begun in the microcosm of Luther's inward life.

In answer the Soviet historians agreed that the human personality plays a most important part in shaping the events of history. The effectiveness of any significant historical personality, they insisted, depended upon the ability with which that personality at any given moment in history grasped the basic new problems of his era and proceeded to do what had to be done by creating new solutions which were more in accord with the new social situation. Inevitably the particular person could only understand the problems of his own age in the framework of the conceptual system dominant at the time. This, however, always arose from the basic social and economic system. When was a personality "ahead of his time?" When was he "progressive?"

For example, the greatness of the personality of Lenin rested, they continued, upon his uncanny ability to analyze the situation in Russia in 1917 in accordance with the principles for the correct scientific interpretation of history finally discovered and set forth by Marx; then to formulate what had to be done and, finally, to lead the Soviet people towards the fulfillment of the plan. But it was an error to make a cult out of Lenin's personality (*kult lichnosti*), to ascribe to it some mysterious originating and creative power and then to maintain that the great results that have followed were solely the products of Lenin's genius.

They then turned to the minor question. Luther and his ideas were not unimportant for the beginning of the Reformation, they answered. Naturally, he could only operate within the conceptual categories of his time. These were completely theological and religious, which was natural because in the rural and feudal Middle Ages the church as an institution was the greatest landowner and even the greatest corporate financial institution as well as inevitably being the final arbiter of all education, learning and science. All questions in sociology, economics and government were finally decided by the church. The sanction for the church's authority was religious. It claimed God as the final validation for its authority. Luther was of peasant origin but his father had become a member of the new bourgeoisie. Luther thus represented the rising new middle class which found itself in conflict with the old feudal system. This conflict between the old rural feudal system and the new urban bourgeoisie was reflected in Luther's personal development by inner conflicts about religion. The theological solution which Luther found for his inner conflicts destroyed the power and authority of the medieval church and of the feudal ruling class and made possible the type of competitive, individualistic life which was demanded by the growing development of the bourgeois, capitalist system in its early stages.

In reply the writer insisted that personal familiarity with the religious experience and theological beliefs of Luther prevented acceptance of the Soviet historians' interpretation as constituting more than three quarters of the truth. The world of the spirit has a life of its own. No amount of philosophical, historical or economic analysis will ever succeed in fathoming the mysterious operations of that spirit which creates its own forms and instruments in the material world and is not their creature and which works especially in and through the human personality.

A quotation from the official Soviet guide on the methodology of teaching history in the middle school (ages eleven to fourteen) will be useful at this point. Chapter Four, entitled "The Study of Specific Facts, Their Critique and Generalizing Use in the Teaching of History" includes the following:

> Before the teacher stands the task of leading the students to the Marxist understanding of the historical process and its fundamental problems. This task is achieved through study of the specific facts which are found in the chronological succession (of events).

Is History a Science?

The facts with which we work in the school course are many-sided and varied. Both the feudal system and the insurrection of Wat Tyler are historical facts, but they differ as to their content and character.

The substance of the first fact (the feudal system) acquaints us with the social-economic life and activity of the people. The inner dynamism of this fact depends upon its illustrating the development of labor, its changes and improvements. The feudal system is a phenomenon characteristic of a definite stage in historical development. Here the chief goal is not confined to the description of a definite manor belonging to an actual fief in an exactly given year. The unique (*yedinichnoye*) does not interest us but rather the typical, i.e., the establishing of the most general traits peculiar to a definite type of land holding and economy.

In the second case (Wat Tyler's Rebellion) we have a concrete specimen (*konkretnii fakt*) of the class struggle. Here we study the vividly expressed activity of men seeking changes in social life. The dynamics of the events are the most important things for us here. The fact of the rebellion is studied as a unique specimen, in a definite country, at a precise and exactly determined time, with the participation of a definitely delimited circle of persons who are exactly determinable participants.

Facts of the first type we call *phenomena* (*yableniyami*), of the second type—*events* (*sobitiyami*).[3]

Distinguimus. Phenomena are one thing and events another. We observe the former but we give meaning to the latter. In this Soviet example philosophical interpretation and historical fact are closely linked.

---
[3] N. V. Andreyevskaya, *Ocherki Metodiki Istorii,* V-VII Klassi (Leningrade: Gosudarstvennoe Uchebno-pedagogicheskoe Isdatelstvo Ministerstva Prosvesheniya R.S.F.S.R., 1958), p. 83.

What really troubles the non-determinist historian about this attitude, whether expressed by Marxist or other determinist historians, is not the joining of phenomena and interpretation in sequential relationships which produce philosophical meanings. It is the failure to admit that these meanings are what Kant called *noumena*. They exist in the mind of the historian who is himself always somewhere in the stream of time and place and whose mind, in its organization of the phenomena perceived through the senses, consciously and unconsciously picks and chooses and arranges its observations into "events." When applied to the future they are the stuff of prophecy.[4]

What conclusions can be drawn?

The historian is a scientist in research. In interpretation he is a philosopher. In presentation he is an artist.

The historian has the duty to present his findings and insights as effectively as possible—whether in print, in speech, on film, or through the still newer electronic media which have been relatively neglected by professional historians. That is not to say that he should permit the art of his presentation to dominate the material. He would then repeat the error of those Renaissance historians whose chief goal was stylistic imitation of Livy or Tacitus but whose content was buried beneath a farrago of beautiful, meaningless latinity.

He must be a scientist when determining phenomena through research. Nothing less than the greatest accuracy

---

[4] Pieter Geyl, "Toynbee as Prophet," *Toynbee and History* (Boston: Porter Sargent, 1956). "Toynbee's thinking is revolutionary, 'metaphysical' in the sense in which Burke used that word, abstract. To my view, this is as much as to say *unhistorical*. For all his wealth of detail . . . he is never for one moment captivated by it. . . . "It is not only . . . the looking for laws, the generalizations, even the faulty reasonings, that offend: it is the vision itself in which every age and every civilization is judged by a standard foreign to it, and its importance restricted to what it contributed to an arbitrarily chosen principle (p. 361)."

which modern research tools and critical analysis and evaluation permit can be demanded at the present stage of technological and scientific development in all research fields.

Last but not least, the historian must be a philosopher. He must interpret and profess fearlessly the truth that has grown within the microcosm of his own being as he has scrutinized the macrocosm of human events. This will help him to know himself and should be of use to his fellowmen. But he must realize the individual character of his insights and must never lose his tolerance for differing or opposing interpretations. He must join the humanistic virtues to those of science.

Artist, scientist, philosopher—it is a complex but highly rewarding discipline to which Cleo calls her devotees.

Apollo, Dionysos and the Computer

By Andre Michalopoulos

> Tell ye the king: the craven hall is fallen in decay
> Apollo hath no chapel left, no prophesying bay,
> No talking spring. The stream is dry that had so much
>   to say.

That was the last message, delivered in 360 A.D., by Appollo's oracle at Delphi to the Byzantine Emporer Julian. Since the death of the luminous god the gift of prophesy has vanished from the world, and it is with a sense of tragic irony that we now read the impressive words of Thomas Jefferson, in my opinion the greatest American of all time:

The mobs of great cities add just so much to the support of pure government as sores do to the strength of the human body. . . . I think our governments will remain virtuous *for many centuries,* as long as they are chiefly agricultural; and this will be as long as there are vacant lands in America. When they get piled upon one another in large cities as in Europe, they will become as corrupt as in Europe.

Jefferson was a wise statesman and philosopher but prophetic vision was denied to him. He could not possibly foresee the Industrial Revolution, the orgasm of scientific discovery, and the population explosion which have swept over the world in the fourteen decades since his death. But his prediction of the evils that would ensue when the mobs got "piled upon one another in large cities" is valid.

If Jefferson were alive today he would no doubt be horrified by the extent to which the western world is becoming urbanized, and by the prospect of the whole eastern seaboard of the United States soon becoming one vast, sprawling metropolitan area from Boston to Washington, as we are told.

This massive urbanization, the piling up of millions of people upon one another, the acceleration of industrial production to meet their needs, and the rapid advance of science to serve the requirements both of industry and of destruction have completely changed the way of life of civilized man. Despite academic denials, the powerful trends of progress are bound to effect changes in the basic values of our civilization.

Among the "values" upon which emphasis seems to be laid today are "progress" and "security." Etymologically the word "progress" denotes forward movement. The assumption that all forward movement unchecked by moral controls is desirable, is fallacious and dangerous. On the other hand, the blind acceptance of the kind of security offered by a materialistic civilization is motivated either by lack of imagination or by fear. Both are negative qualities and if they gain supremacy over the youth of today which is the hope of tomorrow they will bring about the dissolution of a civilization based on imagination, individual enterprise, courage, and faith.

It is a frightening thought that the irresistible sweep of materialistic progress might be a biological urge like that which propels a swarm of locusts—unreasoning, uncontrollable; and might inevitably end in the self-destruction of our civilization. I am sincerely happy that I do not possess the scientific qualifications to present this passing thought as a probable theory. However, it is an incontestable fact that the advance of science has placed at the disposal of the two great powers—controlling the world and opposing each other with hostile ideologies—devastating weapons which, at the touch of a button, could unleash total destruction upon humanity. We belive that reason and fear will combine to prevent such a catastrophe, and we rely more upon fear, since history has proved that in power politics reason has ever provided the excuse for wars that greed and passion have brought about and which reason itself has never prevented.

Scientific invention, the harbinger of progress, claims, not without sincerity, that its purpose is to benefit mankind. Yet, like an electric current, it has its negative as well as its positive pole. Its benefits seem always to be linked with its capacity for destruction.

On October 5, 1908, when I was eleven years of age, I flew with Wilbur Wright at Le Mans, in France. My light weight gave him the opportunity of establishing a record in his flimsy machine for a flight with a passenger. He was successful, for we flew for four minutes and fifty-four seconds. Wright, who was not only a great inventor, but a warm human being who knew how to endear himself to a small boy, said something to me which I did not fully understand at the time but which impressed itself upon my mind. He said: "My brother and I have perfected this machine just so far as can be done in one generation; but in your lifetime, my boy, you will see our invention carried to a point where it will serve the needs of mankind beyond anything we can imagine now. But also I am afraid that men *will use it to destroy themselves.*" Within six years the airplane was being used as a weapon of destruction in World War I. Today it is a superb means of communications; it is also a devastating instrument of war.

It is not with the scientist or the inventor that we should quarrel; but it is perhaps a dismal truth that progress, like Circe's wine, is too heady a draught for human beings to take.

The fact is that under the stress of scientific progress a universal climate of fear has spread over the peoples of the earth. It has crept up on us gradually and we who are older and have known freer days may not be so acutely aware of it. If I may be excused my Nestorian reminiscences, I would say that when I was seven or eight years old and learning the history of the Greek War of Independence, I asked my father whether Greece would ever again be invaded by the Turks. Europe was then basking in the peace, security, and prosperity of the post-Victorian period; there had been no major war for half a century; there was no fear; there was a general anticipation of continued halcyon days. My father replied: "Son, we are living in the twentieth century. Wars are barbaric, they are a thing of the past." Many people really believed that.

I took part in the First World War; I witnessed the invasion of Greece by the Nazis and took part in the Second World War. During my lifetime horrors have been committed by human beings beside which the barbarities of the Middle Ages appear insignificant. Yet I am still conditioned to the moral values, the hopes and ideals of my sheltered boyhood. I do not *feel* the fear which I perceive around me.

Fortunately, nature has invested youth with a driving vital force which rejects pessimism and fear and looks forward to the future with hope. Herein lies the promise of survival. Nonetheless the young people of today are suffering from a double handicap unknown to those of my generation. First, they are not far removed from the influence of those who were deeply scarred and disillusioned by the Great Depression. The insecurity it bred has never been totally eradicated from the collective memory of Americans. Second, the youth of today are the children of those who went through World War II—a necessary war for the free nations, but one which solved none of the problems of humanity, but, on the contrary, left it in a state of political and economic chaos and in a vacuum of faith.

Thus, in the prevailing climate of instability, it is not surprising that the normally hopeful and trusting instincts of the young are all too frequently driven into the negative channels of cynical materialism and protective opportunism. Cooped up in over-populated areas, breathing polluted air, aware of the lack of idealism in their parents, and witnessing the remorseless struggle for gain around them, they live in a sad, closed world where the clear winds of freedom and adventure never blow, and their principal flight from tedium is afforded by the violence of television. Being deeply insecure they worship one deity alone: the goddess Security.

Where in this modern, computerized, sophisticated world are the Sirens, the Circes, the Calypsos, the Cyclopes, the stormy seas of adventure to challenge the courage and ingenuity of an Odysseus—the prototype of the completely integrated man?

It is, of course, perfectly normal for a person to wish to be secure and the pursuit of material prosperity is quite legitimate. Training geared to its achievement is useful and, in contemporary society, very necessary. But the man who sets his sights exclusively on material well-being and attains it by neglecting the spiritual side of his nature, the development of which is vital to his happiness, ends up in a terrible vacuum of frustration which in "successful" men cannot but lead to aggressive and even violent self-assertion and to excruciating loneliness.

It is in this context that I find the emphasis laid upon security to the exclusion of deeper moral values to be alarming.

The votaries of the goddess Security find the doors of progress wide open before them. Magnificent educational facilities are available to the young in this country. But how many of the students entering a university have been taught by their parents or trained by their high-school teachers to regard the education they are about to receive on the higher level as a moral and intellectual endowment for permanent contentment and happiness throughout their lives? Is it excellence for the sake of excellence that they seek with the knowledge that when it has been attained it is a powerful asset for success? Or is it the sad truth that a very great proportion of students care little for excellence and think of education only in terms of credits to be ground out to a stipulated total or of specific technical skills to be acquired as a passport of entry into a vast industrial machine? They are assured that under the auspices of the goddess Security a degree certifying specific abilities, unrelated to the wider domain of wisdom or maturity, will secure them immediate employment, an adequate salary, and regular promotion. They thus enter upon the inexorable path of "success." They apply themselves diligently to a routine for which they have been adequately trained. In most cases imagination is not required—indeed it might be harmful; the routine of business must not be disturbed by originality. Conformity is of the essence, extending to the private lives of the employees. Often before they can attain executive eminence even their wives are investigated to ensure that they too conform to the rigid pattern of propriety. The houses in which they live must be approved; they must join the proper country club; the cocktail party becomes the spiritual hub of their lives.

Then there are the paler votaries of the goddess Security, those who do not aspire to any degree of executive eminence, but who are content to eke out their lives in dull proficiency, performing their routine tasks with assiduous competence, and proceeding smoothly along the path of promotions and salary increases until they reach the age of retirement and are put out to pasture with an adequate pension. These people find themselves utterly lost for lack of inner resources. Having led mechanical lives within the protective walls of some great impersonal organization, they find themselves suddenly alone in the wide world. Refuge in a hobby is of little avail because a hobby is a game, not a serious occupation. Some contemplate enjoyment of a well-earned rest. Such can be seen in numbers on the esplanade of St. Petersburg, Florida, reading the Florida *Times* or dozing in the sun. Within two or three years they are dead, because neither spirit nor body can thrive in a vacuum, and for these wretched creatures nothing but account books, vouchers, and monthly statements could fill that vacuum.

The popular magazines are full of articles on the problems of the modern career woman. To expatiate upon this well-worn theme would be otiose. The stolid, sensible Swiss have saved their womenfolk from the agony of psychological turmoil by refusing them the vote. In the rest of the free world women have given up their paramount influence over men in exchange for the miserable mess of equalitarian pottage. In a predominantly middle-class society, the reduction of the home from a comfortable house to a two- or three-room apartment has divested woman of her matriarchal role. Economic stress sends her out to work in the markets of men. She is often successful, because, as Plato says, woman's intellect is equal to man's, but it is none the less true that her independence has made her psychologically insecure. The emancipation of the female has destroyed the family as a social unit. The unit is now the individual, male and female. With the sanctity of marriage and the family, over which Zeus and Hera once presided, becoming obsolete, divorces become casual conveniences, and the increase in divorce brings with it inevitably an increase in general insecurity.

Still the wheels of progress must turn and the universities provide ample instruction for bright, eager, hopeful young females courageous enough to go out into the world and fend for themselves. It is, however, sad to note how many young women show a preference for courses in psychology, the most useless and, in my reactionary opinion, immoral of disciplines, since its aim is to reveal how other people's minds work in order the better to diddle them.

In this connection, I am much impressed by the words of Dr. Robert Coles, a research psychiatrist at Harvard, in a review published in *The New York Times Book Review* section on February 26, 1967. Dr. Coles writes:

> There are times when I become convinced that millions of Americans are utterly mad, and that the "sickest" patients I treat, those utterly disenchanted with the world and for that reason living in a hospital, are in fact the most sane. Certainly no patient of mine has ever written a book like "Psycho-Cybernetics," and none of them would find it anything but ridiculous; though I fear that all of them would find it handy evidence for their contention that ordinary "normal" people can (and do) subscribe to the most incredible nonsense, while the "mentally ill" have to justify their every idosyncrasy and eccentricity.

Why indeed anyone should write a book on "Psycho-Cybernetics," and a popular book at that, is one of the mysteries of contemporary civilization.

Many indeed are the mysteries of contemporary civilization to people of an older and quieter generation like myself. Yet it is wrong to take a negative attitude toward progress which, in any case, cannot be arrested. We are carried along with it and must adapt to it, not resist it.

If I feel that the obsession with security may be soul-searing, I cannot overlook the fact that the overall operation of the American system has produced the most powerful, positive, imaginative, creative, and generous civilization the world has ever known. Science and industry have produced a poetry of their own. Poetry is derived from the Greek word *Poiesis* meaning "creation," and perhaps there is nothing more harmonious and beautiful than the creation by a combination of multiple skills of a superb machine composed of a thousand parts functioning perfectly with a dynamic purr and serving the need, the pleasure, or the explorative urge of the human intelligence. Scientists, inventors, researchers of the hidden mysteries of the universe are the poets of today; the poets of words have become singularly discordant.

The atomic psysicists have had their moment of glory, and having shown us how to blow the world to pieces, have little left to say. But the molecular biologists have now come to open a new area of discovery by suggesting an explanation for one of the great mysteries of existence—the origin of living matter. This is not the place to discuss DNA, the molecule wich may hold the secret of life. The point is that man's insatiable curiosity which took Odysseus triumphantly through his voyage of adventure is still driving him to unravel the wonders of the universe which are as infinite as the universe itself.

The system which absorbs at the center the vast mass of

the mediocre and the unimaginative in its drab, protective, perhaps unhappy scheme of security and conformity, explodes in light at the top, wherein lies the hope of the future, and in rebellion at the bottom.

The explosion of rebellion among young people in all the free nations of the world today, which is so disturbing to many, is, in my opinion, a sign of social health. It is a sign that the spirit of adventure, free man's most precious heritage, is unquenchable. The more imaginative among the young are in revolt against drab conformism, and manifest their restlessness in various ways: in extreme forms of dancing, for instance, which older people find offensive. When I was young my elders objected to the tango. Age finds it difficult to adapt to new patterns of Dionysiac exhuberance; but Dionysos is a god that never dies. Sometimes youth resorts to violence. This is again a Dionysiac protest of young human beings reaching for the sun out of the dark streets and alleys of the urban slum. Poverty, not youth, is to blame.

On the other hand, the state, through its admirable Peace Corps program provides a splendid outlet for the adventurous and inherently generous spirit of young people.

At the base of progress stand the universities of America. Since the state institutions are mostly free and the private colleges by means of scholarships and endowments provide substantial financial facilities to students, higher education is now accessible to virtually everyone who needs it. In no other country are opportunities offered on so vast a scale to the younger generation. It is to be noted that in recent years both industry and the universities have become aware of the disadvantages of narrow specialization in studies, particularly in the technical field. They have come round to the wise view expressed by Montaigne in his essay on education to the effect that a teacher should have "a well-rounded head rather than a well-filled one," and that the aim of education should be to make the student "an accomplished man rather than a man learning . . . and that both things should be required of him, but character and understanding rather than learning."

Industry has come to realize that a man trained exclusively in technical skills is less valuable than one whose education has embraced a wider field. Thus greater emphasis is now being placed upon the liberal arts and this new direction is certain to endow young graduates with maturer judgment, greater inner resources, and a capacity for a richer enjoyment of life. There should be, in the future, fewer old men in retirement fading away on the benches of St. Petersburg.

Perhaps the most outstanding example of a dynamic modern university is that of Fairleigh Dickinson University, where I am proud to be teaching Classical Literature to students majoring in all disciplines, most of whom will be channeled into industry. We are celebrating the twenty-fifth anniversary since Fairleigh Dickinson was founded as a small college in Rutherford, New Jersey. During a brief quarter of a century, its dynamic president, Dr. Peter Sammartino, a practical visionary, has seen his dream of a great educational institution serving the industrial complex of the Garden State become a splendid reality. The small Rutherford college has grown into a vast university with three main campuses at Rutherford, Teaneck, and Madison, and two subsidiary establishments, and a total enrollment of over 20,000 students. There is also a graduate campus at Wroxton Abbey, near Oxford in England, and a Marine Research Laboratory in the Virgin Islands. The climate of the university is morally strong and healthy. It attracts students from many foreign lands and many states of the Union, but mainly from the robust middle-class families of the industrial seaboard of New

Jersey. I am particularly impressed by the cheerfulness and optimism of the students of both sexes; their outlook on life is positive and eager; campus activities are vigorous and constructive; such restlessness as may exist is normal—the healthy restlessness of youth looking to the future as to a glorious adventure. This buoyant atmosphere is enhanced by the quality of the faculty, the younger members of which, in particular, are animated by exemplary zeal and understanding.

The ten years I have spent at Fairleigh Dickinson University have been the pleasantest of all the exciting years I have enjoyed during a long and somewhat adventurous life.

World War II, a Watershed in the Role of the National Government in the Advancement of Science and Technology*

By Kent C. Redmond

That World War II wrought a major and fundamental change in the national attitude regarding the role of the United States in World affairs is a commonly recognized fact. Nazi successes in the spring of 1940 had compelled the American people and their government to recognize the hidden realities of national security and to adopt measures necessary to the protection of the North Atlantic approaches to the continent.[1] Between April 9 with the invasion of Denmark

---

*The thesis proposed in this brief historical essay is the by-product of a case history in post-World War II research and development upon which the author is presently engaged in collaboration with Professor Thomas M. Smith of the History of Science faculty of the University of Oklahoma.

[1]Richard W. Van Alstyne, *American Diplomacy in Action* (2nd ed., Stanford University, 1947), pp. 418-424.

and June 22 with the fall of France, Hitler had made himself master of Western Europe and his forces stood on the Channel's shore poised for the thrust against the United Kingdom, the last obstacle to Atlantic dominance. In response to this threat of imminent Nazi victory, the United States under the leadership of President Franklin D. Roosevelt turned its back upon Isolationism and embarked upon a course which after Pearl Harbor was to lead to total involvement in the war against Japan and the Fascist powers, membership in the United Nations, and leadership of the free world.

That, however, World War II also wrought a significant change in the national attitude concerning the responsibility of the Federal Government for the advancement of science and technology especially in areas relevant to national security is a less well recognized fact. By its dramatization of "the critical place of research and development in the Nation's military security program," [2] the War compelled the American people and their leaders to reevaluate the role of science and technology in the national life and to revise a national posture which in the pre-War years had been marked by the absence of any popular insistence that the Federal Government formulate and implement a national policy to encourage, coordinate, and sustain comprehensively science and technology as an area of vital concern to the national welfare. This reevaluation was given added impetus by the subsequent rise of the Cold War and, amidst its tensions, by Russian advances in military science and technology. From World War II and its aftermath of hostility, the American people and their leaders learned that they could ill afford to be overtaken, if not surpassed, by powers inimical to American interests. In an age of total war, the consequences could be total disaster.

In the first decades of the Republic's formation, some rec-

---

[2] U. S. Bureau of the Census, *Historical Statistics of the United States, Colonial Times to 1957* (Washington, 1960), p. 609.

ognition had been accorded the importance of the relationship between science and technology and the national welfare. However, shortly after the verification of American independence by the War of 1812, what interest had been present gradually disappeared as the people and their elected leaders became preoccupied with the exploitation of the wealth of the continent and the rise of the common man. The century of relative international stability which followed the Treaty of Vienna in 1815 had permitted the American people to equate security with isolation and, as a result, to concentrate upon matters of domestic and continental concern. Consequently, from those early days of the Republic until World War II, no serious or lasting popular or official consideration was given to the establishment at the national level of a comprehensive policy purposed to encourage, coordinate, and sustain science and technology in the national interest.

Americans had been neither incurious nor imperceptive. Seeking immediate and tangible returns, they had been more concerned with the application of existing scientific knowledge to continental development than they had been concerned with the exploration and advancement of the frontiers of knowledge. Thus they had cultivated the materialistic, empirical, and pragmatic facets of an evolving national character. Proposals which had sought sponsorship of pure research had in the main been rejected by both public and private institutions, including educational. Not until late in the nineteenth century was public or private support for pure research to develop and then such support was to be found principally in the university and the private foundation.[3]

---

[3]Committee on Science and Public Welfare (Isaiah Bowman, Chairman), *Report,* reprinted in Vannevar Bush, *Science, the endless frontier* (Washington, 1945 & 1960), pp. 81-87; A. Hunter Dupree, *Science in the Federal Government, A History of Policies and Activities to 1940* (Cambridge, Mass., 1957), pp. 296-299.

The Federal Government, however, in response to the pressure of dominant economic blocs, had established and sustained agencies and programs purposed to render assistance to particular domestic needs, before the Civil War primarily commercial and agrarian. The Coast Survey, organized in 1807 to give aid to commercial and naval shipping, had become by the Civil War, "the best example of the government in science." After the War, as the Coast and Geodetic Survey, its mission was expanded to include the mapping of the West, becoming one of several government agencies engaged in this task;[4] an instance which in itself illustrates the inability of the Federal Government to coordinate programs of vital importance to the national development. In response to pressures from New England maritime commercial interests, the United States Exploring Expedition between 1838 and 1842 searched the Pacific for safe harbors accessible to merchant and naval vessels. A few years later, on the eve of the Civil War, the United States Surveying Expedition to the North Pacific Ocean explored waters which "would 'soon become the preferred route of the immense commerce that is now anticipated to grow up between the Eastern Coasts of Asia and the Western coast of America.' "[5]

The needs of agrarian America had similarly been attacked by programs and agencies designed to advance the technology of agriculture and to open new lands to cultivation. In 1839, the Patent Office under Commissioner Henry L. Ellsworth had undertaken a program of aid to agriculture which was to continue with limited financial support from the Con-

---

[4] A. H. Dupree, *Science in the Federal Government*, pp. 100-105; Carroll W. Pursell, Jr., "Science and Government Agencies," *Science and Society in the United States*, David D. Van Tassel and Michael G. Hall, eds. (Homewood, Ill., 1966), pp. 226-227.

[5] R. W. Van Alstyne, *The Rising American Empire* (New York, 1960), pp. 126-127, 174-175.

gress until a Department of Agriculture was created in 1862. The Department, raised to Cabinet rank in 1889, was the first government agency to undertake extensive research, and continued for some time the leading research institution in the nation. By 1916, no other economic interest in the country could boast such a research establishment.[6]

What had been true for civil areas within the national organization had been true also for military areas. In times of crises, programs to improve existing weapons or to develop new ones had been established, but no consistent and integrated program to provide coordination and direction to military science and technology had been created and maintained by the Federal Government. Military support had been provided the oceanic and continental explorations which had been salient facets of governmental scientific activity during the pre-Civil War years, but such assistance had been a service function of limited benefit to the advancement of military technology. Nor did the Civil War effect any major or lasting change in popular or official attitudes regarding the interrelationship between science and technology and the national welfare although both services during the War had sought to pull themselves abreast of the profound changes which had occurred in military technology. Changes which made the Civil War the "last of the old wars and the first of the new." [7]

Civilian scientists in government service had sought to make use of the Civil War as an opportunity to involve the government in a comprehensive program to support, sustain, and coordinate science and technology. To this end, they secured

---

[6]Bowman Committee Report, reprinted in Bush, *Science, the endless frontier,* pp. 70-135; A. H. Dupree, *Science in the Federal Government,* pp. 110-114, 159-183.

[7]A. H. Dupree, *Science in the Federal Government,* pp. 120-130.

the establishment within the Navy Department of a consultative body for "all subjects of a scientific character" in which the government might possess an interest. More importantly, in collaboration with colleagues of Cambridge, Massachusetts, they secured passage of legislation incorporating the National Academy of Sciences, a quasi-governmental advisory and consultative body. Creation of the Academy, however, marked neither a recrudesence of earlier governmental concern nor recognition by the contemporary government of any need for a national scientific and technological central body. At best, passage of the legislation demonstrated the parliamentary competence of the bill's sponsor, Senator Henry Wilson of Massachusetts.

The Academy's role during the Civil War and succeeding decades failed the hope and expectations of its sponsors, for at no time did it become incorporated into the governmental structure as a dynamic and vital organization, providing leadership and support at the federal level for science and technology.[8] The failure to realize the potential inherent in the National Academy of Sciences was symptomatic of the national attitude which was to persist until the needs of World War II made a reversal imperative. Acute problems were met by the establishment of *ad hoc* bodies; chronic problems by government bureaus or departments, functioning individually and without established channels of communication or direction which would have permitted the elimination of unnecessary redundancy and the exchange of information so vital to intellectual and creative achievement.

The military continued the general pattern. Both services within normal channels and procedures had advanced their respective technologies. Dedicated Signal Corps personnel had investigated the applicability of the airplane to military use,

---

[8]*Ibid.*, pp. 135-148.

but no major progress was achieved in the years before World War I primarily because of apathy and indifference in the higher echelons of command. Such apathy and indifference mirrored the usual resistance to innovation, but more significantly it reflected popular and Congressional reaction to the expenditure by the Army's Board of Ordnance and Fortification of public monies upon experiments in heavier-than-air flight conducted by Samuel Pierpont Langley. Experiments which in 1903, just a few days before the Wright brothers' success at Kitty Hawk, had ended ingloriously in the Potomac River, causing the War Department considerable embarrassment.[9] Later the Board, sensitive to public reaction, rejected the offer of the Wright brothers to demonstrate a practical flying machine on the grounds the Board could not authorize the expenditure of public monies for experimental purposes.[10] The Navy was more successful in keeping itself technologically current, but its progress was the result of borrowing from abroad rather than the product of a comprehensive and intensive program of research and development.[11]

World War I effected no major change in the national attitude even though from the beginning it had demonstrated that military technology in the twentieth century was becoming highly advanced and sophisticated. Eager to remain aloof, the United States continued purblind, rejecting the

---

[9] Report, Board of Ordnance and Fortification to Secretary of War, November 14, 1908, pp. 279-280 (National Archives); Mark Sullivan, *Our Times, the United States, 1900-1925* (6 vols., New York, 1932), vol. II, *America Finding Herself*, pp. 557-568.

[10] Major General J. C. Bates, President, Board of Ordnance and Fortifications, to Wilbur and Orville Wright, October 16, 1905 (Wright Brothers Papers, MSS Division, Library of Congress); Proceedings of the Board of Ordnance and Fortification, Vol. XVII, January 5, 1905 to December 7, 1905, p. 40 (National Archives).

[11] A. H. Dupree, *Science in the Federal Government*, pp. 301-305.

demonstrated examples of the potential and significance of new weapons such as the airplane and the submarine, although limited recognition of the potential of the airplane was given by Congressional establishment of the National Advisory Committee for Aeronautics. However, no major or significant contribution to military science and technology was made by the United States during the war. The approach to military research and development was typical: a belated, expedient, and inadequate attempt to resolve pressing and immediate problems. The consensus was accurately expressed in 1919 by the Army Chief of Staff's—General P. C. March—observation that "Nothing in this war has changed the fact that it is now, as always heretofore, the Infantry with the rifle and bayonet that in the final analysis, must bear the brunt of the assault and carry it on to victory." [12] The implication in March's comment was given substance by the nation's effort, once the war had ended, to return to research and development as in everything else to "normalcy," paying no heed to the advice of elder statesmen like Elihu Root who warned that "Competency for defense against military aggression requires highly developed organized scientific preparation." [13]

Although efforts to establish a national comprehensive program of support for science and technology had consistently failed in the years after the Civil War, the pace at which separate government bureaus and departments had been created to meet specific national needs markedly accelerated, especially after the turn of the century. Between 1900 and 1940, more than forty agencies were established at the federal

---

[12] Clarence G. Lasby, "Science and the Military," *Science and Society in the United States,* David D. Van Tassel and Michael G. Hall, eds. (Homewood, Ill., 1966), p. 261.

[13] "Industrial Research and National Welfare," *Science,* N. S. XLVIII 1918, pp. 532-534, reprinted in A. Hunter Dupree, *Science and the Emergence of Modern America, 1865-1916, The Berkeley Series in American History,* Charles Sellers, ed. (Chicago, 1963).

level: such bureaus and laboratories as the Bureau of Mines, the Bureau of Standards, and the National Institute of Health. This phenomenon was paralleled within the nation's industrial and educational institutions, implying that the nation, although still recognizing no need for a comprehensive and integrated governmental program, was responding to the profound industrial changes which had occurred in post-Civil War America.

Government expenditures for research and development during those four decades would appear to give substance to this implication, for such expenditures increased from approximately $3,000,000 in 1900 to $88,000,000 in 1940. Despite, however, the increase in expenditures, the ratio which research and development expenditures bore to total government expenditures was the same in 1940 as in 1900. In both years, the ratio was less than one percent. At no time during the four decades did it exceed two percent. The peak was reached in 1915; five years later it had dropped below one-half of one percent. The conclusion which must be drawn is that Americans continued to be expedient and utilitarian in their approach to science and technology. The increase in expenditures constituted, admittedly, an acknowledgement of the increased technical complexity of the industrialization which had occurred after the Civil War and an attempt to respond to the needs created. The failure, however, to increase the ratio between total research and development expenditures and total government expenditures demonstrated anew the nation's inability to perceive and comprehend the intimate relationship between science and technology and the national welfare.

Although government expenditures for research and development were increasing at a greater rate than similar expenditures by either industry or education, nevertheless toward the end of the 1930's, the government's annual expenditures were still but one-third of the amount spent by industry alone. In 1939, they were only two and one-half times greater than those of the Bell Telephone Laboratories.[14] For government and industry, the emphasis continued to be placed upon applied research; the nation's universities, however, were finally applying the major portion of their research budgets to pure or basic scientific research.[15]

Historical statistics of research and development expenditures are of recent origin and for the pre-World War II period give at best but approximations and trends. Before the war, compilation of such statistics was purely incidental and subordinate to "such broad national issues as economic recovery, reemployment, and national planning." They were primarily compiled as "illustrative background materials" to investigations into major national issues and must be treated as such. Not until after the establishment of the National Science Foundation in 1950 was a determined program undertaken to compile and publish accurate statistics, marking a recognition of "scientific research and development both as a permanent component of a successful defense policy and as an essential element in peacetime economic growth and cultural achievement." [16]

During the four decades noted, research and development expenditures in areas pertinent to national defense would appear to have fared a bit better. From a low of approximately $25,000 in 1900, annual expenditures climbed to a pre-war

---

[14]U. S. Senate, Subcommittee on War Mobilization of the Committee on Military Affairs, *The Government's Wartime Research and Development, 1940-44* (Washington, 1945), Part II, pp. 9-10, 21 (Senate Subcommittee report 5, 79th Cong. 1st sess.).

[15]Vannevar Bush, *Science, the endless frontier*, pp. 86-87.

[16]U. S. Bureau of the Census, *Historical Statistics of the United States, Colonial Times to 1957*, p. 609.

high of approximately $40,000,000 in 1940, accelerating markedly in the decade of the '30's. Again, however, the amounts expended can be misleading, for the ratio between research and development expenditures for national security and total government expenditures was the same in 1940 as it had been in 1900, slightly less than one-half of one percent. There was, however, a significant increase in the ratio between research and development expenditures for national defense and total research and development expenditures. The former rose from approximately eight percent in 1900 to forty-five percent in 1940.[17] Nevertheless, despite what appeared to be a growing awareness of the relationship between research and development and the national welfare, the conclusion stated in 1938 by the National Resources Committee only too accurately described the general situation: "Research has never been a large factor in the expenditures of the Federal Government and still remains insignificant in the work of many Government agencies." [18]

The increase in government bureaus and laboratories between 1900 and 1940 reflected the industrial explosion which characterized post-Civil War America. It also demonstrated that industrial America was just as willing, as had been commercial and agricultural America before it, to seek government aid when it encountered problems and difficulties beyond its own capacity to meet. It was also true that industrial America was no more cognizant of any need for a comprehensive national policy in support of science and technology than had been commercial and agrarian America. The failure to utilize the National Academy of Sciences was

---

[17] National Science Foundation Charts, reprinted in A. H. Dupree, *Science in the Federal Government,* pp. 331-333.
[18] National Resources Committee, Report of the Science Committee, *Research—A National Resource, I, Relation of the Federal Government to Research* (Washington, 1938), p. 66.

symptomatic of the national indifference. A Congressional commission, organized in the 1880's to study existing agencies, ambiguously "affirmed the worth of government science" even as it "denied the validity of a separate department for it" and came to grief in an era dominated by concepts of *laissez faire*.[19] Industry, under the control of finance capitalism, resisted technological innovation lest "financial arrangements" be disturbed.[20]

The desire of American industry for limited government assistance even as it opposed a comprehensive program was demonstrated by the embryonic aircraft industry in the mid-1920's. Testifying before a Congressional Committee, Charles L. Lawrance, president of the Aeronautical Chamber of Commerce, recommended that the government "adhere to the principles laid down by Alexander Hamilton when he said, in effect, 'It is fundamental that the Government should not engage in any business which private enterprise can do as well or better." Subsequently, Lawrance noted for a presidential board of investigators, this sentiment had been incorporated into an agreement reached between the aircraft industry and the military services, the first item of the agreement noting that "The Government shall encourage and promote the design and manufacture, by other than Government agencies, of aircraft, aircraft engines, and equipment. The Government shall not engage in such work in competition with the aeronautical industry."[21] Nor as one might suppose

---

[19] A. H. Dupree, *Science in the Federal Government*, pp. 215-231.

[20] Thomas C. Cochran and William Miller, *The Age of Enterprise, A Social History of Industrial America* (revised ed., New York, 1961), pp. 119-128, 198-201.

[21] U. S. House, Select Committee of Inquiry into Operations of the United States Air Services, Hearings pursuant to H. R. 192 and H. R. 243, 68th Cong., 1st sess., p. 1002; U. S. House, Committee on Interstate and Foreign Commerce (69th Cong.), Hearings before the President's Aircraft Board (Morrow Board), September-October, 1925, p. 1166.

was the National Advisory Committee for Aeronautics an exception to this understanding, for it confined its investigations to "fundamental problems of flight . . . basic to the entire industry," performing no research in fields believed adequately covered by the aeronautical industry.[22] In fact by conducting its investigations at public expense, the Committee constituted a substantial subsidy to the infant aircraft industry, providing a splendid example of the type of controlled aid industry obtained from government even in the days of *laissez faire*. This general understanding and the limitations placed upon research by the NACA may make clearer why on the eve of World War II, as General H. H. Arnold described the condition, the Army Air Corps had "plans but no planes." [23]

World War II brought home to Americans the intimate relationship between science and technology and the national welfare, for it demonstrated beyond all shadow of doubt that the scientific and technological requirements of modern war demanded the total and dedicated cooperation of the scientific and engineering community. For the first time, scientists and engineers "became full and responsible partners . . . in the conduct of war." [24] Annual expenditures for research and development catapulted from less than $100,000,000 in 1940 to a peak in excess of $1,500,000,000 in Fiscal Year 1945.

The true significance, however, of the change in government policy was not to be found in the increased expenditures

---

[22]National Resources Committee, Report of the Science Committee, *Research—A National Resource, I, Relation of the Federal Government to Research*, pp. 28-29; II, *Industrial Research* (Washington, 1941), pp. 134-136.

[23]*American Military Thought*, Walter Millis, ed. (New York, 1966), pp. xl-xli.

[24]Vannevar Bush, *Modern Arms and Free Men* (New York, 1949), p. 6.

which were to be anticipated as the nation edged toward war, but in the establishment at the national level of government agencies empowered to direct, coordinate, and finance much of the wartime research and development effort. The first step in this direction was the creation in June, 1940 of the National Defense Research Committee under the leadership of Vannevar Bush, charged with the responsibility for monitoring the "research and development of new weapons and instruments of war."

A year following the organization of the National Defense Research Committee, the president by executive order supplanted it with the Office of Scientific Research and Development authorized to coordinate "the efforts of scientists and technical men in connection with many phases of the war effort." To the new office, also placed under the direction of Vannevar Bush, was assigned the functions of its predecessor plus responsibility for medical research. As the War approached its end, the OSRD was spending money at the rate of $175,000,000 annually, operating "entirely by contracts with existing academic institutions, industrial organizations, and government agencies." Concurrent with its coordination of wartime research and development, the Office worked out "new patterns for the federal government's relation to science." [25] Patterns which were to be carried over and incorporated into post-War programs which continued government support for science and technology. Programs which were mounted, coordinated, and sustained through such government agencies as the Navy's Office of Naval Research, the Air Force's Air Research and Development Command, the Atomic Energy Commission, and the National Science Foundation.

---

[25] Don K. Price, *Government and Science* (New York, 1954), p. 43; Vannevar Bush, *Endless Horizons* (Washington, 1946), pp. 110-111.

After the War's end, research and development expenditures did begin to decline, but under the impetus of the Cold War, this trend reversed itself.[26] At no time, however, did these expenditures even threaten to drop to pre-War levels. No longer was the issue one of propriety and need for government involvement, but rather discussion was to focus upon the nature and extent of such involvement, for agreement had been reached that government involvement was essential to the nation's welfare and security. The corner had been turned and the nation was to commit itself increasingly to positive and comprehensive support of science and technology as an area of vital national concern. So firm had this commitment become by January of 1961 that President Dwight D. Eisenhower, even as he acknowledged in his farewell address the necessity of government involvement, felt compelled to warn the nation to "be alert to the . . . danger that public policy could itself become the captive of a scientific-technological elite." [27]

---

[26]National Science Foundation, *Federal Funds for Science*, VIII, *The Federal Research and Development Budget, Fiscal Years 1958, 1959, and 1960* (NSF-59-40, Washington, 1959), p. 24.
[27]*American Military Thought*, Walter Millis, ed., pp. 511-512.

Guideposts of Scientific Education

By Harold A. Rothbart

PERSPECTIVES IN THE SCIENCES

A progressive science and engineering college of any university requires continuous information feedback from industry, research laboratories, governmental agencies, and other academic institutions because these groups form the community that we serve. The graduates of our college will generally affiliate themselves with one or more of the above groups and very likely maintain some contact with all.

Would not the administration of a college be remiss in its obligation to the student and to the community if it were not cognizant of the present problems and future plans of industry, research, and government establishments? In fact, in view of the time lag between the implementation of an academic program and the production of its first graduate, it is more often necessary for the college administrator to set his sights years beyond the range of present plans made by the administrators of any of the groups that the graduate might join. Thus, the educational institution should harbor a keener awareness of the future course of technology than perhaps any group in our society.

The developments in science and engineering over the past two decades can only be described as fantastic. Not only have the technologies of the classical disciplines been enormously enlarged but the birth of disciplines which transcend classical lines of demarcation has been abundantly evident. Bio-engineering, human factors engineering, space physics, electro-mechanical systems materials science, behavioral sciences, and language laboratories, are all outgrowths of cross-fertilized technological development which we have witnessed in our generation. The future promises similar technological growth, albeit with changes in emphasis. We in education must ask, "In the light of the present trends in our modern world, how can we best prepare our students to assume their rightful role in their disciplines? How shall we provide our graduate with an adequate breadth of background so that he can contribute to any of the hybrid technologies that the future will bring?"

Perhaps the first issue to be determined is what the future holds for the scientist or engineer. We must look to industry, government, and research establishments for their plans and perhaps extrapolate four years to formulate our own. Currently, industry and government have been weighing the effects of a diminution of benignant government defense spending on the economy at large. Will this mean the end of technological advancement and are all our technological needs defense oriented? I think not. Although the immediate government-industry projection portends de-emphases and shifts in emphasis which might prove difficult, the longer range view, which the educator must take, sees protracted if not accelerated technological growth. Problems of water and air pollution, desalinization of sea water, improved communications, development of new foods and food sources, prediction and control of meterological phenomena, biological and physiological investigations, development of novel and more efficient power sources—all remain unsolved and wanting for research and development. Obviously, there is more than enough to challenge our technological potential and to reward non-defense oriented scientific and engineering applications.

As in many of the current defense technologies, the nature of the future technologies is such that established disciplinary lines are crossed. The pedagogical problem seems apparent. The educational curriculum must enable the graduate to accommodate himself to a wide variety of problems which may entail considerable technological scope. Even with a ten- to twelve-year program, the science and engineering educator couldn't hope to provide total preparation, and yet the educational program for reasons of expediency should probably not exceed four to five years.

At first thought, it would seem that a logical educational scheme might be to provide a fundamental program with enlarged breadth at some sacrifice of depth. The graduate of the program could then encompass a range of scientific disciplines in his professional endeavors. However, it is not enough for the science or engineering graduate to be able to understand original work that others have done; he must himself be able to create, design, or "engineer."

To understand the inadequacy of such a plan, one must look to the community served by a college of science and engineering. What function does the engineer or scientist serve on a successful industrial or research project which is interdisciplinary in nature? How is the project responsibility delineated? Almost universally, we see that the usual industrial or research project is not a one man effort but a coordinated team endeavor. Each member of the team contributes according to his own specialization. Of course, the project is generally supervised by a single individual and each member must have some appreciation of related specialized facets, but no one man need know all. Industry rarely needs the completely interdisciplinary man. Rather, the man whom industry seeks is a specialist who is able to understand the efforts of the other specialists with whom he works.

The implications for science and engineering education are obvious. We cannot, in fairness to the student, give him a general technical education devoid of any specialization which is virtually required by industry. However, we must not overemphasize the specialty to the extent that the new graduate would not be able to appreciate the interdisciplinary applications of his field.

In years gone by, after the advent of Sputnik, the reactive temptation was to drift away from the classical engineering and science curricula entirely and offer programs entailing a broad spectrum of courses in science. While it was true at that time that a greater appreciation for technologies outside the student's major discipline was desirable, recent events have also shown that education in the major disciplines was required to even greater depth than before.

We see, therefore, that for current and future technological efforts, the trends in undergraduate educational programs paradoxically should not drift too far away from the established disciplines, must continue to pursue them in greater depth of fundamentals, and provide an appreciation of related scientific disciplines which are or may become relevant to the work of a later-day scientist or engineer. At first glance, these requirements would seem almost impossible to fulfill with any single undergraduate program. But recent changes in graduate school curricula and the rapid progress in high school education have rendered this ideal undergraduate program nearly attainable.

Much of the introductory study which was once the province of an undergraduate technical curriculum is now relegated to secondary schools. College algebra, and the calculus, are studies in high schools. Many high schools have established programs for gifted students wherein higher level courses in science may be undertaken with an eye toward advanced standing on the collegiate level.

Graduate schools have assumed responsibility for bringing detailed study of recent technological advancements into the classroom. Often, because of the novelty of the subject matter, textbooks are unavailable and familiarity with current research and development periodicals is mandatory.

Thus, there remains the entire scope of fundamental technological education which must be thoroughly treated on the undergraduate level. The freshman student comes to us better prepared than ever before. The graduate, whether entering industry or graduate school, must be better equipped than ever before. He must be able to contribute to the immediate industrial needs with which he is concerned, to keep pace with the technological progress which reflects his future concern, and to adjust to and promote shifts in the technology with which the nation is concerned.

Our concern rests with the individual. It is through concentration upon the education of the individual that we strengthen the community and insure national security—not alone for defense but for continued progress in peace.

IMPACT OF SCIENCE

There can be little doubt that many of the blessings and much of the difficulty and tension associated with life in twentieth century America can and should properly be ascribed to the fantastic advance of science and technology. It is difficult to find any aspect of contemporary life which is not influenced to some extent by the implementation of scientific achievement. The degree to which this has permeated our society and its real implications demand a second look.

Modern medical research and application more and more require the interdisciplinary effort of the physician, biologist, biochemist, and pharmacist with the engineer and physicist. New developments in prosthetics, electronics as a diagnostic tool, laser beam surgical techniques, and chemotherapy are announced each day, to mention just a few.

In the field of agriculture, modern chemical technology coupled with high production farm machinery have led to the establishment of the world's most productive agricultural system.

The impact of nuclear weaponry, in particular, and defense and aerospace technology, in general, upon life today is measured not only in terms of national security and the commercial by-products of massive research and development, but in the monumental economic importance with respect to the millions of individuals and the billions of dollars involved.

We have witnessed in a few short years the emergence of a colossus in the field of computer technology used in a great variety of areas ranging from the preparation of payrolls, inventory control, statistical inference in health research, economic analysis and forecasting, to the solution of the most complex missile guidance equations. In terms of its potential, the computer is in its infancy.

Modern technology has led not only to new and improved products, but to advances in processing and fabrication techniques which now make automation both a hope for the easing of man's burdens and the improvement of his lot, and at the same time a cause for serious concern because of the massive social and economic adjustment which it makes necessary.

Modern techniques are applied not only to products and processes, however. The systems approach to the organization and control of the most complex mechanical and electrical assemblies is more and more being implemented in the management of men and capital, in the efficient operation of research and development programs, and as an important tool in decision making. The use of modern systems and computer technology in commerce and industry is mushrooming.

If one looks back at the advance of science from Archimedes in the third century B.C., to Newton's Principia in 1687, to the quantum mechanics of the twentieth century, one conclusion is at once clear. Each century has brought forth much more than the one preceding it. We have no reason to believe that the trend of the centuries will be reversed.

Have we not in this nation come to a time when fuller recognition should be given to the inevitability of the continued advance of science and technology. Toward this end should we not consider the establishment of a cabinet position in Science and Engineering in the Federal government of the United States?

Ours is a society characterized by self-assurance and vigor. We have come to expect, and indeed to demand, success in all our undertakings. The pace and rhythm of contemporary life often lead to impatience with detail and planning, and perhaps an overconcern with the solution of immediate problems. In our haste, our judgements are sometimes hurried; we tend to attack symptoms.

Providing what is probably the most significant stimulus

to the advance of our culture are science and technology. As elements of the scientific-technical-industrial matrix, we are not immune from the possibility at least of impatience and haste. Consider several examples:

So often we read of the announcement of scientific breakthroughs which are all too soon forgotten, or whose magnitude greatly diminishes in the light of further examination.

Consider a manufacturing concern which has decided to create a formal research function and to invest a fixed percentage of sales in this activity. Because of the pressure of competition and the desire to project an improved image, money is sometimes allocated with great rapidity to activities not of a truly creative nature, which are nevertheless classified erroneously as research. More often than not, haste in organizing for research bears little of lasting value.

Even in a situation in which time has been taken to carefully establish a research base in men and material, there is the ever present danger of expecting too much, too soon.

It is incumbent upon us to examine and re-examine our findings and to ask whether enough of the consequences of our work have been investigated. The chemist seeking to eradicate a specific insect must have more than a superficial knowledge of his compound's effect upon other living things, including edible plants, animal life, and man.

We place a premium on doing things quickly to satisfy the myriad demands of our civilization.

In this context, real courage is required to seek the surer answer. There is dynamism too, in patience and thoroughness.

THE SYSTEMS CONCEPT IN EDUCATION

The word "system" is fast becoming as much a part of the day-to-day vocabulary of science and engineering as "nuclear" and "quantum." By system we mean that which is identifiable as existing within a given boundary or interface. It is subject to various inputs which are operated upon by internal processes to produce system outputs. Systems Engineering, which has emerged as a more-or-less formal branch of technology, has as its purpose the design and analysis of systems, the outputs of which bear a prescribed relationship to a set of performance functions determined by goals.

The Systems Engineer finds it useful to treat "components" as "black boxes," each with its characteristic transfer function. This approach greatly assists in the organization of thought and is especially valuable in the analysis and synthesis of complex systems. While mere knowledge of the output-input characteristics of a "black box" or an entire system does not necessarily shed light upon the internal processes, one cannot quarrel with the fact that there are many advantages to this approach. The designer makes an attempt to utilize existing components, items upon which he can rely, under specified environmental conditions. Thus, the system designer is often that fellow who interprets system requirements in terms of available components and who will use filtered data, smoothed data, data processed in one way or another, special corrective loops, and so on, to correct shortcomings, inherent in components. One cannot afford to lose sight, however, of the fact that the processes taking place within the various components are fundamental to the system output. Too often, our enthusiasm is directed toward the manipulation of systems mathematics and the application of corrective devices and away from further study and improvement of the fundamental process. Thus, in future spaceflight system, use of "man-in-the-loop" will require more and more knowledge of the physical and mental processes of man, his internal processes. This must ultimately lead to a more satisfactory mission performance as well as an expanded knowledge of ourselves.

Another hazard often encountered relates to choice of system boundary. While in a burst of enthusiasm one may begin a system discussion by stating that the interaction of the entire universe may be considered, one often settles for a substantially more modest "chuck", often neglecting even those influences which are quite significant. There is a great tendency to linearize, to simplify, to exclude that which causes us some degree of pain. There is a real danger in taking too much comfort from analysis which represent our "rose-colored" opinions of nature. Let us rather delve more deeply into the inner processes, improving them where possible. In the decades ahead, progress will be made not only by improvements in the implementation of systems concepts, but in the fundamental process building blocks as well.

The systems concept not only finds its application in the world of science and engineering but also is fertilely applied in all other fields of creative and analytical endeavor. The business analysist, the biologist, the writer, the actor, the artist, if at all productive, are consciously or unconsciously applying the total viewpoint to their successes. They must not only study the specific essences under consideration but also the effect of other related factors on it. Microscopic and macroscopic shifts in creative and cognitive perspective are imperative to the proper personal expression of their efforts.

WHY THE HUMANITIES?

It is not uncommon for the young person about to embark upon university study in engineering and the sciences to question, somewhat plaintively, the necessity for formal coursework in the humanities. Often, these thoughts persist throughout the undergraduate years, the student harboring suspicions of a conspiracy, the probable objective of which is the making of life even more difficult than it is. Let us "set the record straight."

What we mean by "the humanities" are courses such as history, literature, sociology, philosophy, economics, music, and art. Courses of this type are common to nearly all curricula in the United States, whether in business, liberal arts, engineering, or education. English composition, in the depth usually presented in a first-year sequence, should probably be omitted in a listing of the humanities. In any event, a study of English composition hardly needs any prolonged justification. Brief but honest introspection on the part of most undergraduates would probably bare a feeling of inadequacy with respect to written expression, a feeling borne out by reality. The technical student is probably well aware of the need for clear and interesting presentation of his ideas and his findings, to layman and scientist alike, not only because it will be required of him as a professional, but also because it is often an important element in his advancement. Why then, the humanities?

Never before in the history of mankind has the impact of science been more profound. Even a casual examination will reveal that the fruits of scientific endeavor are important factors in shaping the very character of the society in which we live. The influences in a culture such as ours in communications, travel, medicine, armament, agriculture, production, and construction are manifold. The rate of development of the emerging nations will, in the long run, be determined by their ability to exploit the enormous leverage afforded by modern technology in solving their particular problems. More and more in our society, we see scientists and engineers, formerly limited to purely technical tasks, now serving at all levels of managements, as directors of our largest corporations and as government officials.

Because the influences of the scientist-engineer upon society are so far reaching, he has a special obligation and responsibility to be cognizant of its needs and best interests. Thus, as we have discussed previously, he must look beyond the immediate effects of his scientific findings. He must consider the human values which are an important part of every scientific problem, and to which he may be insensitive. How can the future technologist better prepare himself for such service than to couple his scientific preparation with study in the humanities.

The above argument advances what is essentially a moral obligation to society. Let us not ignore what should be fundamental in the analysis of any scientific problem. In assessing the relative importance of the various factors influencing a technical problem, one must take into account as many of these influences as possible. Humanistic values and ramifications must not be relegated to minor positions because we are ill prepared to recognize and evaluate their importance. In addition, the application of scientific methodology to the solution of social problems has achieved only a small fraction of its full potential.

It almost goes without saying that preparation in the humanities will help prepare the technical graduate for richer adult life as a contributing, mature member of society. He will also appear more interesting to others.

SCIENCE FOR THE NON-SCIENTIST

Previously we supported a proposition which is resisted primarily by its immediate beneficiaries: that students of science and engineering should study the humanities and benefit significantly from such study. The matter is not only one of assuring the emergence of the "complete" University graduate, but indeed one of practical necessity. But what of the reverse situation . . . science education for the non-science major.

There can be little argument against a non-science major learning something about science, in much the same way as a scientist learns about literature, history, music, and art. One aspect of such study is gaining an understanding of the roles played from the beginning by the technologists and the scientists in the development of all human endeavor, bringing us, for better or worse, where we are today. The student thus learns about man's dissatisfaction with learning only of the practical arts and of the beginnings of theoretical science with the Greeks in about 600 B.C. He learns of man thus seeking to know why the world was as he saw it and of his striving for the pattern of the universe. The student learns about the failure of Greek science to bear the test of time and of the evolution of a new science several hundred years ago, based more upon observation than fanciful theories created out of weak evidence.

But more than this, our non-scientist must be brought to a point where the important concepts of science do not overwhelm, intimidate or frighten. As much as is feasible, the student of the humanities must gain an understanding of the physical universe. It is important for him not only to relate science to everyday experience but also to relate one scientific discipline to another. In this way, the words and phrases in news accounts and in the latest books will be ever more meaningful and vivid.

We have not yet gone far enough for, in addition to learning about science, the non-science major should also participate in science. Drawing a parallel, the engineering student should not only learn about art and literature, but should also actually experience creative activity. He not only reads literature but is given an opportunity to learn and apply the techniques of creative written expression.

Similarly, the student of the humanities should learn the techniques of science. For science to have its most profound influence, it is not enough for the student to learn of the accomplishments of others. It is not enough to listen to lectures and watch demonstrations. The student must himself experience science. This entails actual experiment, measurement, observation, error analysis, and appreciation for test limitations and controls. In so doing, he sharpens his powers of objectivity and of critical examination. He questions and generates new questions as the old ones are answered. The student now finds himself cultivating a new respect for the enormous power of language, helping in the long run to fulfill a compelling need in an already complex world for the clear, unambiguous statement. How often have we witnessed difficulties arising out of what has to come to be known popularly as "communications breakdowns," many originating with imprecise or overly subjective statements.

What we propose is that the study of science can assist in the making of rational assessments of a given event, scientific or otherwise, and indeed in formulating accurate representations of what has been observed. In so doing, the value of science education goes far beyond the yielding of cultural and historical benefits which in themselves provide ample justification for such study..

CREATIVITY IN EDUCATION

Of the many criticisms which are levelled against educational systems in general, perhaps the most serious (and most justified) is the claim that creative growth is not in any significant way encouraged, nor is the proper environment provided for its development.

Contemporary institutions of learning, embracing education at all levels, are in large measure oriented to development of logic, problem solving, analysis, data collection, and similar activities which focus on what already exists, rather than what should, or could, exist. Too little time, effort, attention and concern is given the fostering of creative activity. Believing that creativity is impossible to promote, our institutions are often denuded of any creative life which might, with some effort, be developed.

It is our belief that most human beings, who may not outwardly appear in any way extraordinary, possess generally untapped creative potential. If this premise is valid, it follows that the educational experience could be immeasurably richer and significant if it at least attempted, in a meaningful way, to prepare students for more intuitive, creative thinking. What we propose is that an important avenue for achieving this goal is through direct contact and experience with the creative arts. We believe that such experience will lead to substantial benefits in other, seemingly unrelated, areas of creative endeavor.

In fact, it may be stated that art is indispensable to a full life, and we believe that a direct experience in the creative arts may lead to the emergence of a more sensitive and aware human being. Too few educators today are aware of the fact that dance, music, painting, drama, and sculpture are forms of knowledge in their own right.

Far too often we are apt to forget that man's means of expression is not confined to words. We tend to forget that all languages had their origins in some form of graphic expression.

It is of lesser value to instill familiarity with great artists and works of art, by organizing "art facts" or cataloging "culture" than to acquaint the student with the actual creative process so he in turn may learn how to release his own latent possibilities.

It is not our purpose to stress techniques, but rather to

discover the artistic personality of each student and strive to establish a definite emotional connection between the student and the created object, whether it be a painting, sculpture, or dance.

Psychologists have found that the creative impulse may originate as serving a fantasy of the individual, but to the extent that it may emerge and be released from personal conflicts, a true process of creative communication may be initiated. Needless to say, this process once established may lead to concrete achievement, some in the fields of arts, others devoted to problem solving, inventiveness in science, or to the enrichment of the individual's existence.

William Blake has described the act of creation most spiritually:

"Trembling I sit day and night, my friends are astonished at me
Yet they forgive my wanderings, I rest not from my great task
To open the Eternal Worlds, to open the immortal eyes of men
inward into the worlds of thought, into Eternity
Ever expanding in the Bosom of God, the Human Imagination."

The Challenge of Technology

By Harriett Spagnoli

The present generation has experienced advances which have wrought great changes in the life pattern of modern man. Technology has opened many exciting vistas: space travel, long-term underwater habitation, increasing freedom from disease, and remarkable replacement surgery for the human body. Additional material comforts and leisure time have been made possible as programmed information and decision-making have been increasingly utilized as energy-saving devices.

With the advent of this growth in knowledge and technological expansion, man has had to become increasingly specialized. The breadth of interests and contributions of a Leonardo da Vinci can no longer be encompassed by one man. Technology has tended to reduce man's individuality and to place him into readily manipulated groups. The excitement shown by the younger members of our society for "computerized dating" bears ominous overtones. It is necessary, thus, for man to apply his creative intellect to the study of this technology so that he can define the major problems and assets it holds for him.

To this end, it will be imperative for men of diverse interests—philosophers, artists, scientists, historians—to develop closer cooperation with each other. Their basic goal is the comprehension of the continued evolution of man, and his special human traits, in an automated society. Intelligent, concerted action can then be taken to insure the maintenance of his moral fiber and creativity as the sinew of that society.

At this point, some clarification of the term technology, as it will be used in this discussion and its historical development is in order. To date, technology has tended to be defined fairly narrowly in terms of the development and use of the machine. Every school child has had to learn of the significance of the machine to the Industrial Revolution of the nineteenth century in the Western world and its effect on the leisure time of man and his arts as well as his working conditions. With the development of huge manufacturing organizations and the consequent growth of unions and urban concentration, his personal relations became much more involved. The machine lay at the center of this increasingly complex environmental niche. Today, every school child has felt the twentieth-century impact of a Technological Revolution initiated by the machine in the past but already established as a force in its own right. It has superseded the machine. As Ellul has pointed out, man learned to deal with the machine and yet retained his independence; he has not yet learned to deal with technology and retain his independence. Within organizations a greater efficiency of operation has occurred as man's personal relationships have been replaced by computerized cataloguing.

The causes involved in campus revolts may in large part be related to the recognition of this energy-saving, demoralizing efficiency. As the student attempts to establish himself as a mature, controlling element in society, he is faced with the gnawing sensation that his presence in this society—as typified by the university body—may amount to little more than a grade-point ratio totalled on an IBM card which bears his student identification number. Adult society can profit from an analysis of this student revolt. To capitulate to the student by granting him a non-voting seat in the university administrative councils and a pittance of pay for editing the school newspaper does him an injustice. It would be more realistic for the faculty body to help the student realize the universal nature of the problem and the special contribution which the candor and energy of his youthful mind can make in solving it. Student and teacher could share the complexities of defining individual and group action in relation to this relentless technology which treats the scholar in the hallowed university hall with the same disregard as the patient in the hospital corridor or the personnel of the Pentagon conference room.

Ellul sounds the note of alarm in this technological mastery: "But when technique enters into every area of life, including the human, it ceases to be external to man and becomes his very substance. It is no longer face to face with man but is integrated with him, and it progressively absorbs him. In this respect, technique is radically different from the machine. This transformation, so obvious in modern society, is the result of the fact that technique has become autonomous." [1]

It is evident that man must retain the upper hand in the integration of this technology with society. The recognition of the Technological Revolution by today's school child and the challenge it holds for his future is the major task of today's educator, no matter what specialty he has embraced.

---

[1] Ellul, Jacques, *The Technological Society* (translated from the French by John Wilkinson), Alfred A. Knopf, New York, p. 6. 1964.

Worse than the present campus insurgence could be the next decade's campus complaisance with this "game of numbers"—the catastrophe of a generation subjected to the impact of a technology still casually regarded by its elders as an instrument subject to their immediate control.

Technology is thus used in its broadest sense in this discussion. It includes the large-scale production and organizational skills which have developed as a distinct component of technology and which have been essential in its growth.

The results of technological expansion in the sciences and on the material well-being of society are obvious. Its effects on man's intellectual development and daily pursuits are also becoming more apparent. Less obvious, but of fundamental importance, is its effects on man's creative and spiritual life.

Gombrich illustrates the effect of technology in the arts as he speaks of the "victory and vulgarization of representational skills" of today's society.

Gombrich contrasts these present-day technological skills with the individual creative talents exercised by early artists who first developed and utilized representational skills. He speaks of the subtle destruction of general or public appreciation for the creative effort in the preface to "Art and Illusion": "Perhaps even the crude colored renderings we find on a box of breakfast cereal would have made Giotto's contemporaries gasp. I do not know if there are people who conclude from this that the box is superior to a Giotto." [2]

A growing number of writers of the day feel that the superiority of the cereal box has already been acclaimed by a large segment of society and that the number joining this group must inevitably increase in the technologically dominated scene. The power of large-scale merchandising tech-

---

[2]Gombrich, E. H., *Art and Illusion,* Pantheon Books, Inc., New York, p. 8. 1956.

niques to dilute the public taste for creative ability was also demonstrated clearly in the recent rage for op art. The artist, then, must become integrally involved in the problems of technology. What common grounds does the artist share with the scientist in his attack on these problems?

The development of knowledge of, and experience with, materials will obviously affect the artist's work. However, the creative product of the individual at any point in the history of art retains its own quality and significance. To compare the primitive art of early man to a child's art of today is senseless, as Gombrich has pointed out. In each era, the heritage of learning and technical development of the society as a whole will affect the individual artist's observations and interpretations. Recognizing this, the artist observes and studies his subjects critically and compares them with previously observed subjects. He does not accept his first perceptions, as Gombrich has cited, but probes them further before rendering a completed work. This is similar to the approach of the scientist who will observe, hypothesize, test, and continue with further observations as he attempts to extend his knowledge.

It is thus meaningful for the scientist and the artist to establish close communication in meeting the challenge of technology. The effects which all of the senses as well as previous experience may have on interpretations of visual observations are sometimes overlooked by the scientist. Acknowledgment of these effects helps the scientist to maintain a sensible perspective concerning his findings and their limitations. In an age in which it has been proposed that science and technology are becoming "religions in themselves" the wise man will not overlook the significance of the whole of human experience and its inevitable value to the human effort. Gombrich has clearly expressed this as he cites the limitations common to the working artist as well as the scientist: "This inductivist ideal of pure observation has proved a mirage in science no less than in art. The very idea that it should be possible to observe without expectation, that you can make your mind an innocent blank on which nature will record its secrets has come in for strong criticism." [3]

For the technician, these words evoke pessimism: to the creative scientist they are reassuring—they open additional avenues for concerted exploration with other men. The pool of human resources, present and past, is available to all who will maintain communications beyond the confines of a narrow discipline.

Historically, the biologist was trained to respond to all of nature. He was expected, on the basis of broad observations of all living organisms—their interrelationships and their nonliving environments—to discover the natural laws which governed his existence. As data was accumulated, specializations within the biological sciences grew. The exhortation of the famed naturalist, Louis Agassiz, to the study of nature rather than books, was almost forgotten. Refinement of techniques for the exploration of sharply defined segments of the organism produced a mass of detailed knowledge. This in turn caused the demand for more techniques for greater subdivision of the whole. The total organism in its environment was often overlooked as the investigator moved with zeal, electrode in hand, Geiger counter at elbow, into the innermost reaches of the cells. DNA began to divulge its secrets. No reasonable man would belittle these dramatic, brilliant discoveries. However, it became increasingly apparent to the reasonable man that it was important to recall what had always been known: the organism is not just a sum of its parts. Men like René

---

[3]Gombrich, E. H., *Art and Illusion,* Pantheon Books, Inc., New York, p. 321, 1956.

Dubos, Theodor Dobzhansky, George Wald, Albert Szent-Gyorgyi urged that broader studies be undertaken. The effects of the changing environment on the organism as a whole must be correlated with the information gleaned on its parts. The special qualities of man which have distinguished his evolutionary development require clearer definition. The long range effects of man's manipulation of the environment and his utilization of natural resources have to be assessed. These effects reach beyond the biomedical sphere of man into his political, economic, and artistic life. Studies have led to recognition of the increasing population as a prime cause for the continued exploitation of the environment. It has been observed that the burgeoning population and the ensuing expansion of technology tend to engulf the individual, with the result that a collective apathy threaten to replace his creative vigor in the face of mounting social problems.

The focusing of studies on the nature of the population increase and its effects is thus a serious concern of men active in the humanities as well as those engaged in scientific pursuits.

In the stream of evolution, it has been common for successful organisms to reach abundant levels of population. Man is no exception. Just as genetic variation and natural selection have been effective in increasing the numbers of other successful organisms, they have played a part in man's successful evolution. However, from prehistoric man onward, cultural activities have assumed a dominant role. Welding of tools, experiments with fire, development of communication symbols and language, the refinement of the machine have all contributed to the successful spread and increase of the human race. But the greatest period of population increase has developed with the advent of the Technological Revolution. Advances which have brought extensive development, production, and dissemination of drugs and medicinals have lowered death rates in all ages of the population. Similarly, technological innovations in hospital administration, in establishment of governmental agencies for support of large scale inoculations to control epidemics, as well as the support of the aging and indigent have also reduced death rates. These effects have tended to be worldwide through the efforts of such agencies as the World Health Organization and the United Nations Educational Scientific and Cultural Organization.

In addition to reducing death rates in the public health area, technological advances have tended to increase birth rates. In the expanding economies and growing military establishments of nations such as pre-World War Germany and Russia, increased population became a national necessity. The world witnessed the less-than-human condition in which children became a national resource so vital to the needs of the expanding technology that the state assumed major control of the youthful segment of its society. Birth rates also increased in the United States and other nations experiencing higher living standards during military build-up. Meanwhile, birth rates have remained continuously high in underdeveloped countries where the national literacy remains at a low level.

Recent figures show that world population has doubled since 1900 and at the present rate of growth will almost be doubled again to reach a seven billion figure by 2000 A.D. The child of today will experience this impact in his lifetime. The irony of the situation is that the technology which so strongly influences this population growth must in turn be expanded to meet the varied demands of this increasing population for shelter, conveniences, and nutrients. Natural raw materials and open land for agricultural uses, forestry and protection of wild life are being rapidly depleted on a worldwide basis to meet these demands. This is the feedback mechanism which must concern every thinking scientist. As methods of curtailing birth rates are explored, the means for maintaining natural resources must be implemented.

The 1966 report of the Ford Foundation Grants in Population outlines the broad areas of research being applied to reproductive biology and fertility control. Studies at several research centers are aimed at improvement of the periodic continence method, the development of hormonal and biochemical preparations and the production of physical devices which may be useful for long-term periods of control.

The International Institute, which was established at Columbia Medical Center, collaborates with the Population Council and carries on basic research on human reproduction and its clinical applications. The Institute also—through cooperation with an internationally staffed Advisory Council—develops programs for family planning and fertility control activities. Educational programs have been established in some underdeveloped nations and many more are needed. Vast numbers of people throughout the world are illiterate and many of these also maintain distinct religious and cultural mores which oppose control of human reproduction. It is thus obvious that biological advances and technological devices will have a limited effect on the population problem if the leaders in the humanities ignore the problem. Interpretation of man's moral responsibilities within the framework of his spiritual beliefs must be the task of the religious leader and the philosopher. Even in the enlightened Western world society, criticism of unlimited family size is usually made with respect to the underprivileged only. That a large family is a luxury which socially responsible individuals of any socioeconomic level can ill afford must be impressed upon the minds of all men. The courageous, vigorous leadership of an Old Testament styled, informed, modern Joshua may prove to be most influential in effecting universal control of birth rates.

The other phase of the population problem, the increasing food and natural resource needs, must also be attacked with determination. Appleman scores the meaning of the poverty and famine prevalent in the heavily populated Asiatic area as he describes the thousands of families sleeping in the streets, using manure for fuel, competing with dogs for refuse for food, bathing and drinking in the same canals which serve as open sewers for the cities.[4] Sanitation methods, agricultural techniques, teachers may be provided, but the enormity of the population to be served makes this an impossible task for any single nation. Extensive universal support of the growing populations in terms of food and raw materials is required. To maintain a world reservoir for such support, certain areas of research activity must be greatly expanded. Since many natural resources still available lie in the underdeveloped countries, it is essential that investigations be marshalled on an international level.

Ecological studies of land-living as well as water-dwelling organisms must be broadened and increased. Maximum utilization of all possible resources which may effectively increase food supplies is necessary. To illustrate—the exploration of uses for sewage can be cited. The vast amount of sewage produced by human activity has become an important ecological factor in our waterways. To regard sewage as a waste product is as ill-afforded a luxury as is unlimited human fertility. Reclamation of sewage products as agricultural fertilizers has long been carried out. It is necessary now that much more analysis be made of the effects of various elements

---

[4]Appleman, Philip, *The Silent Explosion,* Beacon Press, Boston, 1965.

of sewage on the multiplication and growth of all types of aquatic plants and animals, many useful, others deleterious to human welfare. The typhoid bacillus has been shown to be destroyed within three days in sewage-infected river water, although it will live for seven days in relatively unpolluted lake water. On the other hand, the cholera spirillum cannot live in purified water. Thus, chlorine, so useful in breaking down organic molecules into simpler substances which can be removed by carbon beds or simple exposure to the atmosphere, must be intelligently used if the normal balance of nature is to be maintained. It is obvious that the formulation of realistic regulations of sewage treatment and disposal into waterways is a complex problem.

The increasing amount of sewage resulting from the population growth may also provide an important means of replenishment of resources in the open seas. As man depletes the ocean bottom and shore lands to meet the increasing demands for minerals, oil, and still undiscovered resources, he must assume responsibility for replenishment of these deposits. This will require additional elements needed to support levels of plankton which will maintain and increase the population of shellfish, sea corals, and other living organisms whose detritus forms a large part of these deposits. The eel grass and living plants which are key factors in the retention of normal shore lines and fresh and salt water marshes, which serve as breeding grounds and refuge for innumerable organisms and their young, must be protected. No less important will be the continued support of living plants and animals which serve as direct foods for man or as important links in food chains.

To achieve intelligent, universal sewage usage, scientific efforts and technological skills must be applied in the broadest sense. Additional machinery for definition of sea ownership and area controls by national governments must be established. Water currents, gulf streams, outflow at river mouths have far-reaching effects on oceanic resources so that man-engineered marine operations on offshore lands of one nation have distinct effects on those carried on at distance marine locations controlled by other nations. The *modus operandi* for extension of flexible controls of the sea, as well as land and outer space, must involve the historian, the economist, and the politician in addition to the scientist—all working at international levels. Key areas must be set aside throughout the world to serve as important natural depots for continued ecological research and experimental manipulation of the organism and his environment. National boundaries must increasingly be ignored in the search for those areas best suited to this research.

Equally important is the establishment of other key areas to meet the recreational requirements of the expanding population with more leisure and transportational facilities which have reduced mileage gaps to metric proportions. These areas become essential to the continued development of man's creative, spiritual, and intellectual capacities as the per capita allowance of living space is continuously limited by the ever-expanding population and its technological counterpart. The impact of this need can be brought to the active attention of society and its governing agencies only by the concerted efforts of many men engaged in the arts, the humanities, and the sciences.

To return again to the problem of food shortages, it has been shown that the sea can also serve as an indirect source for more food production on the land. Studies on saltwater agriculture recently reported by Hugo Boyko (1967) have opened up exciting possibilities for the reclamation of the arid lands which form a third of the earth's surface.[5] Irrigation of sandy

---

[5]Boyko, Hugo, *Salt Water Agriculture, Scientific American*, v. 216, March, 1967.

soils with sea water and the culture of plants which tend to accumulate salt are the basic principles involved. In addition to food-producing plants such as the sugar beet, barley, and wheat grass (used for animal fodder), plants useful as sources of medicines, rope, paper, and wood have been successfully grown by these methods. Again, it is evident that application of these studies to the elimination of world famine cannot be achieved by the biologist or the scientist alone. In fact, even more basic than the application of such studies is the recognition and acknowledgement—by more scientists—of the need for the initiation of much more original research designed to deal with the major, universal problems facing modern man. Non-scientists can function actively in forcing this recognition of special research needs. Under the avalanche of scientific information, the scientist may be loathe to shift his research and teaching activities from less relevant studies to those which may be more relevant to the human needs of today. Paul Kramer cites the need for some soul-searching on the part of the scientist in a recent editorial:

Modern science has developed in a laissez-faire atmosphere where individuals have been free to start work on anything which seemed interesting. Also, most scientists appear to regard basic research as inherently more important and higher in status than research on applied problems. However, the increasing number and urgency of biological problems and the increasing cost of research may force a reconsideration of this attitude and require more effective mobilization of research toward the solution of pressing problems. Perhaps scientists ought to have a sufficient sense of social responsibility to be willing to devote part of their time and skill to research which contributes to the welfare of the society which supports them. Also, as research becomes more expensive there will be increasing pressure from the taxpayers who finance it to justify the cost in terms of solutions for practical problems in the realm of health, food production, and abatement of pollution.[6]

Without question, many scientists and biologists have demonstrated directly in their research this social concern. To expand their number, particularly among the young scientists, who understandingly may take for granted the continuance of the public support which has in many cases provided part or all of their training, is a goal which merits the attention of the sociologist as well as the man of letters. Men active in the humanities must reasonably assume a large part of the responsibility for recognizing significant human problems and for forcing an awareness of the urgency of them on the scientist.

The creative efforts of the scientist, thus, are integrally related to the creative efforts of the humanist. Emphasis on this has been the goal of this paper. Some attempt has been made to recognize those capacities which are intrinsic to the creative individual in any discipline and thus make possible the cooperative attack on human problems. Cited as major problems are overpopulation and the stultifying effects of technological forces which are, at once, essential aids in satisfaction of the physical needs of the population, and, ironically enough, contributing factors to the continuance of overpopulation. In view of this dual role, it seems most expedient for man to focus his attention on this technology.

Technology has afforded increasing comforts and leisure to man. It cannot be regarded as mere coincidence that great advances in science, music, art, literature, and philosophy in past centuries, as well as in the present one, have occurred in nations as they advanced technologically and became wealth-

---

[6]Kramer, Paul J., Editorial: "Biology in a Changing World," *BioScience,* v. 17, p. 78. February 1967.

ier. But, as has been pointed out, technological forces have become increasingly powerful in the present age and intelligent application of them must involve conscious, effective controls. In the main, the practical aspects of the role of the humanities in applying technological techniques to the solution of problems related to population increase have been discussed. There has been no discussion of the use of human eugenics involving selective breeding and voluntary insemination to continue genetic lines from the greatest contributors to society and to limit propagation among the physically and mentally weaker members of society. It must be noted that eminent, highly respected scientists in the medical and biological fields have raised the need for exploration of these areas in research as an additional means of maintaining a strong society in the face of the ever-expanding population. Unquestionably, such information should be brought to public notice and related researches continued. However, the writer feels that the major reasons for population increase lie in the cultural and technological area rather than in natural selection and biological "survival of the fittest"; and that the attack on the population problem should be mounted, primarily, at the present, along the lines expressed.

In closing, note must be made of the special role of the humanities in preventing these essential technological forces from overpowering the individual. This role involves the continual exercise of value judgments based on a commitment, first and last, to the continuance of human dignity. The humanist is best equipped to distinguish the subtle timing which must be maintained between technical progress and the human capacity to deal with this progress.

The decisions and judgments which will be asked of those engaged in the humanities—because of the striking developments in science—are great. Does man have the right to control life by his replacement surgery or eugenics? If so, what factors must be considered in the decisions to apply these practices in individual human situations? What ethical principles must be applied in medical experimentation on human subjects and what safeguards are necessary and permissible? As nations are unable to maintain their populations above starvation levels, crime will increase and mental development—along with general health—will decline. Will man be forced to ration food supplies in order to maintain physical and mental vigor in certain societies; and what criteria should be applied in this event? Technological advances will result in more devices for lie detection, programmed crime solving, and crime detection. To what extent may these be used—if at all—in terms of individual rights and privacy on the one hand and the protection of society on the other hand? The list might be extended considerably but this is not necessary: the need for the development of a continuous, flexible plan for human evolution can be seen to emerge.

The tendency for many scientists to turn, in the latter decades of their careers, to philosophy and religion testifies to the working relationship which may exist between the humanist and the scientist. The curiosities of the scientist and the humanist; the one in search of meanings and values which can be applied to the advancing frontiers of knowledge produced by the other, would seem to be the key factors in providing the cornerstones for a vigorous society in constant evolution.

Pioneers of Social Science and the Humanistic Tradition in America

By Willis Rudy

What is the role of the humanities in the training of specialists for our predominantly scientific-technological culture? Strenuous efforts to base educational theory and practice upon empirical social science makes this question all the more urgent.

The whole trend of the past six or seven decades has been toward the development of a defensible "science" of education, one which would apply inductive techniques of diverse types to the investigation of laws of learning and principles of educational administration. All to the good, many will say. Not entirely so! This line of development could prove in the end to be dangerous for our civilization if, through some mischance, it comes to be permanently separated from the humanistic tradition.

We must be careful, in our justifiable eagerness to train

more efficient sociological research workers, child psychologists, statisticians, and experts on administration, that these people become something more than technicians. We must be sure, in our zeal to amass scientifically verifiable information about society, that our knowledge does not become so narrowly specialized and contemporary that we find ourselves losing all concept of its connection with the main currents of human civilization.

In the late nineteenth century those scholars who pioneered in developing the idea of social science in America faced no such difficulties. They customarily approached their work from the vantage point of a broad humanistic tradition and with a deep concern for human welfare. They were not aware of rigid alternatives, such as "objective science *or* humanism" or "pure knowledge *or* applied research."

A review of the careers of leading social science pioneers makes clear their essential breadth of vision. Lester Frank Ward sought to "humanize" the brand of Social Darwinism which William Graham Summer and his followers had introduced in America. Ward's "Reform Darwinism" saw sociology as more than an abstract science for the study of the processes whereby the "fit" survived in society. Ward was actively interested in the improvement of the quality of human life. His disciple, Edward Alsworth Ross, was fond of saying: "Suckled on the practicalism of Lester F. Ward, I wouldn't give a snap of my finger for the 'pussyfooting' sociologist." [1]

Another sociologist who reflected Ward's point of view was Albion W. Small, who went to the newly founded University of Chicago in 1892 to head the first department of

---

[1] Russel B. Nye, *Midwestern Progressive Politics* (East Lansing, Mich., Michigan State University Press, 1951), pp. 150-152; Richard Hofstadter, *Social Darwinism in American Thought* (Boston, Beacon Press, 1955), pp. 67-84.

sociology to be established in any major American university. To Small, as to Ross, social science was a humane and ethical study, not a dispassionate and neutral assemblage of factual data. He attacked over-emphasis on pure science which overlooked immediate social benefit. His contemporary, George E. Howard, expressing the same view, called the motive of seeking knowledge for its own sake "very much of a humbug." [2]

The same outlook may be found among the people who during these years were launching the American Economic Association and developing university departments of economics. Richard T. Ely of Johns Hopkins and the University of Wisconsin, perhaps the best-known of this company, rejected the idea of isolated or abstract economic "laws" and insisted that human economic development was only meaningful when studied in a historical and cultural context. A sincerely religious person, Ely was active in the "Social Gospel" movement which aimed to involve the Protestant churches in the creation of a more just social and economic order.[3] "That which makes life worth living in our world," wrote Ely in 1902, "cannot be presented in tabular form and the work of the men of exact science could not be done, and if it could be done, would not be worth while, had not the humanitarians preceded them and did they not in later times work with them." [4]

One of Ely's most faithful followers in the academic world, a person who had taken a doctorate at Johns Hopkins under

---

[2] Laurence R. Veysey, *The Emergence of the American University* (Chicago, University of Chicago Press, 1965), pp. 76-77.

[3] Sidney Fine, "Richard T. Ely, Forerunner of Progressivism, 1880-1901," *Mississippi Valley Historical Review,* Vol. 37, March, 1951, pp. 599-624; John R. Everett, *Religion in Economics* (New York, King's Crown Press, 1946), pp. 75-97.

[4] Richard T. Ely, "A Sketch of the Life and Services of Herbert Baxter Adams," as quoted in Vesey. *Emergence of American University,* p. 76.

his supervision, was Edward W. Bemis.[5] Bemis, an expert on municipal government and an economist of some stature in his own right, wrote to his mentor in 1890 that he believed his latest campaign against a gas monopoly was more necessary than writing for academic publications, although he conceded that it was "less scientific."[6]

Other economists of this pioneering generation, such as Simon Patten of the University of Pennsylvania, shared Bemis' outlook. In his 1887 monograph, *The Relation of the State to Industrial Action,* Henry Carter Adams of the University of Michigan (another disciple of the "German Historical School") expressed his disbelief that economics could be completely divorced from ethics and social philosophy.[7] Thorstein Veblen, the non-conforming Norwegian-American whose penetrating works created a whole new school of economic thought—the "Institutionalist"—during these years, was another thoroughgoing "cultural organicist." He insisted always upon the necessity of studying economic institutions in close relation to other aspects of human culture, not abstractly or formally. For this reason Veblen employed whenever necessary the tools of history, of anthropology, of cultural analysis. He "looked to temporal antecedents and cultural concomitants." [8]

The political scientists of the era also showed a decided humanistic bent. Charles A. Beard of Columbia University, who was destined to create a sensation in 1913 with his

---

[5] Daniel M. Holmgren, *Edward Webster Bemis and Municipal Reform* (Unpublished doctoral dissertation. Western Reserve University, 1964).
[6] Edward W. Bemis to Richard T. Ely, May 15, 1890. *Richard T. Ely Papers.* State Historical Society of Wisconsin. Madison, Wisconsin.
[7] Lazar Volin, "Henry Carter Adams: Critic of Laissez-Faire," *Journal of Social Philosophy,* Vol. III, 1938, pp. 235-250.
[8] Morton White, *Social Thought in America: The Revolt Against Formalism* (Boston, Beacon Press, 1957), pp. 21-27.

volume, *Economic Interpretation of the Constitution of the United States,* never viewed political developments abstractly or in isolation. During student days in England, Beard had come under the influence of John Ruskin and F. York Powell, Regius Professor of Modern History at Oxford. These men stimulated him to evaluate the political and economic order, not merely by "scientific" and objective criteria, but in aesthetic terms of beauty, function, and style.[9] In his little-known first book, *The Industrial Revolution,* Beard wrote: "The Political Economists who regarded society as composed of a group of independent and warring units did not long occupy the fortress of knowledge unassailed. Owen, Carlyle, Maurice, Kingsley, Ruskin—the humanitarians—impeached in eloquent, if not always logical, English the old assumptions." [10]

Professor J. Allen Smith of the University of Washington, a colleague and close friend of the literary historian Vernon Louis Parrington, spent his whole career as a teacher of political science in a crusade to revitalize Jeffersonian ideals in twentieth-century America. In 1912 Smith rejected the Progressive Party's offer to nominate him for the Governorship of Washington in order to remain a university teacher. Although his published work paralleled Beard's in its investigation of the economic forces which played a historic role in the formulation of the American Constitution,[11] one of his students recalled in later years, "Smith's real impact upon

---

[9] Arthur W. MacMahon, "Charles Austin Beard as a Teacher," in Mary R. Beard, *The Making of Charles A. Beard* (New York, Exposition Press, 1955), pp. 92-93.

[10] Charles A. Beard, *The Industrial Revolution* (London, Swan Sonnenschein, 1901), p. 81.

[11] J. Allen Smith, *The Spirit of American Government* (New York, Macmillan, 1907); *The Growth and Decadence of Constitutional Government* (New York, Henry Holt, 1930).

American life was in the zeal with which he imbued his students for public service and its betterment." [12]

One of the most influential political scientists in America during the late nineteenth century and early twentieth century was John W. Burgess, a moving force in the establishment of the graduate school of Columbia University and for many years its head. Burgess participated enthusiastically in the movement to develop social science courses so that they would be considered just as respectable academically as traditional classical fields of study. In later years, however, Burgess came to have mis-givings about the non-humanistic direction which he felt some social sciences were taking. In a summation of Burgess's views at this point, William R. Shepherd wrote:

The tendencies that appear to accompany in recent years the evolution of the fields of study, more or less related and yet more or less distinct, which have been grouped under the general designation of social science, Burgess regards with a measure of mistrust. They reveal at times, he believes, a disposition to convert an intrinsic interest in fundamental principles into a zest for manifestations of easy inexactness in thought and expression. Rather than producing actual sciences that require precise knowledge, sound reasoning and correct definition for their understanding and elucidation, their development would seem to indicate the presence of a bent for gathering multiplicities of detail and the absence of a zeal for coherent organization and logical formulation. Too much is being assembled in the shape of things of transience which float about on a readily perceptible surface, and too little of the things of permanence which lie deep-rooted beneath. Instead of displaying a vital

---

[12] As quoted in Thomas C. McClintock, "J. Allen Smith, A Pacific Northwest Progressive," *Pacific Northwest Quarterly*, Vol. 53, April, 1962, p. 59.

concern for ascertaining the really basic relations of man to the state and to society, sciences of opinion would appear to be the outcome—not categories of consecutive thought derived from accuracy of information. Quantitatively, their output may be impressive; qualitatively, they are apt to exhibit the earmarks of a pseudo-science animated by mental and often sentimental emotionalism. The net result thus would be the fostering of a cult of generalities in loose and impulsive utterance, of an acreage of pages, of the unlimited expanse of speech.[13]

Similar misgivings were expressed in 1938 by Harry Elmer Barnes and Howard Becker in their massive work, *Social Thought from Lore to Science*. The authors noted the growing scarcity of historically oriented sociologists in the United States after World War I and the growing reaction against nineteenth century social evolutionism. "If we are not to be dragged hither and yon by slogans," they wrote, ". . . sociologists must cease to restrict themselves to the study of current events and history-less preliterate societies." Continuing with this critique, Barnes and Becker noted: "The most common epistemological notion seems to be that there are 'lots of facts' lying about which when sorted into piles and counted will enable us to discover 'laws' that exist independently of the observer. . . . Pure Induction is a god to whom the appropriate genuflections must always be made. . . .Ironically enough, the most belligerent exponents of this metaphysical and epistemological conception are precisely those people who know nothing of metaphysics and epistemology and have no desire to know anything. . . . 'Don't think—try!' may be an excellent motto for some types of natural-science research (al-

---

[13] William R. Shepherd, "John W. Burgess," in Howard W. Odum, Editor, *American Masters of Social Science* (New York, Henry Holt, 1927), pp. 7-8.

though we doubt it), but it is certainly pernicious when transferred to the field of the social science." [14]

Luther and Jessie Bernard, reviewing the history of sociology in America, speculate that the failure of the social sciences to maintain an integrated existence and a humanistic concern in the years following the First World War was due not so much to an inability to achieve their ideal and aims as to the fact that their growing success compelled them "to divide and specialize" their "forces of reform on the practical side and also to divide and specialize" their "theoretical endeavors into the various special social sciences." [15] Whatever the reasons, the resultant "schism in American scholarship" has been reprobated as recently as October, 1966, in an article by John Higham, a historian. Higham notes that in the period between 1917 and 1960 "students of man in American universities" became "segregated into rival camps, one labeled 'humanities,' and the other labeled 'social science.'" This situation contrasted markedly, he observes, with that prevailing during the same span of time in Western Europe. It was an essentially artificial division which in some respects was "both modern and indigenous." [16]

The masters of social science in its pioneering period in America established no such dichotomy, however. Instead, they left a message which we would do well to heed. The social science pioneers tell us that researchers, while pushing back frontiers of knowledge in special fields, must view their discoveries in the rich and varied context of human achieve-

---

[14] Harry Elmer Barnes and Howard Becker, *Social Thought from Lore to Science* (Boston, D. C. Heath, 1938), pp. 997-998.

[15] Luther L. Bernard and Jessie Bernard, *Origins of American Sociology: The Social Science Movement in the United States* (New York, Thomas Y. Crowell, 1943), p. 845.

[16] John Higham, "The Schism in American Scholarship," *The American Historical Review.*

ment. They ask us to retain historical perspective and relate particular investigations to the important and eternal problems of existence.

In short, we must see man scientifically, but we must also remember to see him whole. And to do this we must utilize whatever insights into human life poets, philosophers, historians, novelists, and dramatists have succeeded over the centuries in unfolding. The question is not one of science *or* humanism; the problem is to achieve the most efficacious synthesis of science *and* humanism. This is the all-inclusive ideal of wisdom whose glories the poet Shelley celebrated:

> I am the eye with which the Universe
> > Beholds itself and knows itself divine;
> All harmony of instrument or verse,
> > All prophecy, all medicine is mine,
> All light of art or nature;—to my song
> > Victory and praise in its own right belong.[17]

---
[17] *Hymn to Apollo.*

History, Accidents and Monsters

By John C. Warren

"Man," declared Solon, wisest of Greek statesmen, "is wholly accident." According to Herodotus, he was warning Croesus, king of Lydia, against the reckless self-confidence which the Greeks called *hubris*. Croesus did not think much of Solon's advice. Reassured by oracles that convinced him destiny was on his side, he took one chance too many, lost his kingdom, and nearly lost his life. Then in his extremity he called out Solon's name, declaring that every ruler should hear and heed his words. The value of Solon's admonitions lay precisely in his emphasis on accidents, the unforeseen, unforeseeable crises against which prudence is the only defense. Fate may be master of gods and men, but men whose brakes fail at a speed of twenty miles an hour are better risks than those who are going sixty.

However, ever since Herodotus the emphasis of history has been on the explicable, not the inexplicable. By finding the causes of accidents, men can prevent them. We suppose that only those who do not know history are condemned to repeat it. This attitude has been reinforced during the past century-and-a-half by the prodigious triumphs of the physical sciences. It appears more and more possible to know and to control nature, and if nature, why not man? It is now more than a hundred years since Henry Thomas Buckle and Auguste Comte set out to find laws which governed the affairs of men as Newton's laws dictated the orbits of the planets. Progress has been slow, and mistakes have been many. It is easy to ridicule Henry Adams for invoking the Second Law of Thermodynamics to explain the malaise of the *fin de siecle* or Spengler for equating the life-cycles of civilizations with those of vegetables. Arnold J. Toynbee erects an eleven-volume edifice of splendid theory, only to confess in a twelfth book that the empirical foundations were inadequate.[1] On the other extreme cautious gentlemen who were once called antiquarians and might now be classified as writers of mini-history continue to speculate on which Indian killed General Custer, or to edit the diary of some worthy deputy-customs collector in Maine, without venturing to draw any profound inferences.[2]

Still, even those who most fiercely attack perversions of the scientific method and are most skeptical about its results to date in the historical realm have no doubt that scientific history is the right kind of history. After devoting a whole book to the evils of pseudo-scientific history and premature hypothesizing Karl Popper proposes only to start over again more modestly, taking greater pains and seeking more limited objectives, a 'piecemeal' approach rather than a rash attempt

---

[1] *See* Arnold J. Toynbee, *A Study of History*, v. 12, *Reconsiderations* (New York: Oxford University Press, 1961).
[2] Arthur Spear, ed., *Journals of Hezekiah Prince, Jr., 1822-28* (New York: Crown Pub., for the Maine Historical Society, 1965).

at a synthesis.[3] Historicism is dead. Long live scientific history.

No modern man can quarrel with the scientific method. It has made us. It is part of us. However, as will be seen, there are good reasons why it cannot for a long time, if ever, bring such order and certainty to history and the social sciences as it has in the physical and biological fields. Meanwhile, addiction to it may make the historian inclined to a materialistic and rationalistic approach and to treat as meaningless and therefore unimportant all that does not fit into a simple pattern of cause and effect. In other words, he ignores or rejects Solon's maxim about the importance of the accidental.

Even in the physical sciences man's ability to comprehend and to predict is still in many respects embarrassingly inadequate. One example would be our knowledge of the weather. The atmosphere is a blend of a few elements, so simple a mixture as to be readily memorized by schoolchildren. Transparent, passive, spied on all over the globe by space-vehicles, tested daily from top to bottom, it has no secrets. Yet the experts dare not predict more than two days in advance what the weather will be, and the forecaster predicting a sunny day may even now see snow or rain falling outside his window.

In contrast, human society is almost infinitely complex. Hundreds of miles of records in filing cabinets, dozens of miles of books, from this twentieth century alone defy the student to master them, even though much of human life is still unrecorded. Much of what is recorded cannot be measured. Much of what is measured is so inaccurate as to be worse than useless. For example a simple stiffening of reporting procedures by the police of New York City can increase the

---

[3]Karl Popper, *The Poverty of Historicism* (Boston: Beacon Press, 1957).

amount of recorded crime by 70 percent. Fraud, falsehood, prejudice, and guesswork masquerade as proven fact. What scholar can evaluate the economic statistics of those countries whose businessmen commonly keep three sets of books, one for their government, one for their stockholders, and one for themselves?

As we move into the past, the amount of reliable knowledge shrinks greatly. More has probably been recorded about the daily lives of the headhunters in the Solomon Islands than has come down to us about life in the tenth century. Much of what we have is suspect. Some experts would reject most of what passes as the history of Rome under the kings and even in the first centuries of the Republic. Statistics, the food of the physical sciences, diminish and deteriorate much more rapidly than narrative history. Population statistics for China begin and end with the census of 1953. Even in the United States, where population records go back without a break to 1790, the longest sequence of censuses in the world, nobody knows how many unemployed were walking the streets in 1933.

In our world of ignorance and misinformation, all sorts of accidents can happen, including the mishaps and disasters that vulgarly monopolize that name. Because we concentrate our attention on the known, predictable, and controllable, and because we have such faith in the wonders wrought by science we are always shocked to find an unsinkable Titanic being sunk by an iceberg, or a flawless jet aircraft knocked out of the air by a flock of seagulls. Precautions are taken against the recurrence of past accidents, but we refuse to face the possibility of future accidents. Until they happen they are impossible.

Powerful new insecticides have killed or sterilized whole populations of fish, small animals, and birds. We rely on scientific testing to protect us and will continue to do so until the day when some drug will surprise us with a delayed effect or cumulative action. We and our enemies have enough missiles poised and ready to destroy each other several times over. Though ready for instant retaliation, those missiles are safeguarded against any unintentional release. We shall believe that, too, until the day when a demented colonel or a frightened mouse in a control box demonstrates the contrary. Certainly, faith in science and our power to control events seems to have brought us to a kind of *hubris*. Perhaps old legends would be a better remedy for this than recent history, legends like that of the knight who, swinging his sword to strike a snake, accidentally started a disastrous war.

In spite of Freud, love and hate, and, indeed, all powerful emotions, are still unpredictable. The Romans wondered whether history might not have been different if Cleopatra's nose had been shorter. We in our turn may speculate what course the history of Britain might have taken if Edward VIII had never met an American divorcée named Wallis Warfield Simpson. Certainly in a year of crisis, with Hitler's power swelling to a dangerous height, their ill-fated romance preoccupied the British people to the virtual exclusion of all other subjects. To those who believe that man's fate is determined by the glacial pressures of social and economic forces, the episode may seem preposterous, a tempest in high-society teapots, but in its time it caused more tear-shedding and fist-shaking than patriotic fervor or Marxist zeal.

Petty, personal dislikes can also tip the scales of destiny. The Russians are believed to have lost the great battle of Tannenberg in 1914 because two of their generals were not on speaking terms. Anthony Eden's failure to notify the United States in advance about his attack on Suez would be inexplicable except for the fact that he loathed the very sight of John Foster Dulles, the American Secretary of State. Flinching from an unpleasant interview with Dulles, Eden chose to present the United States with a *fait accompli*. The resultant wrath of the outraged Americans was fatal to his venture and thereby perhaps precipitated the dissolution of the British Empire.

Throughout history the fate of nations has been decided innumerable times by some unpredictable change in the weather. A favoring breeze brought the Normans to England at a moment when the defending forces, which had just fought a battle against Scandinavian invaders far to the northward, were least ready to repel them. A "Protestant wind" wafted William of Orange across the Channel in 1688, while giving the British Navy an excellent excuse for not intercepting him.

The vast Allied invasion of Normandy in 1944 was almost cancelled by a summer storm; but a lull in that storm, which the Germans could not predict, gave the invaders the inestimable and unhoped for advantage of complete surprise. Later that summer, when the Nazis were on the verge of complete collapse, a few days of squally weather enabled them to regroup and go on with the war. On September 17 British airborne forces had been set down in Indian summer weather on the German side of the Rhine. Once across that barrier in strength the Allies could not have been stopped. Instead, a minor weather disturbance swirling capriciously in from the Atlantic halted the airlift, giving the Germans time to counterattack and drive the isolated paratroops back across the river. Thus three days of squally weather added eight months to the war, time enough for the Red Army to bring Communism to Central Europe. Three more sunny days over Arnheim would probably have brought German collapse while the Russian forces were still east of Warsaw, in which case

Czechoslovakia, Hungary and perhaps other nations of central Europe might have been saved from Communist domination.

Modern industrial production is almost independent of the vagaries of the weather, but farming has always been and still is very much at its mercy. Two partial failures of the monsoon rains have brought India to the brink of a general famine. If the rains failed again the government of the world's largest democracy might succumb, a victim not of the maladies posited by Marxian determinists but of a spell of unfavorable weather.

In short, history teaches that man, if not "wholly accident," is accident-prone. While wise men proceed with the task of explanation and control, it is well to bear in mind that understanding and control are far from complete and that we need some margin for error. Otherwise we may end in the same situation as the speeding motorist on a dark night who suddenly finds that the road ahead of him ends at a washed-out bridge.

If, as has been argued, accidents are very much a part of the natural course of events, monsters are not. Variously defined as fabulous, abnormal, or gigantic, they are by any definition extraordinary. Those who play an extraordinary part in history may in this sense be classified as monsters. Magnified by legend, they become fabulous. As Rilke wrote, "Kings in legends are like mountains in the evening." The legend of an Augustus or a Charlemagne may be mightier than the living man. Such men are also atypical, if not abnormal. Ordinary men are not chosen to positions of power. Even a Harding or a Millard Fillmore, when carefully examined, will prove exceptional, though not necessarily impressive. In time of crisis unique and formidable men are chosen, as Winston Churchill was in World War II; or seize power as Lenin did in World War I. Also, great stress and great power twist human character in inimitable ways. Twenty years of struggle against the Vikings tempered King Alfred's character to a singular strength. Without the corrupting temptations of being emperor, Nero might have passed his life as a harmless eccentric. Conversely, the tensions of extreme psychic maladjustment may drive a man to achievement. Thus Erikson's brilliant psychological study of the young Luther explains his revolt against the Catholic Church in terms of a traumatic conflict with his father, his doctrine of justification by faith as an antidote to the black despair of a manic-depressive.[4] These Promethian psychoses, like vultures at his liver, tortured Luther's genius into action.

There are monstrous events, too, so different from the ordinary that in ancient and medieval times it was generally believed they would be heralded by supernatural phenomena. Thus it was said that before Caesar's assassination dead men walked the Roman streets and "fierce fiery warriors" battled in the clouds. A reliable medieval chronicler reports that in 793

> ... dire portents appeared over Northumbria and sorely frightened the people. They consisted of immense whirlwinds and flashes of lightning, and fiery dragons were seen flying in the air. A great famine immediately followed those signs, and a little after that in the same year, on 8 June, the ravages of heathen man (Vikings) miserably destroyed God's church on Lindisfarne with plunder and slaughter.[5]

wick: Rutgers Univ. Press, 1961), p. 36.

The Northumbrians had had good cause to be frightened. Coming events had cast their shadows before. Today, though the skies are crowded with flying saucers, dragons are obsolete. Still, books and articles asserting that Nostradamus

---

[4] Erik H. Erikson, *Young Man Luther* (New York: Norton, 1958).
[5] Dorothy Whitelock, ed., *The Anglo-Saxon Chronicle* (New Bruns-

prophesied our world wars four centuries before they happened have found avid acceptance, and there are those who seek portents for the death of a president as their ancestors would have done for the death of a Caesar.

Signs there are for those who can read them. Monstrous events which have no parallel in ordinary times often have a recognizable kinship with each other. Sir Lewis Namier, scrutinizing the history of modern England with microscopic care, could have searched forever without finding anything remotely comparable to Stalin's purges. Turn to ancient history and read Suetonius' account of the Emperor Tiberius and his purges. The resemblance is astonishing. Both men were masters of maneuver and dissimulation. Both men were psychopathically suspicious and vengeful. Most important, both men had come to power as the unglamorous successors of charismatic usurpers, a Lenin and an Augustus. Both had to win or crush a jealous elite, Old Bolsheviks or Roman Senators, which as a group they dared not openly oppose. Both had been conditioned by a recent era of assassinations, civil wars and mass proscriptions. It is thus not altogether surprising that Stalin behaved more like Tiberius than like William Ewart Gladstone.

A pleasanter parallel might be that of John Wilkes and Adam Clayton Powell. Wilkes, a notable ladies' man, a dandy and leading member of the Hellfire Club, was accused of libel, expelled from Parliament and had to take refuge on the Continent to escape conviction. Returning to England, he made himself the champion of the discontented masses in the London slums. Thrice elected to Parliament, he was twice expelled, and on the third occasion his badly beaten opponent was declared the winner. Thriving on this treatment, Wilkes became a national hero. Admiring supporters raised the equivalent of a half million dollars to pay his fines and his debts. Finally, in 1774 when he was again elected to Parliament, the Establishment which he had so affronted, gave up the struggle and let him take his seat. To crown his triumph he was also elected to the prestigious position of Lord Mayor of London. Whether the Reverend Powell will reach Gracie Mansion remains to be seen, but if his opponents keep trying, they may get him there. The careers of Wilkes and Powell are at least as strange as fiction. That there were two so similar is even stranger.

The moral of the tale is that there is much to be said for old-fashioned history with its old-fashioned emphasis on extraordinary events and the personalities of great men.

Where scientific classification will not work for lack of evidence, old-fashioned analogies will have to serve. One must match phoenix with phoenix, hero with hero, monster with monster, a Roland for an Oliver.

On the Origins of Art

By Gene Weltfish*

INTRODUCTION

History begins where we are in time and space and, in our looking backward, gives us our only clues to our tomorrows. If we are to understand where we are going, we must carefully explore the long road down which we have come, for the past is all that we can really know and the future can best be guessed at through the perspective we have gained from the past. Art too is a continuum, inseparable from all that we think and feel, now and in the past, as far back as we care to go. And so the two categories I propose to explore are by no means self-evident and by the problem of *the Origins of Art* I mean, "What is there in the experience of a human

---

*I want to express my gratitude to Professor Ralph Solecki of the Anthropology Department at Columbia for his critical reading and suggestions concerning the paleolithic data.

[1]Cole, Sonia, 1963, 1965, *The Prehistory of East Africa*, The Macmillan Co., New York; 1965 Mentor Books, The New American Library of World Literature, New York.

being in the process of his living that appears as what we have called art in different times and places?"

In the present-day world, the life patterns of peoples vary in an enormous spectrum from the remote Amazon headhunter, isolated by time and space in his tropical jungle, to the intense Manhattan "sophisticate" upon whom all history has crowded. This range of living patterns we will try to focus on, as well as successive time periods, seeking additional light on some universals and particulars concerning our question.

IN THE BEGINNING

With recent findings in archeology, we now have a pretty good estimate of the broad progress of man's living from his very beginning, albeit with wide gaps in time and a vast lack of particulars at all stages. At present writing it appears that the recently uncovered *homo habilis* of Olduvai Gorge in East Africa, potassium-argon dated 1,800,000 years old, is a fair representative of our first ancestor. To many people who had hoped for a first ancestor of heroic proportions, he is a disappointing specimen. He was a small man about 4 feet tall, weighing about 90 pounds, with a small-capacity brain case not much roomier than that of a modern ape. The apparent similarity, however, is deceiving, for between our *homo habilis* or "handy man" and the four-footed ape and monkey there was a crucial difference. Instead of using all four limbs for walking, our homo walked upright full-time, on his two hind legs, leaving his forelimbs free. These he used to good effect, coordinating hand and brain to produce a knife-edge by chipping stones. This was a major turning point on the way toward his humanity; for all other primates have had to depend almost entirely on vegetables, while our homo, lacking tooth and claw, could still use the meat of any animals he could get hold of dead or alive and avail himself of a high-energy food—through the growth of his mind rather than of his body. Here began man's nearly two-million-year quest for a better and better knife as one of the primary elements of his tool kit. With this mental exercise along with the other activities that evolved along with it, man's brain expanded in size. In the past we thought that first the brain expanded to a notable degree because of a relatively sudden mutation in the structure of the genes and that only then did man have the capacity to make tools and to organize his life intelligently. The Olduvai material has disproved this long-held hypothesis, for it is clear that as the skill of man's hands increased, his brain expanded accordingly, the two factors moving along in close interrelationship in the subsequent course of history, pointing to the fact that the progress of thought and action were never very far apart.

The scene shifts to a time more than a million years later. Man is now an accomplished hunter of the largest kind of game—elephants, rhinoceri, bison, bear, oxen, wild boar, giant deer, elk, and other animals of somewhat less formidable size, but large enough when compared with the size and strength of the hunter. Tens of thousands of generations had passed with knowledge shared and transmitted over and over and over again. These experiences gave man the skill and strength to survive when glacial ice and torrential rains visited the planet, continuing for hundreds of thousands of years.

The pioneer work in prehistoric archaelogy that was carried on by the scientists of Western Europe gave us our first systematic knowledge of Ice Age Man—the Big Game Hunter.[2] In just the last decade, the Leakeys in East Africa have lead the way in pushing back our time horizons almost three-fold in dealing with man's career. This new vista sug-

---

[2]MacCurdy, Geo. Grant, 1924, *Human Origins,* vol. I and II, D. Appleton and Company, New York; Burkitt, Miles, 1963, *The Old Stone Age,* Atheneum revised edition, New York University Press, New York.

gests that East Africa was the heartland of early man as he was emerging from the sub-human primate stage of evolution.

How was it then in that time of human beginning? Our evidence points to early man living on the shores of a pond or lake where other animals were also likely to congregate. Squatting on the ground he tossed away the leavings of his meals as well as the simple stone tools with which he had cut up the animals, including the waste chips of stone that fell off when he pounded the tools into shape. The material evidence of such an encampment was uncovered by a very careful archeological procedure. After an encampment is deserted, it will be covered up with mud and dirt, so that eventually all evidences of the camp will be buried and a new land surface will have formed on top of it. People will then again settle down on what looks like an empty and desirable spot and the sequence of events will repeat itself. Layer by layer, the archeologist will remove the superimposed living surfaces from the top down, carefully recording what he finds in each to give us a picture of man's successive residences on that spot, over the millenia that have passed since he first settled there. One of the earliest of these floors at Olduvai was a circular area about 15 square feet, covered with bone and stone debris such as we have mentioned above, the largest pieces on the outer edge of the circle as if they were tossed over the shoulder. There were no whole animal skeletons. Most of the bone material was broken splinters. In some cases the ends of the long bones were found still joined and there were broken parts of the lower jaws of the animals that the early men had eaten. From the kind of material that was there, it would appear that the meat was carried to the mud flats beside the lake to be eaten after having been collected by scavenging from the prey of carnivores.[3]

---

[3]Sonia Cole, *op. cit.*, p. 116.

But even while man may have purloined the meat from the carnivores while he was unable to hunt for himself, he still could not have used it effectively for his food until he had a knife in order to cut it up into bite sizes and to get out the marrow and juice of the bones, for the human being lacks adequate claws or even efficient tearing teeth. Like his primate cousins and ancestors, man's teeth were adapted for biting and grinding, sufficient equipment for tough leaves and vegetable food, but not for tearing meat and cracking bones. Faced with the challenge, man did discover the substitute. All around the area of that ancient lake, there were large almost fist-size pebbles that had been rolled about by the rising waters of the lake. Hitting one against the other, our early man learned to direct his blows so that he had a jagged edge at one end of the pebble.[4] This was the beginning of our industries and of our many conveniences.

Then the lake rose and fell and silt covered the abandoned camp of this ancient little group. This happened repeatedly in the next half a million years, piling one layer of silt on top of the other and one "living floor" over the other. The time was from 1,750,000 years ago to 1,230,000 years ago.[5] The new residents had no intimation that deep beneath their feet lay buried a very ancient encampment, long covered up by a deep deposit of silt and earth. In that half a million years man had progressed considerably. He was hunting for his own game animals. At his excavated camp site we find the remains of adult animals as well as young ones as evidence of his achieved hunting prowess. In tool-making he had not really progressed; he was still making his cutting tool by striking off a few flakes from the working end of a large pebble. His learning had apparently been concentrated in the area

---

[4]Sonia Cole, *op. cit.*, p. 120.
[5]Sonia Cole, *op. cit.*, p. 111.

of his hunting strategy. Probably, he now joined in groups that would work together to drive a large animal into a swamp where they could pelt the trapped animal with strategically aimed rocks and stones. Such rocks have been found embedded in the clay in the archeological deposits for this period.[6] From the way the bones of the animals were found in the excavations, the men of this period must then have hacked off the lighter parts of the animal and carried them to the butchering site, leaving the heavy limb bones standing in position.[7] Apparently it was also the practise, as it had been half a million years before, to abandon the cutting tools and to "travel light" to the next hunting episode. From this time forward, man's hunting skills progressed. His body became more agile, his walking and running more efficient, as he occupied himself with the hunt. In the next three-quarters of a million years, by about 400,000 years ago, the more advanced form of man known as *homo erectus* makes his appearance. He has become larger, taller, has a larger brain capacity and has certainly become more the master of himself.

THE SCULPTURED FORM BECOMES AN IDEA AS A RESULT OF AN ADVANCE IN STONE TOOL MAKING

In the last half-million years, "Cave Man" was coming into being on three continents—Africa, Europe and Asia—and intervening areas. Neanderthal man (125,000 to approx. 38,000 years ago) in his fully evolved form was a large person with a heavy bony frame and a skull with a massive bone structure. Though not particularly tall in terms of our above-medium height, he was strong-muscled and heavily built with a deep barrel chest. He lived in the ice-box climate of Europe on the edge of glaciers and in the high winds and torrential

---

[6] Sonia Cole, *op. cit.*, p. 116-7; 131-2; 124.
[7] Sonia Cole, *op. cit.*, p. 131.

rains of Africa.[8] He was a hunter of the largest animals[9] and he also began to improve his tool-making skills, that had remained stagnant for more than a million and a half years. The first step was an improvement in the old pebble tool which had one cutting edge at the end.[10] He now chipped the pebble so that there were two knife edges near the head end, one on each side, converging toward the top. From this first improvement, with the passage of another half a million years by about 55,000 years ago, the implement was perfected. It had evolved into an almond-shaped tool, symmetrical in form, with clean, straight edges instead of rough, jagged edges of the earlier tools. It was indeed a work of art with all that that implies, deliberately motivated by aesthetic values—the first clearly identifiable art object of man's career.

As observed by the field archeologist:[11]

In many cases the implements show little signs of use; in certain areas they are found in such incredible numbers that, remembering that the Stone Age population was small, it would be inconceivable that they had all been used. The perfect finish of some of the later specimens makes it seem that the craftsmen took an artistic pride in their work beyond the needs of pure utility. When they were displeased with a tool, they discarded it and started afresh.

This cutting tool, known in French prehistory as coup de poing, emerging as a new form, appears at a site in Olduvai

---

[8]Less severe climates prevailed for solo man in Java in Southwest Asia, Uzlekistan, and Kwang Chi Chang.

[9]At the present time there is an apparent, unexplained discontinuity in the hunting habits of Neanderthal man, who appears to have concentrated on hunting less monumental animals, e.g., cave bear, goat, deer, and horse, while his predecessors *homo erectus* and his successors, *homo sapiens*, hunted the mammoth regularly.

[10]Sonia Cole, *op. cit.*, p. 135.
[11]Sonia Cole, *op. cit.*, p. 128.

Gorge as a specialty among the customary pebble tools. At this site there were only 22 coup de poing among 575 pebble choppers.[12] The long, slow process in which man mastered his material (490,000-55,000), with the image becoming free of its context in his mind, can only be understood as the growth and emergence of art as we conceive it.

The evolution of the coup de poing proceeded in a similar time period in Africa, Europe and western Asia. The types of stone used varied widely. In all cases, the pebble had to be hit with a hammerstone and shaped by dislodging flakes or chips from the surface, leaving a negative, shallow, cup-like scar. Another blow directed adjacent to the first, dislodged a second chip and left another scar on the surface. In striking the successive blows, the maker would have to have in mind the shape he wished to produce and a knowledge of the structure of the stone so that he would achieve what he planned. In the early stages of its evolution, the blows were struck only near the point end, leaving the base of the flint pebble intact. In postulating what the steps in the manufacture of the tool might actually have been, after a certain amount of technological experimentation, it was concluded that the blows were struck alternately, the first on one surface, the second on the other, and so on, so that the cutting edges had a scallopped appearance. In view of this trimming on both surfaces, these tools are referred to as bifaces. As the technique was finally perfected, both surfaces were entirely worked, removing all of the surface crust of the original pebble. In its final form, the technique of manufacturing the coup de poing was so thoroughly mastered that the edges were perfectly straight and sharp all around the whole tool and in some cases the virtuosity of control was so

---

[12]Sonia Cole, *op. cit.*, p. 130.

great that an "S" twist was deliberately produced on the side edges.

That the coup de poing was a unique invention is borne out by the fact that a stone industry which evolved in Paleolithic China and Southeast Asia followed an entirely different course. No such symmetrical forms were produced. The shaping of the stones was entirely functional. Standard shapes of wide distribution and long-standing trends of evolution did not appear. Rather we see that wider varieties of stones were handled, probably with increasing facility, but the standardization of shape was clearly not the main emphasis. On the other hand, the coup de poing almond-like form does have a tremendous though circumscribed geographic distribution, i.e., south-north from the tip of South Africa, East Africa, the Sahara, the Mediterranean, Italy, Spain, France, and England, and west-east from France to southern India. At the present state of our knowledge we cannot establish priorities in one place or another. Radiocarbon or potassium-argon dating will eventually make this possible. What was shared was the formal image of the tool, for as observed by Cole, "the nature of the raw material seems to have had little influence on the technology, for many of the most perfect specimens are made from a coarse-grained quartzite. 'Here at Olduvai,' wrote Leakey, 'we have people . . . who in part, at least, were using materials quite as intractable as those by Sinanthropus at Chouktien (China), yet they achieved as high a perfection in their workmanship as did the hand-ax men in those areas of England and France where flint of the finest quality was available.' " [13] Until all the local areas where the coup de poing is found are accurately dated, we will not be able to reconstruct the process

---

[13] Sonia Cole, *op. cit.*, p. 138.

by which this shared art form including its successive developmental stages was transmitted over such an enormous area of the then-inhabited world. In Europe these are discontinuous; in Africa the sequential development is continuous. In Europe there are no clear antecedents to the coup de poing; in Africa it emerges in the context of the old pebble tool.

The term coup de poing was first applied to the stone tool by French scholars for it was discovered and recognized for what it was for the first time in France. The detailed studies of the development of the tool over time through archeological sequence and technological experiment gives us insight into the technological developments that were instrumental in producing the form. The coup de poing is denoted in terms of two major archeological stages—the Chellean, now termed Abbevillian, and the Acheulean, the perfected version of the tool. These names refer to localities in France where the tools were first excavated and identified. These names are now generally applied to comparable tools found in other world areas. The term coup de poing is commonly interpreted in English as hand-ax or hand-hammer; neither term is appropriate as it is now evident that the tool was used as a knife. In the earlier Abbevillian stage, the tool is deeply scarred with chip marks and the cutting edges are ragged, giving an irregular scalloped effect. The later Acheulean tool has chip marks all over the surface that are far shallower; the tool is generally flatter and thinner and the edge is regular and continuous all around. This result is a direct reflection of an improvement in the technological procedure. The Abbevillian coup de poing was chipped by striking with a blunt-pointed stone hammer, the Acheulean with a slim pencil-like striking tool of antler or boxwood, about the thickness of a broomstick handle, ten or eleven inches long, hit directly on the edge of the tool.[14] Here we face the problem of which motivation predominates—beauty or utility. It is clear that the earlier Abbevillian coup de poing was much longer in evolving than the later Acheulean form, and in its evolution the Abbevillian was trending toward bilateral symmetry. The clear realization of this aspiration is in the Acheulean tool. On the other hand, the achievement of a continuous sharp edge was of major technological significance for people who needed a good cutting edge. Here the two values, use and beauty, are inextricably intertwined as man became master of his materials and his techniques, and in his exuberance achieved a new value—a deeply satisfying form and texture.

After the Acheulean period, technological progress in stone tool-making accelerated. We can now identify the "Cave Man" of France with his work and with his home. The tool he produced known as Mousterian after the first discovered French site is a masterpiece of technological skill. By a series of very intricate technical steps he struck off a large flake from the pebble so precisely that it had a standard shape and size, much like the coup de poing but smaller and finer in proportions. In a later variant of his technique, he produced a second type of tool, thought to have been used as a skin scraper with a blunt back and one sharp edge on the long side. It is clearly the first model of the commonest type of knife that we use, with a blunt back, a sharp edge, and a curving end. These type tools were produced in Europe, Asia, and Africa. Along with the new flake tools, however, in some sites the Mousterian industry includes a version of old coup de poing, smaller and more squat in shape so that it some-

---

[14]"The Origin of Language," Dounak, pp. 104-5, in: *Les Processus de l'hominisation,* Pars, 19-23, Mai, 1958. Paris Centre National de la Recherche Scientifque. Colloques Internationaux. Sciences humaine.

what resembles a heart. Possibly it was made as a tour de force or in a transition stage of borrowing the new flake technique. Dating techniques will help us to resolve the question. In either case its presence in the same deposits establishes the continuity of the two types of technology, the new flake and the older worked pebble. In France, Neanderthal man, along with his technical competence had developed a settled way of life. High on the cliff above the plain, in the shadow of the overhanging rocks that marked the entrance to the cave, he made his hearth and his home. Inside the cave he made a grave for his dead with offerings of tools and food. The meat of the large animals he hunted was brought home and the bones used for fuel. He had gained this home place in a contest with the formidable cave bear that he managed to permanently displace.

ANIMAL BONE, A NEW MEDIUM FOR TOOL-MAKING;
A SCULPTURE PROCESS BY ABRASION CONNECTED
WITH IT; THE SCULPTURED HUMAN FORM PRODUCED
BY AN ANALOGOUS PROCESS.

Thirty-three thousand years ago (radio-carbon date, begining of Aurignacian period), man began to give animal bones a definite shape as tools and implements. The first of these was a long thin shaft of bone that served as a spear head. Another early bone implement was a flat spatula whose use we are unable to reconstruct. Later the bone industry grew; harpoon points with barbs along the sides, shaft straighteners and fine bone needles with eyes, bone buttons, toggles were among the objects made. Neanderthal man had used pieces of bone as an industrial accessory, but he made only a very few crude attempts at shaping it into a tool. The deliberate bone-shaping process required a new type of stone tool for its regular operation. Long, thin blades of flint were

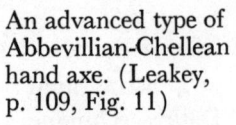

Pebble tool or chopper of Olduvan culture. Bed I, Olduvai Gorge, East Africa. (Sonia Cole, *The Pre-history of Africa*, p. 120, Fig. 9, Mentor Books, 1965)

An advanced type of Abbevillian-Chellean hand axe. (Leakey, p. 109, Fig. 11)

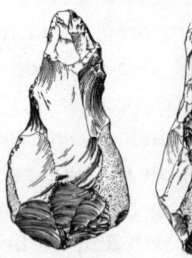

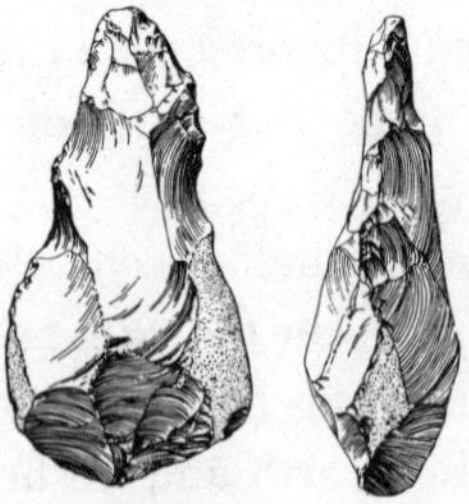

An early Abbevillian hand axe. (Period also known as Chellean.) (L.S.B. Leakey, *Adam's Ancestors*, Longman's Green & Co. N Y 1934, p. 100, Fig. 9)

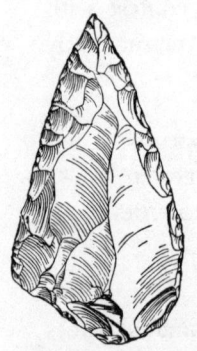

Mousterian flake tools, point and side scraper. (Leakey, p. 141, Figs. 24A and B)

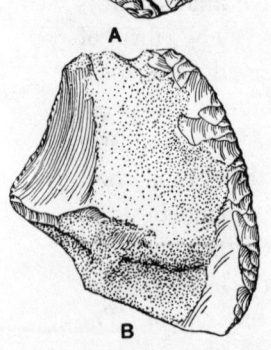

An advanced form of Acheulean hand axe with specially designed "S" twist edge. (Leakey, p. 117, Fig. 15)

A

B

Figure I: Hand axes or coup de poing, paleolithic chipped stone tools.

struck off from a prepared cylindrical blank, the ends of the blades being reworked into a wide variety of engraving tools or burins with a sturdy, sharp point. A fine, small, blunt-backed knife with a sharp edge was also made on the same type of blade. The engraving tool had its main utilitarian function in chiselling out slivers of bone for reworking into the new lance points by abrasion with another rough stone or by scraping with a knife. This operation, however, was not confined to producing lance points. Small sculptures of women were made, three or four inches high, out of lumps of soft stone such as limestone, talc, and soapstone, that clearly had a utility other than industrial. We refer to these little figures as "Venuses" on the tacit assumption that they represent an ideal of Ice Age beauty. It would appear that they are individual portraits as there is considerable variation in style and detail and apparently in the models in view of the variety of their physical attributes. On the lance points themselves, the artist-craftsman engraved pictures with his burin—chiefly naturalistic subjects, conventionalized versions of plants and human and animal figures.

OIL PAINTING EMERGES OUT OF THE PALEOLITHIC CONTEXT IN FRANCE

The period of little sculptured figures of women was followed by figures done in low relief on slabs of limestone representing women, men, and animals. The usual explanation is that the motive was largely "religious" or magical. I doubt that this was the predominant impetus to their initial production although these functions may have become attached to them thereafter. I think in many cases they were no more religious than the symmetrical coup de poing. Aesthetic satisfaction must have been a long-established value by 33,000 years ago. Most of these bas reliefs were appar-

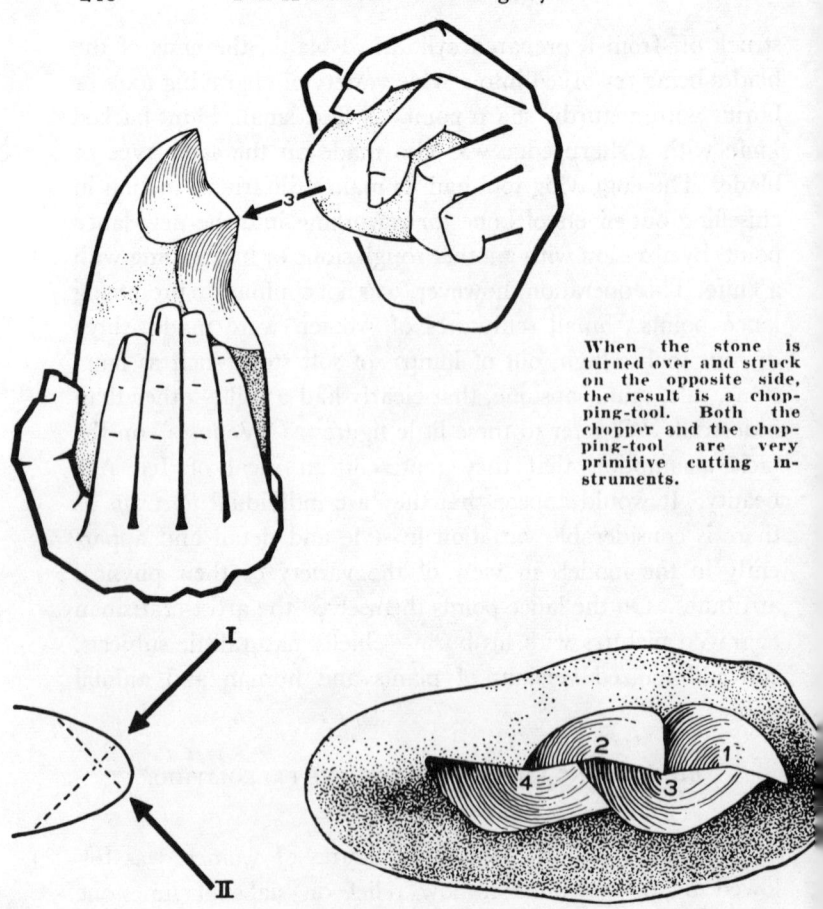

When the stone is turned over and struck on the opposite side, the result is a chopping-tool. Both the chopper and the chopping-tool are very primitive cutting instruments.

Figure II: Making a bi-face stone tool by striking with another stone. (André Leroi-Gourhan, *Prehistoric Man*, Philosophical Library, New York, 15 East 40 St. N.Y. 16, p. 54)

ently placed around the home bases high on the cliffs under the rock shelters, indicating "interior decorating" rather than worship.

The first two-dimensional representations were made by dragging the fingers through the thin layer of wet clay that covered the floors of the caves in their interiors, curving the path of the fingers so that a series of parallel spaghetti-like, snaky curves were produced. A whole series of these would be made in one restricted area of the floor and among these random lines, a head and shoulders or a whole outline figure of an elephant or bison would be drawn. This looks suspiciously like a present-day practise of the person that draws a pencil idly across the paper while listening to conversation, talking, or perhaps while absorbed in his own thoughts. It is hardly consonant with romantic expectations, but it appears to be a well-documented fact that in France at least, two-dimensional representative art began in the all-too familiar process of "doodling." Such figures are found in Gargas in Spain and in Pech-Merle in France where three female figures appear drawn on clay with the artist's finger. At Niaux in France a head of a bison appears on the clay floor among the "spaghetti." In the case of Baume-Latrone near Nimes, France, there are archaic animal figures drawn on the walls by dipping the fingers in clay and drawing over the surface in the general mode of the "spaghetti" and other figures that are drawn in the clay on the floors; similar figures are found on the walls of the Andalusian cave of La Pileta.[15]

Then paints were substituted for the original clay for drawing very large outline figures of the animals in profile on the cave walls. Charcoal or magnesium oxide was mixed with animal fat to serve as the medium. In the course of time the

[15]Bandi, Hans-Georg, Bandi, Breuil, Henri; & others, 1961, *The Art of the Stone Age*, Crown Publishers, Inc., New York, p. 45; p. 21; p. 24.

Female figurine height 92 mm. From Foulet de Gazelle, Sireuil, Dordogne.

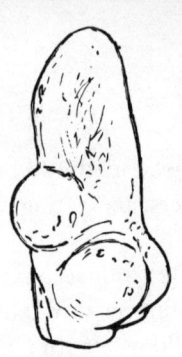

Venus in Steatite, Italy, near Florenc 37 mm, app. 1½ inches high (lackir head or limbs).

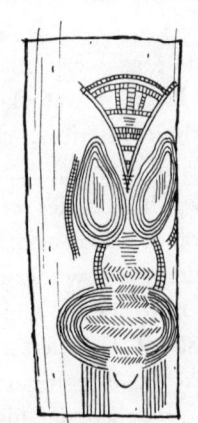

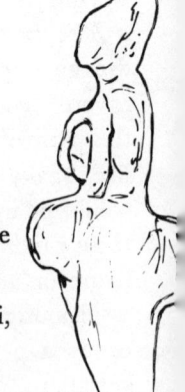

Female figurine "The Polchinello." Height 62 mm. From the Balzl Rossi, Grimaldi, Italy. Carved in crystalline talc.

Drawn after photograph fig. II, opp p. 16. Die Altnordische Kunst, F. Adama Van Scheltema. Mauritius Verlag, Berlin, 1924. Engraving on Mammoth tooth, Predmost, Czechoslovakia.

Venus modelled in clay, Moravia, Czechoslovakia, 114 mm. high about 4¼ inches.

"Venus of Willendorf." Height 110 n Austria, original in Naturhistorisches Museum, Vienna, carved in limestone.

Figure III: THE EARLIEST PORTRAYAL OF THE HUMAN FORM. "VENUSES"–SMALL SCULPTURED FEMALE FIGURES OF THE UPPER PALEOLITHIC PERIOD. (*Old Stone Age* by Stevan Celebonovic and Geoffrey Grigson Philosophical Library, New York, 15 East 40th Street, N.Y. 16. Drawn by Mr. Merill Harvey from Photographic Illustrations)

continuous outline was interrupted, sketching in details such as hair, hooves, eyes. Experiments in developing an impression of depth included deeply engraved outlines to supplement those that were drawn, dotted surfaces and shading of the interior surfaces within the outline with areas of paint to indicate muscles and other surface features. Restricted in area to the caves of France and northern Spain, this art apparently ended with the end of the Ice Ages 10,000 years ago. The retreat of the glaciers was of course not a sudden event. But in sum total, possibly in a period of 2000 years, the large animals became extinct in Europe and the land was scoured of vegetation. Man had to divert a good deal of his energy to finding a new way of life.

In the Levantine region of eastern Spain on the exposed walls of the rock shelters, a representative art also appears. To authenticate its age is well-nigh impossible at this stage of our knowledge. French caves were sealed at the end of the Ice Ages by natural deposits and the objects included in the deposits give us a good estimate of the time when the paintings were made. The location of the Spanish Levantine murals gives us no such assistance. They are in the open. Only their subjects suggest some age. The life portrayed is clearly of a hunting people. Some extinct animals that are shown give it a respectable age. Its technique and what it portrays is markedly different from the French cave art. The individual figures are relatively small and in solid silhouette. In the French pictorial art, a single self-contained animal portrait is the common subject shaded within the outline in iron oxide colors of red, brown, yellow, and orange. Spanish Levantine pictures are of groups of people and animals in lively interplay in monochrome silhouettes. If we conceive that realistic representation is intended in both cases, then the two interpretations of that reality, while both equally

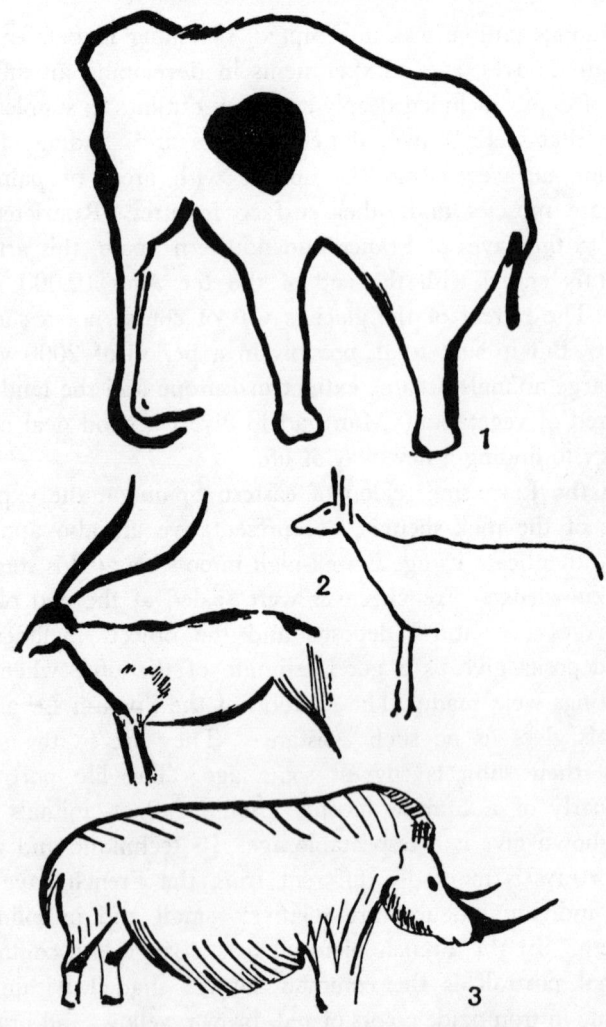

Figure IV: Two early stages in the development of cave painting in France and northern Spain, Phase A and B. 1 Phase A; 2, 3 Phase B. (Miles Burkitt, *The Old Stone Age,* Atheneum, N. Y., revised edition 1963, p. 195, Fig. 23)

valid, are markedly different. For the French Paleolithic artist, the painting is of a solid object as a unit, for the Levantine Spanish artist, it is lively motion carried on by participating figures. Historically in our own art tradition, we are inclined to favor the ancient French view.[16]

WHERE MAT-WORK TEXTILES GAVE RISE TO A DIFFERENT ART IN EASTERN EUROPE

In eastern Europe in the Ukraine, some interesting data of a very different nature has been excavated, dated in the Upper Paleolithic period. At a flint-working station near Mezine, a number of pieces of mammoth ivory were found engraved with a remarkably familiar design, the so-called Greek fret or key. Some of the pieces appear to be fragments of ivory bracelets. There were also five carved figures of birds with the fret design engraved all over the underbody, extending up under the tail. The age of the pieces is certainly between ten and fifteen thousand years. How can this remarkable instance be explained.[17]

By a fortunate circumstance there are American Indians living on the Amazon in the remote jungle areas of South America that can lead the way toward our understanding of the development of these designs. In their jungle home, the Amazon Indians have plenty of palm leaves and strips of cane available which they weave into beautiful baskets and trays with all sorts of intricate patterns appearing in the weave itself as a result of the contrast between the two sets of crossing strands that normally form the basis of all woven textiles. A simple under-and-over weave will ordinarily produce a checker pattern. Twilling which produces herringbone weaves

---

[16]Burkitt, *op. cit.*, pp. 195-239 and Fig. IV in this paper.
[17]Volkov, Theo., Congrés d'anthropologie et d'archeologie préhistorique, Comptes-rendus (Paris), I 415-428, Geneva, 1912.

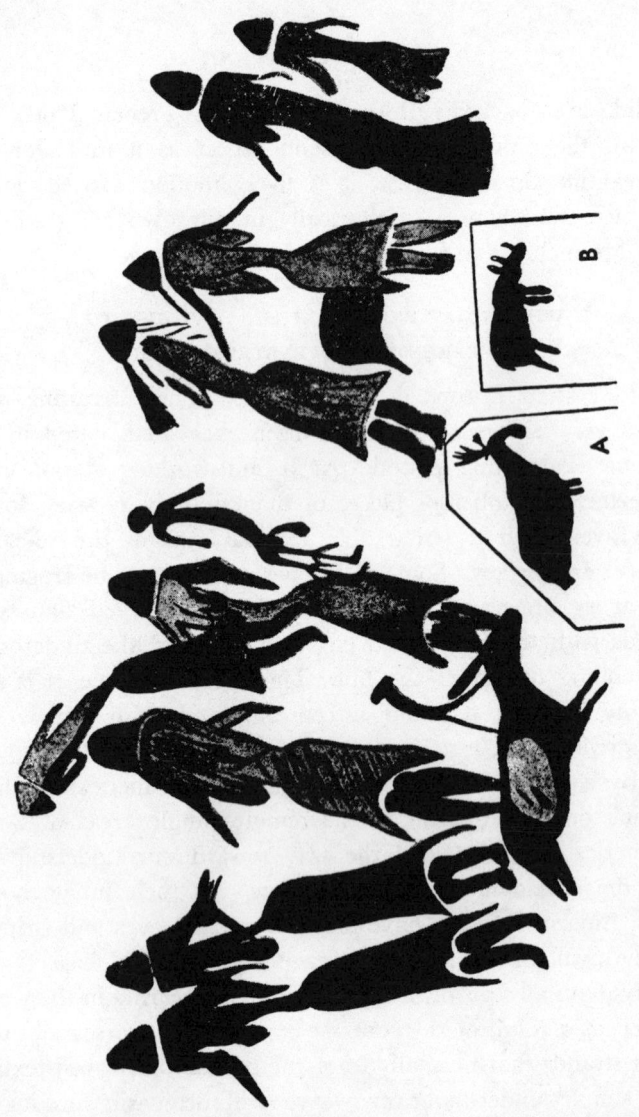

Figure V: Levantine art of eastern Spain. "Women Dancing Around a Young Male." (Miles Burkitt, *The Old Stone Age,* Atheneum, revised edition 1963, Fig. 30, p. 232)

in some of our woolen fabrics can produce a great many more intricate patternings with variations in the order of interweaving the strands. When, instead of spun threads, the weaving elements are wide strips of palm leaf, tall grass or cane splints, the surface effect is quite striking. The Amazon Indians produced these designs partly as a by-product of their work procedures and in part they varied the order of work for the sake of a particular emergent design. These texture designs they reproduced in drawings on their pottery, engravings in clay and reproduced in tapestry, preserving the basketry texture and varying the arrangement of the elements to suit an ideological context which they grafted onto it. The Greek key or fret design is a common element of these arts, and its emergence is to be found within the technological logic of the twilled basket-weaving. Parallel zigzags of a kind found engraved on the ivory bracelet from Mezine, are also common elements of the Amazon Indian weaving industry.

In the barren cold of the Ice Ages why do these designs appear in the Ukraine? Clearly there were suitable grasses and the climate was considerably more moderate than in western or northern Europe of the same period. Subsequent excavations in southern Russia show this to be the case, with the people living in little villages of dug-out houses.[18] Perhaps on the basis of the engraved design alone, its derivation from twilled mat weaving might remain in doubt, but in a recently excavated site at Shanindar Cave in Iraq, Dr. Ralph Solecki tells me that he found a clay impression of a twilled woven mat or basket with the characteristic concentric diamond design. The radio-carbon date of this find is 10,800 years ago.

The characteristic twilled woven texture patterns have

---

[18]Mongait, A. L., 1961, *Archaeology in the U.S.S.R.* Penguin Books, Baltimore, Md., pp. 93-4, housing; "Venuses," pp. 24-6.

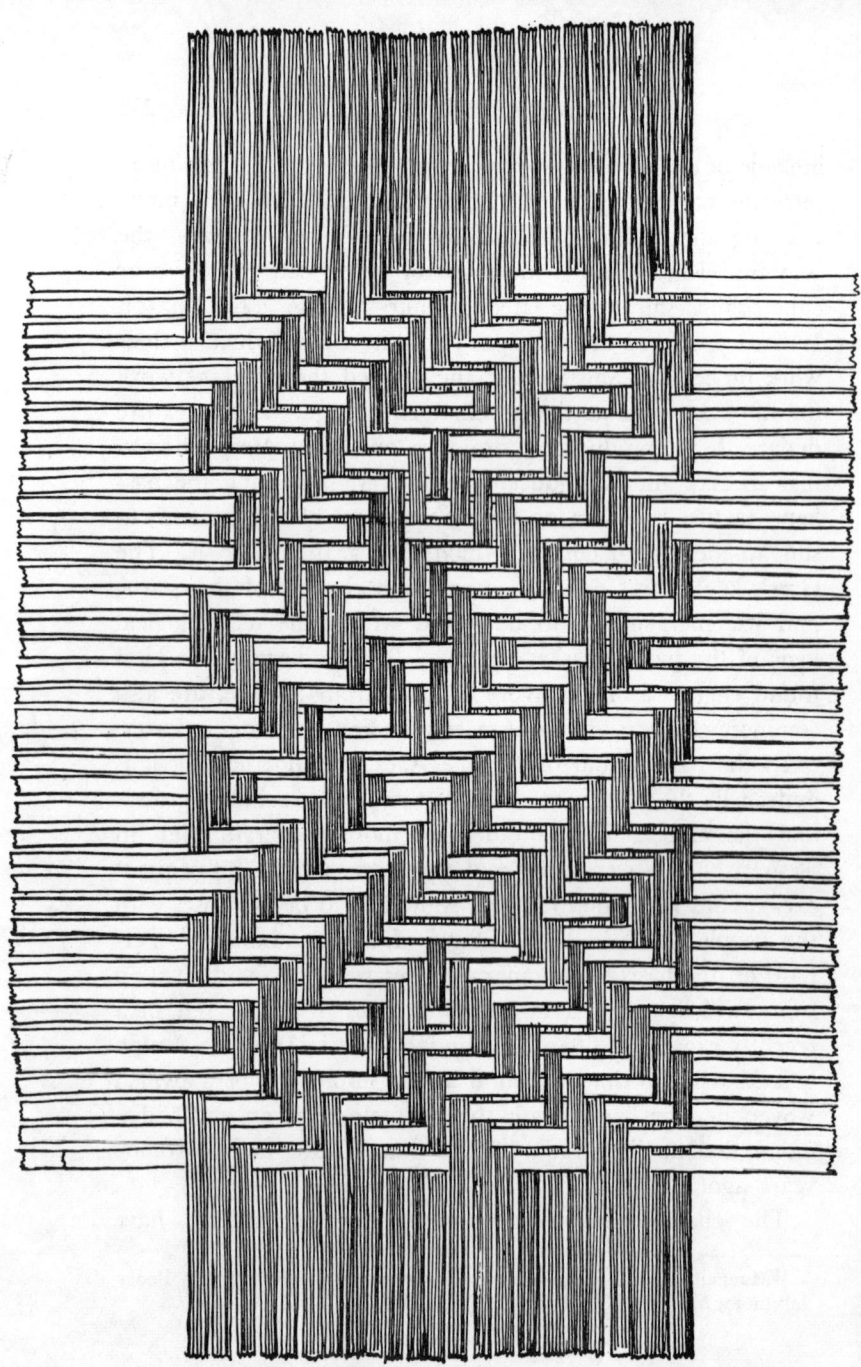

Figure VI: The Emergence of the fret or Greek key design in the texture of woven matting. (G. Weltfish, *The Origins of Art,* Bobbs Merrill Co., Inc., Indianapolis, 1953, Plate I, p. 38)

Fragments of paleolithic bracelet from the Ukraine, Mezine near Kiev, engraved on mammoth ivory—about 15,000 years ago, 150 centuries.

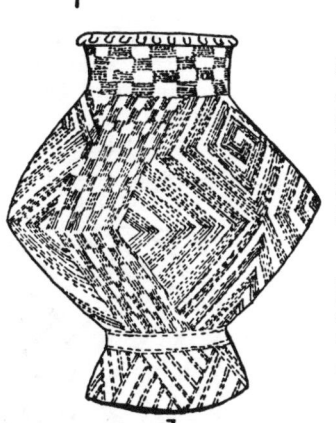

Clay pot with fret design "punctured" into the wet clay probably to simulate stitching on leather. Excavated at Bschanz, Wohlau, Germany (post Hinkelstein period, Danubian II, 2000-1600 B.C. about 4000 years ago, 40 centuries.

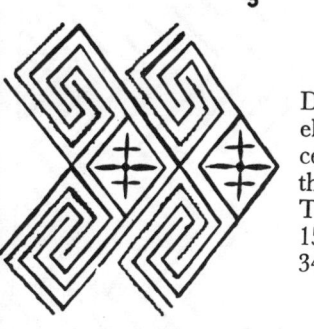

Designs painted in elaborate colors on the ceiling of the tomb of the Egyptian pharaoh, Thutmose III (about 1500 B.C.) 3400 years, 34 centuries ago.

Pottery with black designs painted against a white background. Excavated on Zuni Indian reservation, New Mexico (1000 A.D.) ten centuries ago.

Figure VII: The texture-patterned Greek key or fret adapted as design in other technical media. (Weltfish, *The Origins of Art* Plate II, p. 39)

A piece of textile that is going to be formed into a crown or headring by the Bakairi Indians of the Amazon River in South America.

A piece of mammoth ivory engraved with the woven "herringbone" design of the matting textile–from the Upper Paleolithic Period–excavated near the Mezine in the Ukraine.

Pottery drinking cup showing an adaptation of the zigzag-herringbone pattern. From the Aguano Indians of Northeast Peru.

Figure VIII: Emergence of the zigzag "herringbone" design from the texture of the woven matting; piece of textile that is going to be formed into a crown or headring by the Bakairi Indians of the Amazon River in South America. (Weltfish, *Origins of Art,* Plate XIX, p. 76)

appealed to peoples in a tremendous spread of time and space. They still retain their freshness for us and do not seem to pall. In some of its aspects, the appearance of these design motifs from the texture patterns of twilled textiles suggests our modern vogue for "optical art." Its difference is that these designs represent to the artist, not abstract sensation, but the work of his own hands and the rhythms of his own body at work. Their human content is fundamentally implicit. The occasions when he has gathered the materials, the sounds and sights, the company he was with, his associations with familiar use of the objects—feasts, food, ceremonies—are there for him in the pattern.

Far from the Amazon and far removed in time, two New World peoples serve to illustrate an explicit integration of conceptual themes with formal twilled texture patterns. The one is a people that has long disappeared, but lived for nearly two hundred years from 1150 A.D. to 1300 A.D. in the American Southwest on the Mimbres river in southwestern New Mexico. They shared a common style of pottery with the classical Pueblo cultures known as black-on-white. Round bowls, shallow to fairly deep, were coated with a white slip upon which black designs were painted. This accounts for the name of the pottery style which is associated with the Golden Era of Pueblo civilization with which the Mimbres people are roughly contemporary.

FORM AND DESIGN—THE HUMAN FORM AS DESIGN OBJECT AND DESIGN SOURCE

The most personally involved of all art forms is the decoration of the human body itself. As an object of decoration it may well have been developing concomitantly with the coup de poing. Dating from the upper Paleolithic Period, the Aurignacian of France, 33,000 years ago, we find elabo-

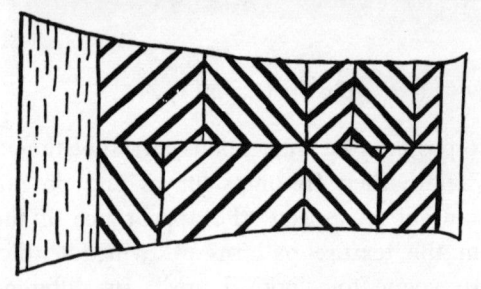

Tubular quiver formed of a piece of twill-woven matwork to hold arrows. Made by the Indians of the Rio Branco of northwest Brazil. The weaving is done in rectangular sections of uneven size. Each section has a simple diagonal twill pattern, but their juxtaposition as the weaving proceeds results in the emergence of the fret-key pattern. There are two sets of weaving sections down the length of the fabric. In the lower row there are four sections next to one another, with a very small fifth one at the end. In the upper row there are four sections also of different sizes.

A piece of pottery from the Icaná Indians of Northwest Brazil; the design is painted in black lines on a white background.

A clay hearth with a fret-hook design engraved on it made by the Icaná Indians of Northwest Brazil.

Figure IX: (Weltfish, *The Origins of Art,* Plate XXI, p. 78)

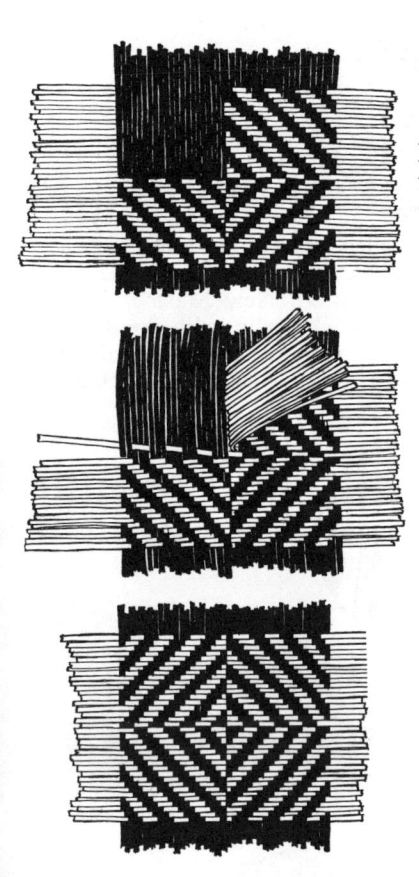

Developing a twilled weave pattern of diagonal inverse symmetry. Constructing the base of a square basket by the Chitimacha Indians of Louisiana in strips of split cane (drawings based on the work process as observed in the field by the author).

Prehistoric cotton tapestry poncho from Nasca Peru adapting the diagonal inverse symmetry pattern to the representation of conventionalized plant and animal figures. Nasca B period, Tiahuanaco style about 1000 A.D., end of Nasca, expansionist period of Tiahuanaco. The highland Tiahuanaco people with an angular textile-oriented aesthetic approach expanded politically so that they dominated the coastal Nasca peoples whose approach was predominantly naturalistic. This design reflects the emergent combination of graphic modes.)

Figure X: (Reproduced from Plate XXVI, *Origins of Art*, p. 83. Original in Walter Lehmann, Kunstgeschichte des alter Peru, Berlin 1924, p. 20 Plate 3). *See:* Max Schmidt, Indianerstudien in Zentralbrasilien, Berlin 1905, Bakairi basket, Fig. 1846, p. 361, Berlin Museum VB 5218, for similar weave)

A painted interpretation of the twilled-weave pattern of diagonal inverse symmetry. Archeological excavation in the American Southwest, Mimbres river in southeastern New Mexico, 1150-1350 A.D. Pottery bowl coated with a white slip, with the design painted in the interior in black, representing an outlier of the classical prehistoric Pueblo Indian style known as black-on-white.

Twill-weave-derived diagonal inverse symmetry designs, representing much further departures from the original texture model. Like the texture itself, the white area is as integral a part of the design scheme as the black.

Figure XI: (Weltfish, *Origins of Art,* Plate XXVII, p. 105)

Mimbres black-on-white pottery; naturalistic animal pictures framed by the texture-derived design, highly adapted and modified. There seems reason to believe that something of the temperament of the animal was implied by the way the framing design was developed. This was called to my attention by an American artist, Ann Margetson.

3, The butting goat with the white design area crazily askew; 5, the hopping grasshopper; 6, the poor trapped rabbit; 7, the fluttery humming bird; 1 and 2, two different fish, the one small and gentle, the other larger and more vigorous; and No. 5, the quail with the design right on his body, signifying his jerky movements in walking. In the original, this bowl (No. 5), shows that the design on the quail's body was constructed by first drawing in the central white strap pattern that can be seen in Fig. XI no. 2 and then painting over it to make the four inversely symmetrical arms of the final design.

Figure XII: (Weltfish, *Origins of Art,* Plate XLI, p. 119)

Neolithic clay pots from Germany. The designs were made by pressing a sharp object into the wet clay. In No. 1, the loop handle is emphasized with a small chevron figure above and below it.

In No. 2, in addition to the placement of the design, emphasizing the rim of the pot, the four protuberances are emphasized with series' of vertical chevrons.

Woman from the Celebes Islands, Indonesia, with a design tattooed on her body; the areas of design serve to emphasize the various structural features of the body itself.

Figure XIII: A fertile source of design ideas is the general human tendency to emphasize points on a surface—handles, nail heads and especially rims, shoulders and other protuberances. Taken out of the original technical context, the general format may be preserved and take on a "life of its own" as a discrete design. The human body was probably the earliest focus of such "form and structural" emphasis, the nature of the body as a bilaterally symmetrical structure both visually and kinetically, perhaps contributing to the almost universal value of this basic aesthetic principle. (*The Origins of Art,* Fig. LVI, p. 143)

Crow Indians. No. 2, Arapaho; No. 3, Blackfoot; No. 6, Gros Ventre; No. 7, Nez Perce.

Figure XIV: Design as structural emphasis in Parfleche containers of the Indians of the American Plains. Designs painted on the rawhide "envelopes" in which the Indians of the North American Plains stored their dried buffalo meat. The designs are built up within the angular surface of the rawhide flaps. First the outline is drawn around the flap; then within this outline a certain number of panels are ruled off in the length and in turn cut down their entire length with diagonals. (Weltfish, *Origins of Art,* Plate LII, p. 139)

Twined basketry of the Pit River Indians of northern California said to symbolize flying geese or wild duck. (*The Origins of Art*, Plate LXIX, p. 202 No. 1 and No. 2)

Figure XV: Angular designs of the Amerindian peoples surrounding the North American plains.

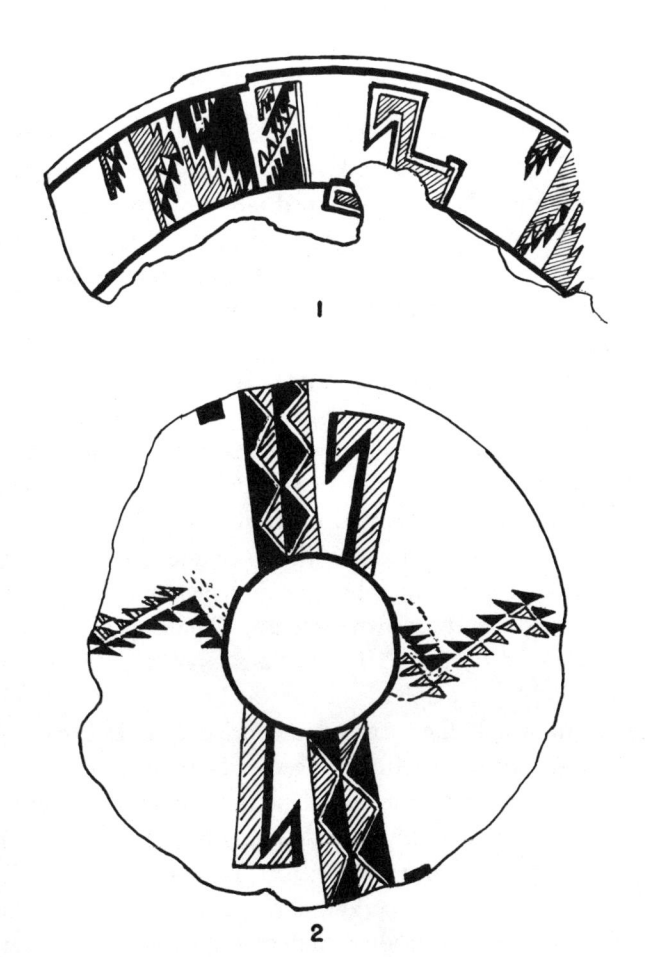

Prehistoric Southwestern coiled basket fragment of a shallow bowl, probably with flying geese motif. The wings are represented by the same sort of angular designs as in the Pit River baskets which lack any obvious naturalistic features. Excavated by Earl H. Morris, Basket-Maker III period, 400 A.D.-700 A.D. near Durango, Colorado. (Weltfish, *Origins of Art*, Plate LXXIV No. 2, p. 207) (drawn from the specimen in the collection of the American Museum of Natural History. Earl H. Morris and Robert F. Burgh, *Anasazi Basketry,* Carnegie Institution of Washington, D. C. Publication 533, 1941)

rate jewelry on the buried skeletons we excavate—necklaces, arm bands, girdles, anklets, and head nets strung with shells and animal bones and shaped pieces of stone in intricate patterns of symmetry. The graves themselves are filled with red ochre, a favorite material for body decoration among tribal peoples today as well as in the known past. Lumps of red ochre have been found in the excavated encampments of half a million years ago in East Africa, suggesting their possible use for body decoration even in this early period. Among modern tribes, painted-on body decorations tend to "underline" certain aspects of the body—the neck, wrists, waist, nose, eyes, forehead. This type of form emphasis is a common source of new design themes that become separated from their original context and become independent designs that are elaborated on their own account. The characteristically angular designs of the Plains Indians may well have their source in the form emphasis of the rawhide parfleche or skin envelope in which they carried the dried buffalo meat that they had preserved for future needs. If in fact man's own body was his earliest "canvas" then the tendency to develop bi-lateral symmetry in the coup de poing may have some relationship to this fact, for long before its perfect symmetrical form in the Acheulean period, the Abbevillian tool maker, with no real skill to produce refinement of shape, was still anticipating a bilateral symmetry in the tool he was making. Man himself as object may be the source of the most important organizing principle of universal aesthetics. Alternatively or in concert, the bilateral symmetry of man's body and of his movements may furnish the basis. The deepest satisfaction of the human being must surely spring from his very humanity.

CONCLUSION

In our search for the origins of art, we have ranged far over the world and deep in time. Even the little evidence we have mustered here shows that art is so deeply involved in so much of human experience that contrary to the common saying, *art* can be all things to all men if we live in an open world. The impress of man is on the material world wherever he touches it or even as he brushes by. Materiality gives way to the patterning of man on every hand. How long will it be before man learns that out of his challenges and of his living he can project his own image and become "captain of his soul and master of his fate," instead of, as he now too readily believes, a slave of his genes and of his chemistry? When will we learn that the greatest work of art can be man himself? Man long freed in the process of his evolution from the bondage of instincts can truly now decide.[19]

---

[19]Weltfish, Gene, 1953, *The Origins of Art,* The Bobbs-Merrill Company, Inc., Indianapolis, Ind., based on research in the museums of the United States, experimental work in the laboratory in the industrial processes involved, and field work with American Indian artist-craftsmen.

Notes on Contributors

CHARLES ANGOFF, A.B. (Harvard), Litt.D. (Fairleigh Dickinson University), is professor of English at Fairleigh Dickinson University. He is editor of *The Literary Review,* sponsored by the University, and vice-president of The Poetry Society of America. He has been an editor of many magazines, among them *The American Mercury, The Nation,* and *The North American Review.* He is the author or editor of about 35 books. The most recent are *The Tone of The Twenties* (*essays*), *Summer Storm* (a novel), and H. L. *Mencken: A Portrait from Memory.* The seventh novel in his series of fictional studies of American Jewry since the turn of the century will be published this spring. It will be called *Memory of Autumn.* His manuscripts, letters, books, and other documents are being collected by Boston University Libraries, of which he is a Fellow.

NASROLLAH S. FATEMI is a graduate of Stuart Memorial College, and has an M.A. from Columbia University and a Ph.D. from the New School for Social Research. He represented Iran at the UNESCO National Conference in 1948 and the International Congress of Americanists in New York in 1949. In 1948–1949 he was Iran's delegate to the United Nations, presenting the case of Iran to the Security Council. He has taught at the Asia Institute at Princeton University, and at Canadian universities. He is professor of social science at Fairleigh Dickinson University, and was chairman of the department in 1960–1966. He is now dean of the Graduate School at Fairleigh Dickinson University. He has written for *Orbis, Islamic Review* and many other American and Persian newspapers and periodicals. He is author of five books in Persian and three books in English: *Diplomatic History of Persia, Oil Diplomacy* and the *Dollar Crisis.*

ROBERT T. FRANCOEUR, M.A., M.S., Ph.D., teaches embryology at the Madison campus of Fairleigh Dickinson University, and is the author of *The World of Teilhard* and *Perspectives in Evolution.* He has contributed essays to thirteen other books and encyclopedias as well as some ninety articles in journals on five continents and in three languages. He has been guest lecturer at more than forty universities here and abroad.

LOYD HABERLY, M.A., LL.D., was educated at Reed, Harvard, and Oxford. He is a veteran printer, illustrator, and binder of fine books, author of a work on medieval pavements, and of a life of George Catlin the Indian Man. He is president of the Poetry Society of America. He has for long been associated with Fairleigh Dickinson University as Professor, Chairman and Dean.

SAMUEL L. HART has been professor and chairman, Department of Philosophy, Fairleigh Dickinson University, Teaneck Campus, since 1957. He has studied at the University of Vienna, where he received the Ph.D. in 1923. His thesis was *Nietzsche, die Vorstufen Zarathustras.* He is author of *Treatise on Values,* and *Ethics, the Quest for the Good Life,* and co-author of *The Frontiers of Social Science.*

EMIL LENGYEL, author and teacher, started his writing career in his native Budapest, as a journalist, continued it in Vienna, as a newspaper correspondent, and in New York, as a special correspondent of *The New York Times,* and correspondent of the *Toronto Star Weekly.* He is the author of more than twenty books, two of them best sellers, *The Danube* and *Turkey*. His most recent book *Mahatma Gandhi: The Great Soul* has just been published. The "two cultures," about which he writes in this volume, aroused his interest many years ago when he interviewed Albert Einstein for *The New York Times Magazine*. He is chairman of the Social Science Department, Fairleigh Dickinson University, Rutherford, New Jersey. Previously, he taught at New York University.

HEINZ F. MACKENSEN, Ph.D., is Dean of the Evening Division of Fairleigh Dickinson University. He holds advanced degrees in history and theology. He has taught history at Fairleigh Dickinson University since 1954 and before that at the College of William and Mary. He has travelled widely and has contributed to several periodicals.

FRANK H. MCCLOSKEY, Ph.D. (Harvard), has taught at Boston University and New York University. He was a Fulbright professor at the University of Karachi, and is now adjunct professor of English at Fairleigh Dickinson. Last year he was Resident Director of Wroxton College, Fairleigh Dickinson University. His publications include *What College Offers, Reading and Thinking,* and *How to Write Clearly and Effectively*. He has prepared a monthly sixteen page insert for the Educational Edition of the *Readers Digest* for twenty-seven years.

ANDRE MICHALOPOULOS, C.B.E., F.R.S.A., F.A.M.S., M.A. (Oxon.), who has been adviser to the Royal Greek Embassy in Washington, D. C., is professor emeritus of Classical Literatures & Civilizations in Fairleigh Dickinson University. He is a member of the Supreme Council of Education of the Greek Orthodox Archdiocese of North & South America. He was formerly a Provincial Governor in Greece, a Banking & Business Executive in Athens, a Member of the Greek Cabinet, and a Greek Minister Plenipotentiary in the United States. His honors and awards include: Commander of the Order of George I of Greece (Civil & Military Division); Commander of the Order of the Phoenix of Greece; Archon in the Order of St. Andrew and Grand Protonotary of the Ecumenical Patriarchate of Constantinople; Commander of the Order of the British Empire; Commander of the Order of Orange & Nassau (Netherlands); Chevalier of the Legion of Honor (France); Fellow of the Royal Society of Arts (London); and Fellow of the Ancient Monuments Society (London). His publications include: two collections of verse, 1923 & 1928; *Greek Fire* (a collection of war broadcasts, addresses and articles) 1943; *Homer,* 1966.

KENT REDMOND, Ph.D. (University of Southern California, Los Angeles) has been Associate Professor of American History at Fairleigh Dickinson University since 1963. He is now preparing, with Professor T. M. Smith, of the University of Oklahoma, *Project Whirlwind: A Case History in Contemporary Technology.* He has published several articles in historical journals.

HAROLD A. ROTHBART, Dean of the College of Science and Engineering at Fairleigh Dickinson University, received his B.S. Degree in Mechanical Engineering from Newark College of Engineering in 1939. In 1942 he received his M.S. in Mechanical Engineering from the University of Pennsylvania, and in 1959 he received his Dr. Eng. from Technischen Hochschule, Munchen, Germany. Before Dr. Rothbart came to Fairleigh Dickinson, he was a Professor of Mechanical Engineering at the City University of New York, teaching graduate and undergraduate courses. He has written two books—*Cams* and *Mechanical Design and Systems Handbook*—in addition to numerous articles. He has presented over 30 papers and lectures before the American Society of Mechanical Engineers, at National Conferences, and has written for technical journals on mechanical systems. In 1966 he lectured throughout Japan, stopping at the Universities of Hong Kong and Hawaii on the way home.

WILLIS RUDY, Ph.D. (Columbia University), is professor of social science at Fairleigh Dickinson University, and Chairman of the Department, Teaneck Campus. He is author of *The College of the City of New York: A History, Higher Education in Transition* (with J. S. Brubacher), *The Evolving Liberal Arts College Curriculum,* and *Schools in an Age of Mass Culture.*

HARRIETT SPAGNOLI, Ph.D. (New York University), is associate professor of Biology at Fairleigh Dickinson University, Teaneck Campus. In addition to teaching, she served as Acting Chairman of the Department for a few years. While in that capacity, she contributed largely to the organization of the Graduate Biology program. Dr. Spagnoli served as a Research Associate in American Cyanamid prior to coming to Fairleigh Dickinson University. She has done research at the Woods Hole Marine Laboratories in Massachusetts. Her most recent articles have appeared in the *Journal of Dental Research.*

JOHN WARREN, Ph.D. (Harvard), is associate professor of history at Fairleigh Dickinson University, Rutherford campus. He served with the United States Army and AAF in World War II, receiving the Bronze Star. He did research and writing for the Air Force Historical Division. He is author of two books on airborne operations and co-author of a history of the Air Force.

GENE WELTFISH, Ph.D., (Columbia), is associate professor of Anthropology at Fairleigh Dickinson University, Madison Campus. She was Research Associate, 1928-1935; Lecturer, 1935-1953, in the Graduate Department of Anthropology, Columbia. She did field work in art, linguistics, technology, and ethnology, among American Indians in Louisiana, the Dakotas, Oklahoma, New Mexico, and Arizona. She has published technical papers in various journals, and pamphlet material on the race problem, including "The Races of Mankind," with Ruth F. Benedict. She was consultant in Science Teaching, Teachers College, Columbia, 1939-1943. Her books include *The Origins of Art,* (1953), *Caddoan Texts (Pawnee Language)* (1937), and *The Lost Universe,* (1965).